Input for Instructed L2 Learners

SECOND LANGUAGE ACQUISITION
Series Editor: Professor David Singleton, *Trinity College, Dublin, Ireland*

This series brings together titles dealing with a variety of aspects of language acquisition and processing in situations where a language or languages other than the native language is involved. Second language is thus interpreted in its broadest possible sense. The volumes included in the series all offer in their different ways, on the one hand, exposition and discussion of empirical findings and, on the other, some degree of theoretical reflection. In this latter connection, no particular theoretical stance is privileged in the series; nor is any relevant perspective – sociolinguistic, psycholinguistic, neurolinguistic, etc. – deemed out of place. The intended readership of the series includes final-year undergraduates working on second language acquisition projects, postgraduate students involved in second language acquisition research, and researchers and teachers in general whose interests include a second language acquisition component.

Other Books in the Series
Age, Accent and Experience in Second Language Acquisition
    Alene Moyer
Studying Speaking to Inform Second Language Learning
    Diana Boxer and Andrew D. Cohen (eds)
Language Acquisition: The Age Factor (2nd edn)
    David Singleton and Lisa Ryan
Focus on French as a Foreign Language: Multidisciplinary Approaches
    Jean-Marc Dewaele (ed.)
Second Language Writing Systems
    Vivian Cook and Benedetta Bassetti (eds)
Third Language Learners: Pragmatic Production and Awareness
    Maria Pilar Safont Jordà
Artificial Intelligence in Second Language Learning: Raising Error Awareness
    Marina Dodigovic
Studies of Fossilization in Second Language Acquisition
    ZhaoHong Han and Terence Odlin (eds)
Language Learners in Study Abroad Contexts
    Margaret A. DuFon and Eton Churchill (eds)
Early Trilingualism: A Focus on Questions
    Julia D. Barnes
Cross-linguistic Influences in the Second Language Lexicon
    Janusz Arabski (ed.)
Motivation, Language Attitudes and Globalisation: A Hungarian Perspective
    Zoltán Dörnyei, Kata Csizér and Nóra Németh
Age and the Rate of Foreign Language Learning
    Carmen Muñoz (ed.)
Investigating Tasks in Formal Language Learning
    María del Pilar García Mayo (ed.)
Cross-linguistic Similarity in Foreign Language Learning
    Håkan Ringbom

For more details of these or any other of our publications, please contact:
Multilingual Matters, Frankfurt Lodge, Clevedon Hall,
Victoria Road, Clevedon, BS21 7HH, England
http://www.multilingual-matters.com

SECOND LANGUAGE ACQUISITION 22
Series Editor: David Singleton, *Trinity College, Dublin, Ireland*

Input for Instructed L2 Learners
The Relevance of Relevance

Anna Niżegorodcew

MULTILINGUAL MATTERS LTD
Clevedon • Buffalo • Toronto

To the memory of my parents
Bogna and Adam Turnau

Library of Congress Cataloging in Publication Data
Nizegorodcew, Anna.
Input for Instructed L2 Learners: The Relevance of Relevance/Anna Nizegorodcew.
Second Language Acquisition: 22
Includes bibliographical references and index.
1. Language and languages–Study and teaching. 2. Second language acquisition.
3. Discourse analysis. 4. Language and education. I. Title.
P53.N57 2007
418.0071–dc22   2006022418

British Library Cataloguing in Publication Data
A catalogue entry for this book is available from the British Library.

ISBN-13: 978-1-85359-938-5 (hbk)
ISBN-13: 978-1-85359-937-8 (pbk)

Multilingual Matters Ltd
UK: Frankfurt Lodge, Clevedon Hall, Victoria Road, Clevedon BS21 7HH.
USA: UTP, 2250 Military Road, Tonawanda, NY 14150, USA.
Canada: UTP, 5201 Dufferin Street, North York, Ontario M3H 5T8, Canada.

Copyright © 2007 Anna Niżegorodcew.

All rights reserved. No part of this work may be reproduced in any form or by any means without permission in writing from the publisher.

The policy of Multilingual Matters/Channel View Publications is to use papers that are natural, renewable and recyclable products, made from wood grown in sustainable forests. In the manufacturing process of our books, and to further support our policy, preference is given to printers that have FSC and PEFC Chain of Custody accreditation. The FSC and/or PEFC logos will appear on those books where full accreditation has been granted to the printer concerned.

Typeset by Techset Composition Ltd.
Printed and bound in Great Britain by MPG Books Ltd.

Contents

Acknowledgements vii
Preface ix

1 The Role of L2 Classroom Input in the Light of Second
  Language Acquisition Models and Relevance Theory 1
  The Role of L2 Classroom Input in the Light of Second
  Language Acquisition (SLA) Models 1
  The Role of L2 Classroom Input in the Light of
  Relevance Theory 12

2 L2 Teaching Perspective on the Role of Instructional Input 23
  The Changing Status of L2 Teaching Methods 23
  Native and Non-native L2 Teachers 24
  Secondary Instructed L2 Learners 25
  The Background of Communicative Language Teaching (CLT) .. 27
  Communicative Practice in the L2 Classroom 29
  Fluency and Accuracy Practice in the L2 Classroom 31
  Feedback and Error Correction in the L2 Classroom 34
  L1 Use in the Monolingual L2 Classroom 36

3 L2 Classroom Discourse Perspective on the Role of
  Instructional Input 39
  L2 Classroom Discourse 39
  L2 Naturalistic and Classroom Discourse 39
  Functions of L2 Classroom Discourse 41
  Patterns of Participation in L2 Classroom Discourse 44
  L2 Teacher Talk and Peer Talk 46
  L2 Classroom Discourse Modifications 50

4 Evidence from L2 Classroom Discourse Research Projects 53
  Jagiellonian University English Department Projects
  on Teachers' Input in L2 English Classroom Interaction
  (1984–2004) 53

5 Classroom Discourse Data Interpreted in the Light of RT: Levels of Expected Optimal Relevance of L2 Classroom Input 93
    Instructional Input in the RT Perspective 93
    Instructional Input: Explicit Teaching 102
    Instructional Input: L2 Classroom Communication 114
    Input for Instructed L2 Learners in the Light of RT: Raw (Primary) and Corrective (Secondary) Linguistic Data Revisited 142

6 L2 Teaching Implications 148
    Conclusion 166

References 169
Index 178

Acknowledgements

I am grateful to my former MA seminar students from the English Department of the Jagiellonian University in Kraków, in particular those who participated in L2 classroom research projects. My special gratitude is due to the seven students, who collected the corpus of classroom discourse data, which has become the database for my analysis in this book. They are: Ewa Kusibab, Anna Kosiarz, Dorota Puchała, Agnieszka Czekajewska, Joanna Mazur, Anna Fryc and Anna Przebinda.

I am also grateful to my colleagues from the English Department, who helped me in many ways; in particular, I would like to thank Dr Maria Jodłowiec and Dr Justyna Leśniewska.

I wish to express my gratitude to Prof. Deirde Wilson for inspiring talks during the *Interpreting for Relevance* Conference 1 at Kazimierz Dolny in 2002, and to Prof. Ewa Mioduszewska from Warsaw University, who invited me to the Conference.

I would also like to thank Prof. Janusz Arabski from the University of Silesia in Sosnowiec, and his co-workers: Prof. Danuta Gabryś-Barker, Dr Adam Wojtaszek, Dr Andrzej Łyda, and other members of the organising committee of annual Foreign Language Acquisition/Learning and Teaching Conferences at Szczyrk, for creating a permanent venue and an inspiring forum for the exchange of ideas focused on the interface of learning and teaching foreign languages.

I would like to thank my Editor, Prof. David Singleton from Trinity College, Dublin, for his encouragement and confidence in my proposed book, and the anonymous reviewer of the book proposal for constructive critical remarks and valuable suggestions. I also wish to express my gratitude to the anonymous reviewer of the original version of this book for his insightful comments. I am grateful to Marjukka Grover, the Editorial Manager from Multilingual Matters, for her invaluable help.

Finally, I would like to thank my family and friends, for their support and understanding.

Preface

This book is an attempt to apply relevance theory (RT) (Sperber & Wilson 1986/1995) to verbal input for instructed foreign language learners. First, I would like to define the scope of my discussion and my understanding of the terms used.

Input is difficult to define in the second/foreign (L2) classroom perspective[1] because, on the one hand, in its general sense, the term stems from information processing theory, where it denotes any verbal or non-verbal information that reaches one's processing system, and on the other, in a more specific sense, the Comprehensible Input and Interaction Hypotheses have linked the concept of input in L2 learning and teaching with Second Language Acquisition (SLA) theory.[2]

However, SLA theorists and researchers who have tried to account for second language acquisition on the basis of an analysis of the linguistic data reaching one's processing system have faced great problems in finding empirical support for the existence of specific input factors conducive to SLA (see Ellis, 1994). The reason for the problems seems to lie in the vagueness of the concept of input itself, as well as in the multiplicity of factors which affect successful language learning/acquisition (see Brown, 1994).

Being an L2 teacher and an L2 teacher trainer, I firmly believe that there is a link between teaching and learning/acquisition. Such a link is demonstrated in teaching and learning practice every day in thousands of L2 classrooms. On the other hand, I must admit that it is very difficult to find unequivocal evidence, conforming to a rigorous scientific paradigm, that some types of teaching, including some types of L2 classroom discourse, are more conducive to learning/acquisition than others.

Searching for innovative theoretical approaches to the aforementioned problems, we can begin our search from the teacher's perspective, and her/his obvious intention to facilitate the process of L2 learning and acquisition. Thus, my intention is to treat input for instructed L2 learners in a different way. In my understanding of the term, 'input for instructed L2 learners' is not any verbal information that reaches the learners' processing systems. It is 'the language intentionally presented to the learners by the teacher or other learners in order to facilitate the process of L2 learning/acquisition'. Such an understanding of the term stems from the nature and basic goals of the L2 teaching process. I do not claim that the teacher's input is always facilitative. I only say that the teacher wants the learners think that it is.

On this view, my intention is to conceptualise the teachers' (or peers') input within the framework of RT, which is a theory of the interpretation of incoming messages. The presentation of the L2 classroom input is understood as following the Principle of Relevance, that is, automatically communicating to the audience (the learners) a presumption of its optimal relevance (Sperber & Wilson, 1986/1995). By the above definition, I mean that the teacher, or the learner in the role of the teacher, according to the Principle of Relevance, makes their audience (the learners) believe that the input he/she provides is optimally relevant to them.

Interpretation of L2 classroom input has become an interesting issue in the light of RT, because the teachers' intentions are not fully explicit. The impact of the Communicative Approach has contributed to considerable tensions within L2 classrooms, particularly those in foreign language learning contexts. Those tensions involve apparent conflicts between a focus on fluency and a focus on accuracy, and in monolingual contexts,[3] additionally, between L2 and native language (L1) use. I would like to interpret those conflicts as stemming from a fundamental tension within the communicative L2 classroom, between a focus on communication and a focus on the target language code.

My intention is to analyse teachers' (and peers') input within L2 classroom discourse in the light of RT. However, before I do this, I would like to give an overview of two other closely related perspectives on L2 classroom input: an L2 teaching perspective and an interactional discourse analysis view.

My classroom data is based on a corpus collected in seven L2 classroom research projects by my former MA seminar students. All the classroom discourse data was collected in secondary school English as a Foreign Language (EFL) classrooms in Poland.

The first chapter presents an overview of the role of L2 classroom input in the light of SLA theory and its critique, followed by my main claims concerning the application of RT to classroom input for instructed L2 learners in a foreign language learning context.

The second chapter gives a teaching perspective on the role of the L2 classroom input in the communicative L2 classrooms. In particular, it focuses on fluency and accuracy practice, providing feedback and error correction, and L1 use in monolingual L2 classrooms.

The third chapter presents the L2 classroom discourse perspective on the role of input and interaction. The approaches involve a discussion on the differences between naturalistic and L2 classroom discourse, functions of L2 classroom discourse, patterns of participation in L2 classroom discourse, teacher talk and peer talk approaches to L2 classroom discourse and L2 classroom discourse modifications.

The findings of seven MA L2 classroom research projects from the years 1984 to 2004 are presented in their original versions in Chapter 4 to enable their reinterpretation in the light of relevance theory in the next chapter.

Chapter 5 analyses L2 classroom discourse samples according to the functional teaching categories: explicit teaching, including explicit presentation of the linguistic data and teacher corrections of learners' language, as well as L2 classroom communication, subdivided into real communication and simulated communication.

In real communication, the analysis is focused on talking about the learning content, including subject-matter teaching, and talking about organisational and social matters. In simulated communication, two types of communicative activities are analysed: role-plays and discussions.

It is suggested that L2 classroom instructional input plays an important role in classroom discourse, because by changing the expected levels of relevance, it indicates to the learners how they should interpret it: as fluency practice, as accuracy practice, or as fluency combined with accuracy.

The final Chapter 6 presents teaching implications of the proposed interpretation of instructional input in the L2 classroom discourse, in particular for the development of fluency and accuracy in foreign language teaching contexts.

This book is first of all intended for L2 teacher educators, L2 teachers and pre-service and in-service teacher-trainees, in particular those working in the countries where English and other foreign languages are taught primarily in educational settings by non-native teachers.

I also believe that the book can be of interest to SLA researchers. In my opinion, a number of SLA researchers, who are predominantly linguists and have little to do with L2 classroom teaching, tend to disregard what actually happens in instructional settings, where the majority of students learn their L2, admittedly not to the level of near-native proficiency.

On the other hand, teachers and teacher educators, by virtue of their teaching focus, may overestimate the impact of instructional factors upon target language development. The two groups of professionals often work in different worlds although their research subjects remain the same – instructed L2 learners. My intention in this book is to link both perspectives on the grounds of RT.

Notes

1. The abbreviated term L2 refers to both second and foreign language. Second language is the language which is acquired/learned naturalistically and/or in the classroom, in the countries where it is spoken as a first language, e.g. English is a second language for non-native speakers in Great Britain. Foreign language is usually acquired/learned only in instructional settings in the countries where it is not spoken as a first language, e.g. English is a foreign language in Poland.
2. L2 acquisition is a term closely connected with SLA theory, stemming from a psycholinguistic claim that language learning (both first and second language) is first of all based on unconscious mental processes. On the other hand, L2 learning usually refers to intentional activities which aim at the development of the learners' L2 knowledge. Frequently, both terms cannot be easily distinguished on theoretical grounds, and it is common to use the combined term L2 learning/acquisition. L2 teachers tend to avoid entering into the acquisition and/or learning dilemma, and they use another term L2 development, which denotes growing communicative competence in L2 use.
3. By monolingual classrooms I mean the classrooms where all L2 learners speak one common native language (L1). Most frequently, L2 teachers in monolingual classrooms are non-native L2 speakers and share the common L1 with their students.

Chapter 1

The Role of L2 Classroom Input in the Light of Second Language Acquisition Models and Relevance Theory

The Role of L2 Classroom Input in the Light of Second Language Acquisition (SLA) Models

Introduction

At first, it should be stressed that the understanding of the term *input* in SLA theory and in Relevance Theory is different. Although my aim is to view L2 input in terms of Relevance Theory, it is impossible to avoid references to L2 input as it is understood in SLA theory. That is why it seems appropriate to outline some current approaches to the role of input in SLA models.

Input is understood in them as raw (primary) L2 data (Gass, 1997) that reaches the non-native audience's perceptual system, that is, the second language which is noticed by the audience. In terms of the L2 classroom, L2 input is the target language spoken by the teacher which is heard by the learners.

The SLA models which consider L2 input as one of the crucial factors in language acquisition, view the process of L2 comprehension as the decoding by the non-native audience of the meanings communicated by the native speakers. By the same token, the SLA models which are concerned with L2 classroom second language learning/acquisition view the L2 comprehension process as the decoding by the learners of the meanings communicated by the teachers.

On the other hand, Relevance Theory is concerned with the interpretation of the already decoded messages, and the main part of the comprehension process follows linguistic decoding. I will discuss the aforementioned difference in the following part of this chapter.

Krashen, Long and Swain (input/interaction/output models)

The first model which treated input, in the above raw L2 data sense of the word, as the main factor in L2 acquisition was Stephen Krashen's Comprehensible Input Hypothesis (Krashen, 1981, 1982). Krashen claimed that the first necessary condition for the input to be acquired is its comprehensibility, which is in turn ensured by its approximate level of difficulty, slightly higher than the non-native speaker's or the learner's present proficiency level. Such input was called roughly tuned input.

The other necessary condition for the comprehensible input to be acquired, according to Krashen, is an accompanying low Affective Filter, which refers to the non-native speaker's or the learner's positive attitude towards L2 learning and everything that entails. According to Krashen's model L2 acquisition will automatically occur when communication and comprehension are successful.

Critics of Krashen's Comprehensible Input Hypothesis point out that his concepts are vague, e.g. it is not clear what is a slightly higher level of difficulty, and it is not explicitly stated whether they apply to all aspects and levels of L2 learning/acquisition (see McLaughlin, 1987). Moreover, Krashen's theory conflates L2 acquisition and L2 comprehension, by claiming that once L2 input has been comprehended, it has also been automatically acquired, which, obviously, is not the case.

A similar SLA model, equating comprehension with acquisition of raw L2 input data was proposed by Michael Long (1983) as the Interaction Hypothesis. Long claimed that the input provided by native speakers for non-native speakers must be adjusted in interaction to become comprehensible. He identified a few types of interactional adjustments in conversations between native and non-native speakers, such as confirmation checks, clarification requests and comprehension checks. Long concluded that there exists an 'indirect causal relationship between linguistic and conversational adjustments and SLA' (Long, 1985: 388).

The indirect causal relationship was based upon deduction: if adjustments result in comprehension, and comprehension results in acquisition, then adjustments should result in acquisition. However, Long's conclusion did not find consistent support in research studies, and even those studies that supported the hypothesis in its first part, concerning the relationship between adjustments and comprehension, did not support the second part, that comprehension equals acquisition (see Ellis, 1994).

In a weak version of the Interaction Hypothesis Long claims that the feedback on errors, received from the native speaker interlocutor during interaction can facilitate L2 development, but probably only in some aspects of L2 learning (Long, 1996), which is a much less radical claim, which could be much more easily accepted by L2 teachers.

In turn, Merrill Swain (1985) in a modification of the Comprehensible Input Hypothesis argued that comprehensible input alone, even in vast quantities, cannot make L2 learners fully competent target language speakers. What she postulated as a necessary condition for achieving native-like competence was 'comprehensible output', that is, the learner's spoken language 'as he or she attempts to create precisely and appropriately the meaning desired' (Swain, 1985: 252).

Swain (1995) further elaborated her hypothesis, in which she distinguished three functions of output in L2 learning: the noticing function, the hypothesis-testing function and the metalinguistic function.[1] In the first and the third functions, learners' output plays the role of input for them. According to Swain, learners' own spoken language, that is, their output, helps them to notice gaps in their L2 knowledge and to reflect upon them. Consequently, learners' output can function as input for conscious reflection.

However, in Swain's output-as-input model, it is not clear how learners can notice gaps in their knowledge if they are not provided with any feedback on their errors. Moreover, even if they are aware of their deficiencies, they may not have time to reflect on them in oral communication.

Nevertheless, in contrast to Krashen's and Long's hypotheses, Swain puts stress on accuracy of target language forms. She realises that meaning-focused instruction does not suffice in acquiring accurate L2 forms.

Gass's model

An integrated model was proposed by Susan Gass (1997) as an attempt at combining the Input/Interaction Hypotheses with the Universal Grammar Hypothesis[2] and cognitive approaches[3] to L2 learning/acquisition. According to Gass, L2 input should be first noticed and related to the existing knowledge. Raw L2 data is claimed to be first filtered by a cognitive mechanism called apperception to become apperceived input.

> Apperception is an internal cognitive act in which a linguistic form is related to some bit of existing knowledge (or gap in knowledge). We can think of apperception as a priming device that prepares the input for further analysis. Thus, apperceived input is that bit of language that is, noticed in some way by the learner because of some particular recognizable features. (Gass, 1997: 4)

The apperceived input is claimed to be understood due to the process of negotiation and input modification, which places Gass's model as an elaboration of the Comprehensible Input and Interaction Hypotheses.

However, according to Gass, comprehended input is different from comprehensible input in that 'the focus is on the hearer (the learner) and the extent to which he or she understands' (Gass, 1997: 5). Gass also claims that in her model understanding may mean anything from general comprehension to detailed understanding of phonological or syntactic patterns.

At the next stage in Gass's model comprehended input is either used for immediate communication and processed at the level of general meaning, or it is processed at the level of morphology, lexicon and syntax, and consequently incorporated into L2 learners' grammar to become intake, that is, acquired language.

Gass's psycholinguistic model seems oversimplified, particularly in that it makes a sharp distinction between general meaning-focused processing for immediate communication (for comprehension) and form-focused processing (for acquisition). Moreover, it is not clear what makes some comprehended input suitable for form-focused processing.

Ellis's model

Another SLA model which places L2 input in the focus of attention and tries to integrate various aspects and stages of the process of L2 acquisition is the Integrated Theory of Instructed L2 Learning proposed by Ellis (1990). The author draws on Krashen's and Long's hypotheses, as well as on Bialystok's and Bialystok and Sharwood-Smith's cognitive models of L2 learning[4] (Bialystok, 1978; Bialystok & Sharwood-Smith, 1985).

From the perspective of instructed L2 learners, Ellis's model is interesting because it treats specific classroom input as an important factor in L2 acquisition. Ellis acknowledges that beside meaning-focused instruction, form-focused instruction has a role to play in L2 acquisition. He is aware of the complex nature of meaning-focused and form-focused instruction in the L2 classroom and the role played by the L2 teacher in shifting the focus from form to meaning and vice versa. In his interpretation, Ellis is close to the ideas expressed by Sperber and Wilson in Relevance Theory.

> The input that derives from these two kinds of instruction [meaning-focused and form-focused] differs with regard to its communicative properties (e.g. meaning-focused instruction is likely to afford the learner an opportunity to listen to and to perform a greater range of linguistic functions than will form-focused instruction) and also with regard to the kind of response it typically evokes in the learner (e.g. form-focused instruction encourages the learner to reflect on the formal features of the language while meaning focused instruction encourages semantic processing [...]. The instructional input in many lessons will be mixed,

affording the learner the opportunity to attend to both meaning and form – to experience language or to study it. Teachers shift the focus as the lesson unravels – at one moment engaging the learners in meaningful communication and at another directing their attention to the linguistic code [...]. Ultimately, of course, it is the learner and not the textbook or the teacher that determines in what way the input is attended to. (Ellis, 1990: 188)

The Integrated Theory of L2 Learning underlines the learners' active role in attending to meaning-focused and/or form-focused input. According to Ellis, learners derive L2 explicit knowledge, i.e. knowledge about the language and conscious concepts, from form-focused instruction. Explicit knowledge is used to 'sensitise the learner to the existence of non-standard form in her interlanguage and thus facilitates the acquisition of target-language forms'[5] (Ellis, 1990: 195).

However, in Ellis's view, it is only implicit knowledge, i.e. subconscious L2 knowledge, derived mostly from meaning-focused teaching, which is responsible for spontaneous L2 use. In other words, L2 is acquired first of all from meaning-focused teaching although form-focused instruction can somehow help the learners in the process.

The cognitive focus-on-form (FonF) approach

The cognitive focus-on-form approach (FonF) is an elaboration of the models which treat input to L2 learning as an important factor affecting cognitive processes of knowledge acquisition. In particular, the FonF model puts stress on L2 language forms as they are learned and/or acquired in communicative L2 classroom contexts. The approach draws on numerous research studies stimulated by the Interaction Hypothesis and its modification, the Output Hypothesis (Swain, 1985), which aimed at discovering input/interaction/output factors conducive to L2 acquisition (see Doughty & Williams, 1998).

It was the lack of native-like L2 acquisition in L2 classroom immersion contexts, where L2 learners had a great amount of comprehensible (and comprehended) input, which resulted in a renewed interest in focusing on L2 form in instructed L2 (Long, 1991).

What should be borne in mind is the distinction between focus-on-form (FonF) and focus-on-forms (FonFs) approaches. While 'focus on form overtly draws students' attention to linguistic elements as they arise incidentally in lessons whose overriding focus is on meaning or communication' (Long, 1991: 45, in Doughty, 2001: 210), focus on forms is concerned with explicit teaching of L2 forms only.

According to Doughty (2001), cognitive processes that are involved in L2 learning can be divided into macroprocesses, one of them being acquisition of input, and microprocesses, such as focus on form.

The crucial question asked by FonF approach is whether and how a microprocess, such as focus on form, which consists of teacher intervention, can influence an inaccessible and automatic macroprocess, such as acquisition of input.

Doughty claims that L2 learners must notice the gap between their non-native-like forms and the target forms made salient by the teacher. Such noticing is possible due to the cognitive resources L2 learners possess, one of which is 'a cognitive preference for re-utilizing recent speech' (Doughty, 2001: 229).

Doughty (2001: 249) makes an interesting case for the existence of 'small cognitive windows of opportunity', through which L2 teachers could intervene by focusing on form in otherwise meaning focused activities. Such an approach is close to my understanding of the L2 teacher's role in the language classroom, to be discussed in the following part of this chapter and exemplified in Chapter 5.

The questions that are asked by FonF researchers concern the time when shifts of attention from meaning (fluency) to form (accuracy) should occur. In other words, when L2 teachers should intervene in communicative activities. Another equally important question refers to the form of teachers' interventions. Both questions have been only partly answered (see Havranek & Cesnik, 2001), but according to Doughty, it seems that teachers' recasts[6] of learners' non-native-like forms following immediately those forms are most useful in cognitive processing at the level of macroprocesses.

The above outlined SLA models make a clear opposition between the focus on meaning and the focus on form. According to them, L2 acquisition is possible when learners are first and foremost focused on meaning (see The Comprehensible Input Hypothesis and the Interaction Hypothesis), or when the focus is on meaning but the learners' attention is simultaneously focused on relevant forms (see The Integrated Theory of Instructed L2 Learning and The Cognitive Focus-on-Form Approach).

Finally, it should be stressed, following VanPatten (1996), that input processing for meaning is claimed to precede processing for form, but it is useful to train 'language learners in effective processing, to make them more able to notice relevant cues in the input so that form-meaning links are more likely to be attended to' (Skehan, 1998: 47).

In the following section of this chapter, I will briefly present some critical views on the role of input in SLA theory. The first type of criticism, referring to input accessibility for processing, treats input in a similar way to the treatment in the above outlined SLA models, that is, as raw (primary) L2 data.

Accessibility of input for processing

The focus on meaning and/or on form must take into account input accessibility to the learners. In the information-processing models, the internal cognitive systems possess constraints that make only some input accessible for further processing.

Such a constraint in Schmidt's (1990) model refers to the notion of noticing the gap. In the model, some sort of awareness of the gap between the learner's present L2 knowledge and the target form(s) is necessary before the learner can change his/her knowledge system.

According to Schmidt's Noticing Hypothesis, input can be noticed if it is salient enough and if it occurs frequently enough. L2 classroom instruction can help in both these aspects: teachers can make input more salient for the learners to notice, as well as they can present it more frequently.

The awareness of the gap between one's L2 knowledge and communicative needs has also been pointed out as a necessary condition for the development of communicative competence through positive strategic behaviour, by e.g. appealing for the interlocutor's help (see Faerch & Kasper, 1986; Niżegorodcew, 1986).

The question of the learner's awareness in the Noticing Hypothesis has been equated with consciousness. The question arises, though, as to the level of awareness needed for noticing the gap (Robinson, 1995). Tomlin and Villa (1994) claim that detection of a feature in the input does not necessarily mean that the detection process must be conscious, as has been claimed by Schmidt. They distinguish between the detecting, orienting and alerting functions of attention.[7]

This distinction seems to be helpful in modelling the focus on meaning and the focus on form not as two discrete processes but rather as a continuum, from the full focus on form without taking meaning into consideration to the full focus on meaning without considering form, with intermediate stages, when the learner is more or less focused either on meaning or on form.

On the other hand, Truscott (1998) claims that the learners' awareness of the gap between their L2 knowledge and the target language is not necessary for the changes in the learners' knowledge to occur. In other words, that L2 acquisition in the sense of competence development does not require conscious attention focusing.

However, conscious attention is needed for L2 acquisition understood as the development of the metalinguistic knowledge (knowledge about the language). Truscott acknowledges, though, that he is concerned only with the acquisition of grammatical knowledge and that other types of knowledge, e.g. lexical knowledge, may benefit from form-focused conscious attention.

Robinson (1995) tried to reconcile different positions on the concept of noticing as follows:

> Noticing can be identified with what is both detected and then further activated following the allocation of attentional resources from a central executive. Rehearsal following detection would be a consequence of the allocation of resources to fulfil task demands [...]. The nature of rehearsal and elaboration would vary according to whether the task demanded data-driven or conceptually driven processing. (Robinson, 1995: 297)

Data-driven or conceptually driven input processing may be equated with two ways in which input is utilised by the learners to build up their L2 knowledge: implicit learning is equated with data-driven unconscious processes, while explicit learning involves conscious reference to higher-order rules (see Bialystok, 1978). Thus, the answer given by Robinson does not fully clarify the consciousness dilemma: if data-driven processing is unconscious, it is impossible to conceptualise the rehearsal and elaboration stages as involving conscious allocation of attention.

Relevance Theory seems to have a better explanation of variable allocation of attentional resources as varying according to the level of expected relevance of the input. Admittedly, in the Noticing Hypothesis (and in the SLA models) input is understood as raw L2 data, and in Relevance Theory input is viewed as resulting from the decoding process. I will discuss the distinction in the section devoted to the relevance of instructional input to L2 learners in the light of Relevance Theory.

Discussion on the role of attentional resources in L2 acquisition, in particular on the role of the teachers in making learners aware of L2 forms, is especially important in instructed L2 contexts. The L2 teaching profession can draw on the developments in SLA theory only if the theory assigns a place for L2 instruction. If SLA theory does not assign any role to L2 instruction, as is the case in grammar instruction criticism (see Truscott, 1998), L2 teachers find such theory irrelevant and uninteresting (see Niżegorodcew, 1998a).

Carroll's criticism of the input question

What is significant, the role of input in SLA models has been criticised both from a more theoretical, psycholinguistic perspective, and from a more practical, sociolinguistic perspective. Obviously, the critical remarks of the two approaches have been diametrically different.

The most serious psycholinguistic criticism has been formulated by Susan Carroll (1999). She questioned the very nature of input as raw (primary) L2 data by focusing specifically on the nature and role of input in the L2 acquisition. Carroll (1999: 337) claimed that what she called the 'standard analysis of the input question' is not interpretable in the absence of relevant theories of 'mental representation, [...] speech perception and language parsing, [...] and language learning'.

According to Carroll, the accepted views of input in SLA models are pretheoretical, which means that they are not explanatory for L2 learning theory. In her view, we must distinguish between input to processing and input to learning. Carroll claims that it is Universal Grammar (internal grammar systems) that determines what is detected in the incoming speech signals and then transformed into mental representations at various levels of analysis.

Thus, Carroll (1999: 361) equates input to processing with a mental representation which can be interpreted by particular processors, and she claims that attention does not pick out 'some part of the stimulus array and feeds it into the learning mechanisms based on objective properties which make some aspects of the stimulus array "salient". [...] Saliency results from the contents of our cognitive representations'.

On the other hand, in Carroll's view, input to learning is automatically triggered when the parsing processes fail, that is, when particular processors are not able to match mental representations with the incoming stimuli. However, both input to processing at different levels of analysis, as well as input to learning are inaccessible to conscious noticing. In other words, L2 learners cannot consciously notice in the language spoken to them what they know or what they do not know. Consequently, Carroll claims that the role of selective attention-as-noticing and attention-as-awareness, functioning as a filter between L2 input and L2 acquisition has to be rejected or modified.

As can be seen from the above brief overview, Carroll's criticism is based on a psycholinguistic theory which is not concerned with L2 instruction and L2 learners' intentional learning processes. However, her insightful comments on the cognitive interpretation of L2 input in terms of cognitive representations rather than conceptualising input as raw L2 data, to be acquired due to its frequency or saliency in the incoming stimuli, are interesting in the light of Relevance Theory, which also treats input in a different sense than the raw L2 data.

Sociolinguistic and sociocultural approaches to the role of L2 input

The SLA models which assume an important role of input and interaction, have also been criticised from a sociolinguistic perspective. In sociolinguistic view, SLA models should takes into account a wider social context in which L2 learning/acquisition takes place. The sociolinguistic criticism addressing the mainstream psycholinguistic SLA theory and research was first expressly formulated by Firth and Wagner (1997), who postulated that the field should be reconceptualised to include a greater awareness of the contextual and interactional dimensions of language use.

In particular, they criticised the oppositions: between the native speaker (the competent language user) and the non-native speaker (the learner), and between the cognitive, mentalistic perspective of L2 acquisition as an autonomic process versus the social and contextual perspective of L2 use and acquisition through shared negotiation of meanings in interactions. Consequently, they postulated a more holistic approach to the study of language, encompassing a wide spectrum of sociocultural aspects of L2 use.

In turn, a number of SLA theorists and researchers working within psycholinguistic frameworks responded to Firth and Wagner's postulates by criticising their position as a misinterpretation of their approaches and a failure to distinguish between L2 acquisition and L2 use (see Long, 1997; Kasper, 1997; Poulisse, 1997; Gass, 1998).

On more practical side, Tarone (2000) provides some research evidence for the influence of the social context on the role of input in the development of L2 grammatical competence (Swain & Lapkin, 1998; Parks & Maguire, 1999).[8] Tarone (2000) claims that those studies do not only provide evidence for L2 use, but also indicate that the learners and non-native speakers in collaborative tasks helped each other by providing input which was gradually incorporated into their L2 knowledge.

Another line of research refers to social accommodation to interlocutors. While L2 classroom discourse does not make learners sensitive to social constraints, in naturalistic discourse, according to Tarone and Liu (1995), L2 learners may be more sensitive to sociolinguistic constraints in the input they receive.

In Tarone's understanding, input is understood as in SLA psycholinguistic models, as raw L2 data. In Sociocultural Theory, however, input is viewed in a more symbolic way. The theory draws on Vygotsky's (1978,

1986) idea of mediation. From this perspective, language input is a symbolic mediator between the world of objects and individual cognition.

L1 acquisition, as well as L2 learning, is mediated through parent or teacher assistance in building up interactional discourse. The process is called scaffolding and it is claimed to be effective for acquiring a new knowledge, including language knowledge, in what Vygotsky calls the Zone of Proximal Development, in other words, a developmental level the child or the learner can reach assisted by the parent or the teacher.

Among earlier SLA models, Evelyn Hatch's Discourse Theory (Hatch, 1978) draws directly on the idea of scaffolding and building up interactional discourse through vertical structures, in other words, learner utterances 'constructed by borrowing chunks of speech from the preceding discourse' (Ellis, 1985: 155).

The question arises, however, if scaffolding or vertical structures are available for spontaneous L2 use, that is, whether they have been acquired as analysed knowledge (see Bialystok, 1978), or whether they are memorised chunks of language or lexicalised sentence stems[9] (Pawley & Syder, 1983).

In a more radical sociocultural approach, L2 input has been replaced by the concept of affordance. Trying to define affordance in what he calls an ecological perspective, Van Lier writes:

> An affordance is a particular property of the environment that is relevant [...] to an active, perceiving organism in that environment. An affordance affords further action (but does not cause or trigger it). What becomes affordance depends on what the organism does, what it wants, and what is useful for it. [...] The unit of analysis is not the perceived object or linguistic input, but the active learner, or the activity itself. (Van Lier, 2000: 253)

As can be seen from the above brief survey, the sociolinguistic critique of the input/interaction paradigm is not concerned only with L2 acquisition, but with language development through use, and the impact of the environment on the emerging language.

Moreover, the concept of input in Sociocultural Theory has been totally reconceptualized. In such an understanding of input as the activities performed by the learner, including his/her language use, the learner's active role, his/her learning and communication strategies regain prominence in the L2 learning process.

On the other hand, the environmental factors affecting L2 use shift the focus of attention in the input from the focus on meanings and/or form(s) to the focus on language functions in discourse and communication. Such a shift is also interesting from the perspective of Relevance Theory.

I will discuss L2 classroom language functions and the role of L2 teachers in the light of Relevance Theory in the following part of this chapter and in Chapter 5.

The Role of L2 Classroom Input in the Light of Relevance Theory

Relevance Theory: A general theory of human communication and cognition

After having discussed the role of input understood either as raw L2 data, or as a property of the environment, or as an activity performed by the learner, let me turn to its treatment in Relevance Theory.

Relevance according to Sperber and Wilson (1986/1995) is a fundamental assumption concerning human cognition and communication. Searching for relevance in the incoming messages is an inherent feature of human cognition. As a cognitive psychological theory based on the theory of information processing, Relevance Theory follows Grice's theory of human communication: that most human communication is focused on recognition and expression of intentions (Grice, 1975).

According to Sperber and Wilson, input is relevant when it produces enough contextual effect for the least processing effort. In other words, in order to comprehend the speaker's intention expressed in an utterance, the hearer has to arrive at contextual assumptions on the basis of his/her present knowledge, without putting too much effort into the process. Contextual assumptions and contextual effect refer to the hearer's use of his/her knowledge in the context of particular communication, that is, taking into consideration the speaker's identity and the circumstances in which the utterance is produced.

Relevance Theory claims that all human beings automatically aim for the most efficient information processing, that is why the information they pay attention to in the input must be optimally relevant, which means requiring the least processing effort to comprehend.

The theory claims that every act of overt communication (verbal or non-verbal) creates in the receiver the expectation of relevance. The hearers interpret the utterances they have heard according to the rationality principle, which postulates that the first acceptable interpretation of an utterance is the only acceptable interpretation. Thus, every act of overt communication automatically communicates a presumption of its optimal relevance. That is what Sperber and Wilson call the Principle of Relevance.[10]

In view of my intention to conceptualise input within the framework of Relevance Theory, which is a theory of interpretation of incoming messages, input must be considered from a different perspective than in the above outlined SLA theories.

L2 classroom input in my understanding of the term refers to the language intentionally presented to the learners by the teacher (or other learners) in order to facilitate the process of L2 learning.

For example, if the L2 teacher wants to focus the learners' attention on a particular grammatical form in an otherwise communicative activity, the learners' processing effort required to focus simultaneously on accuracy and on fluency is greater than in the case when the teacher disregards formal accuracy, or the messages to be conveyed in the activity.

Thus, there is an inherent danger that the learners wishing to put the least processing effort in order to arrive at contextual assumptions, that is, to follow the teacher's requirements, will either focus only on the grammatical form or on communication.

Contextual assumptions in this case refer to the learners' language knowledge (both in L1 and L2) and their knowledge about the world, including their experience of the teaching/learning goals. If the whole L2 teaching is focused first of all on L2 grammatical accuracy, it is very difficult for L2 teachers to persuade the students that they should suspend their automatic focus on accuracy and put more effort into a double focus – on accuracy and on fluency.

Conversely, if the whole L2 teaching is focused first of all on fluency, it is equally difficult for the L2 teachers to persuade the students that they should suspend their automatic focus on fluency and put more effort into a double purpose – on fluency and on accuracy.

Two layers of intention: Ostensive-inferential communication

The above view of human communication (verbal or non-verbal) differs from the code model of verbal communication, which claims that meanings are encoded by a communicator in a given language, to be decoded as accurately as possible by an audience. In the code model of verbal communication, it is assumed that what has been encoded should be decoded, obviously provided the code is known to the communicators and the channel of communication is open. Sperber and Wilson (1986/1995) postulate that linguistic signals are decoded automatically in the language which is familiar to the speakers and hearers.

Sperber and Wilson (1986/1995) claim that the code model of communication is not sufficient to account for how people communicate their intentions in verbal and non-verbal communication. The information which is interpreted as relevant in the input must first be decoded, but the process of decoding is not sufficient to comprehend the information.

The authors of Relevance Theory express the view that 'there is a gap between the semantic representations of sentences and the thoughts actually communicated by utterances. This gap is filled not by more coding, but by inference' (Sperber & Wilson, 1986/1995: 9).

The inferencing mechanism fills the gap between the semantic representation of the heard utterances and their interpretation by the audience. On the other hand, the audience cannot be absolutely certain that their interpretation is correct.

> If comprehension is defined as a process of identifying the speaker's informative intention, linguistic decoding is not so much a part of the comprehension process as something that precedes the real work of understanding, something that merely provides an input to the main part of the comprehension process. (Sperber & Wilson, 1986/1995: 177)

Sperber and Wilson (1986/1995) distinguish between two layers of intention: the informative intention and the communicative intention. The informative intention refers to our wish to inform an audience of something, and the communicative intention – to our wish to inform the audience of our informative intention. Communication is ostensive from the point of view of the communicator and it is inferential from the point of view of the audience. Ostensive-inferential communication is understood as a largely innate endowment of human species.

I believe that these layers of intention can also be distinguished in the L2 classroom. The informative intention refers to the teachers' wish to inform their students of something, and the communicative intention – to the teachers' wish to inform their audience of their informative intention.

For example, if the teacher provides a recast of a student's erroneous utterance, she does not only provide an accurate target language form(s), but she also communicates to the students her corrective intention.

From the learners' perspective, although something can be noticed without noticing the communicative intention, the failure to notice the communicative intention results in the failure to notice relevant information.

For example, if the students fail to notice the teacher's corrective intention, they will interpret the recast as the teacher's echoing of the learner's utterance. In consequence, they will not focus their attention on their erroneous form(s), and will not have a chance to modify them.

If the code model alone was applied to the above example, in which the teacher recasts students' erroneous forms, the students would not be required to infer any implied intentions, and consequently, they would not be urged by the teacher to correct their inaccurate forms. Obviously, on condition that they listened to the teacher, that is, that the channel of communication was open, and that they understood the L2 forms which were used in the recast. In such a case the students would understand the meaning of the recast but not the teacher's corrective intention.

Optimal relevance

As has been said before, verbal communication is not limited to the decoding of linguistically encoded sentence meanings. In order to accurately interpret the speaker's intended meaning, the hearer must supply the encoded sentence meaning with a set of contextual assumptions governed by the Principle of Relevance, in other words, the main part of the comprehension process entails interpreting an utterance as the most relevant one the speaker could have made in a given context.

Sperber and Wilson do not claim that utterances are always optimally relevant; they only say that the speakers intend their audiences to think that they are. Consequently, 'the presumption of optimal relevance [is] communicated by every act of ostensive communication' (Sperber & Wilson, 1995: 158).

Obviously, sometimes speakers fail to be relevant but from the relevance-theoretic perspective the presumption of optimal relevance is communicated automatically by ostensive-inferential communication. As has been said before, according to Relevance Theory, an optimally relevant utterance produces enough contextual effect for the least processing effort.

In the most recent version of RT, Sperber and Wilson define optimal relevance in the following way:

(a) The ostensive stimulus is relevant enough to be worth the audience's processing effort;
(b) It is the most relevant one compatible with communicator's abilities and preferences. (Wilson & Sperber, 2004: 612)

However, Sperber and Wilson (1995) also claim that the expected processing effort may vary depending on the communicator, the circumstances and the relationship between the communicator and the audience. In other words, although according to the Principle of Relevance, an ostensive stimulus is always perceived as optimally relevant to the hearer, what counts as optimal varies with particular communicators addressing particular hearers in particular circumstances.

Jodłowiec elucidates the comprehension process in Relevance Theory by saying that the context for utterance interpretation must be chosen and that the choice of context is (at least most of the time) the responsibility of the hearer, and it is open to changes, revisions and modifications throughout the communication process (Jodłowiec, 1991: 76).

On this view, and in accordance with Relevance Theory, I can claim that the learners involved in communication in the L2 classroom have to choose a context of existing assumptions which are brought to bear on the interpretation of the teachers' utterances. Obviously, they should first decode them, and then they should use the product of the decoding process as an input to what Sperber and Wilson (1995: 177) call 'the main part of the comprehension process'.

Accordingly, I believe that the specific nature of L2 classroom communication, stemming, as has been said before, from a fundamental conflict between a focus on communication and a focus on the target language as a code, can be interpreted in the light of RT as an automatic process of learners' searching for optimal relevance of the teacher's utterances.

Two obstacles to the automatic interpretation of L2 utterances

I would like to claim that the process of inferring meanings from utterances produced by the teacher in L2 is not as smooth as in the case of utterances produced in L1, because there are two obstacles to the automatic interpretation of the products of the decoding process in the L2 classroom: one obstacle is incomplete knowledge of the code, and the other stems from the irrelevance of the semantic interpretation of utterances.

As far as the first obstacle is concerned, the decoding process in L2 is hampered by the learners' lacking in sufficient linguistic competence to process formal representations of L2 utterances automatically, in order to yield their appropriate meaning.

For example, the teacher says: Where did you go on your holiday? And the learner is not able to automatically decode the past tense grammatical form to interpret the question as referring to the past. Instead, he/she interprets the question as referring to the future, i.e. Where are you going for your holiday? In other words, he/she automatically searches for the first acceptable interpretation of the question.

Since, according to Relevance Theory, the search for relevance is a fundamental feature of human cognition, people tend automatically to perceive incomplete or faulty semantic representations as relevant and interpret them according to the Principle of Relevance. Gozdawa-Gołębiowski (2004: 297) suggests, in line with Relevance Theory, that what communicative L2 classrooms need is 'relevance defocus', in the sense of drawing 'the learners' attention to form and away from meaning'. Otherwise, 'meaning-focused activities [...] may lead to interlanguage fossilization at dangerously low levels' (Gozdawa-Gołębiowski, 2004: 298).

In consequence, L2 learners focused on communication disregard correctness of L2 forms as long as they seem to be successful communicators. They even disregard the code itself and code-switch to another code, that is, their L1. Such language uses have been interpreted in terms of L2 learners' communicative strategic behaviour (see Kellerman *et al.*, 1987; Bialystok, 1990).

Thus, the relevance-theoretic interpretation of reasons why L2 learners do not pay attention to form, focus on meaning, and consequently, are frequently satisfied with incomplete or wrong meanings, can shed new light on the empirical findings concerning the role of negotiated input in L2 comprehension (see first sections of this chapter). Even if momentary comprehension is apparently speeded up by negotiation, it is quite frequently superficial, incomplete and/or faulty (see Faerch & Kasper, 1986; Niżegorodcew, 1991).

Besides, human beings do not only search for relevance, but they also tend to protect their face (see Goffman, 1959, 1967). Non-native speakers frequently pretend that they understand the messages conveyed by nativespeakers in order to save their face and continue in their roles of conversational partners rather than learners. For example, a Polish child said frequently *yes, yes* and nodded his head in order to continue conversations with a native speaker, although he did not understand what the native speaker was saying (Niżegorodcew, 1983).

Conversely, the other obstacle in the L2 decoding process is the relevance of the code itself and irrelevance of its semantic representations. In the light of Relevance Theory I believe that if the code, such as L2, is only partly familiar to the hearers (learners), L2 forms can become the relevant focus of attention to the learners, rather than the meanings conveyed through these forms.

Admittedly, according to Sperber and Wilson, in most cases, an utterance interpretation is based on its meaning. However, sometimes the meaning of the utterance is not the most interesting focus, and its formal properties, for example, structural or phonetic patterns replace the meaning focus. This is the case when we pay less attention to what somebody is saying, but rather to how they are saying it.

> The language learner [...] is interested in new ideas and facts – the content of communication to be learned. But he or she is just as interested in the language signs including their structure, which are used in communication to convey meaning. (Dakowska, 2003: 97)

If a learner is interpreting the teacher's utterance as an exemplification of a grammatical tense rather than a meaningful message, the semantic properties of the utterance become irrelevant. Carroll provides an example of an exchange in a supermarket, where a non-native speaker was grateful to a native speaker for correcting the grammatical form of his question, rather than being furious with him for not supplying him with the required information (Carroll, 1995: 78).

Such behaviour is, obviously, very common in the L2 classroom, where one of the main teacher's roles is to provide corrective feedback. It seems, however, that also in naturalistic circumstances, non-native speakers tend to accept native-speakers' role of correctors of their formal inaccuracy. A sociocultural context of communication can play a crucial role in this respect, both in providing formal corrections and in accepting them as natural, in other words, whether a native speaker has a superior, equal or inferior position in relation to a non-native speaker.

L2 classroom discourse and the level of expected optimal relevance

The approach I propose is based upon Relevance Theory and interactional discourse analysis. The key concept in the following discussion is the level of expected optimal relevance.

Relevance Theory elucidates one of the most difficult problems in SLA theory: whether paying attention to the input necessarily involves conscious processes (see Schmidt, 1990; Truscott, 1998), admittedly, Relevance Theory does not treat input as raw (primary) L2 data but as the product of the hearers' decoding processes to be interpreted according to the intentions of the speakers.

If, according to Relevance Theory, human beings pay attention automatically to the most efficient information, that is, the information that will enable them to arrive at contextual assumptions with the smallest expenditure of energy, the process of paying attention is not a conscious voluntary process. What is conscious (or partly conscious) is the result of paying attention, in other words, the interpretation of the input in the act of comprehension.

Furthermore, if we accept the common psychological view that paying attention is a process of narrowing down the input since the cognitive system is able to process only a fraction of the stimuli which reach it at any given moment, and the role of attention is to filter out some of the information which reaches the cognitive system, we can interpret the well-known phenomenon when some information enters the system and is stored subconsciously, to be retrieved consciously later, when it becomes the focus of attention.

Theories of selective attention claim that information can be retained in a weaker form (Nęcka, 2000). According to Relevance Theory, we can say that such input is not relevant enough at one moment, but provided the audience is ready to put more effort and/or find more contextual assumptions, it can become relevant enough at the next moment.

Sperber and Wilson (1986/1995) give an example taken from non-verbal communication. If a disabled person suddenly waves her arms to indicate something, the very fact that she is able to move her arms is more relevant in the context than the meaning of the gestures. After a while, however, the meaning of the gestures can also be noticed by the spectators. We can say that the spectators retained the weaker input (the meaning of the gestures) until later, while they focused their attention firstly on the stronger input (the very act of waving).

Let us take an example from verbal communication. In the monolingual setting of a L2 classroom, the teacher and the learners could immediately understand an utterance spoken by a messenger in their L1 (stronger input): *Przepraszam, czy X może iść do sekretariatu?* (Excuse me, could X go to the secretary's office, please?).

The teacher and the learner would promptly act on the message. Let us imagine, however, that the messenger spoke L2 English and has chosen to convey the information in English. In such a case, the form of the message would be more relevant to the teacher and to the learners than the meaning, because everyone might wonder why in the L1 setting the message was delivered in L2 in the first place. Their attention would, first of all, be focused on the formal properties of the message. The contextual effects of the utterance might not be strong enough to make the teacher and the learner immediately act upon the message.

Later, however, the retained, weaker semantic representation of the input might produce enough contextual effect to (automatically) appear relevant to the teacher and to the learners, who after a moment of reflection, would act upon the message.

According to the latest developments of SLA theory (FonF approach), L2 classroom input is most useful for acquisition when it is focused on meaning and on form (see first sections of this chapter). I would like to expand this view in the light of Relevance Theory, claiming that focus on form in fluency practice in L2 classroom, in other words, focus on fluency and accuracy, can be interpreted as moving to a higher level of expected optimal relevance.

Relevance theory involves different levels of expected optimal relevance, relative to the processing effort needed to reach contextual effects. Simultaneous focus on accuracy and fluency requires an increased expenditure of energy. We could claim that since the expected level of relevance should always be optimal, if the teacher focuses on accuracy, according to the Principle of Relevance, she communicates to the learners that she intends them to believe that she communicates something that is optimally relevant to them. Consequently, although the teacher may not succeed in being relevant, the learners who believe that the teacher at least tries to be relevant are likely to focus on accuracy.

However, if, in a communicative activity, the teacher does not take care of correctness of forms, she communicates to the learners that communication and fluency are optimally relevant at that time.

Additionally, if the teacher uses L1 in metacommunicative utterances (commenting on the communication or on the L2 code), especially repeating in L1 what has been communicated in L2, she indicates that L1 communication is optimally relevant at that moment, in other words, that the level of expected optimal relevance has been lowered, and, consequently, the learners stop paying attention to L2 metacommunication, which automatically becomes less relevant. L1 utterances indicate their own optimal relevance in metacommunicative functions.

From what has been said above it follows that the role of the teacher's input is crucial indeed. It is the teacher who focuses the learners' attention on fluency or on accuracy, on L2 or on L1 discourse. As a manager of L2 classroom discourse and, in particular, communicative activities, the teacher's input communicates its own optimal relevance in a given function of classroom discourse.

Firstly, and most interestingly, when the teacher combines fluency and accuracy practice, and she makes learners attend to L2 forms while simultaneously focusing on a role-play or discussion topic, she communicates to them moving to a higher level of expected optimal relevance. At such a higher level of expected optimal relevance, the learners are informed that the teacher is not satisfied with incomplete or faulty communication, consequently, that the learners are expected to focus on the L2 code as well.

Secondly, through organisational language and metacommunication in L2, the teacher can also communicate to the learners that she wants them to move to a higher level of expected optimal relevance. Thus, as in the above example with an L2 speaking messenger, she can focus the learners additionally on the code, instead of focusing them only on the message.

Furthermore, Relevance Theory elucidates code-switching in monolingual L2 classroom discourse by interpreting such switches as making it clear to the audience that the communicator (the teacher or another learner) is changing the level of expected optimal relevance. In every switch between L1 and L2, a change of the level of expected optimal relevance is communicated.

As far as L2 acquisition is concerned, although Relevance Theory cannot answer directly the questions asked by SLA theory concerning the usefulness of L2 classroom input for language acquisition, it elucidates the question of input interpretation. The teachers in the L2 classroom discourse shift the learners' attention from forms to meanings, and vice versa, and in monolingual contexts from L1 to L2 and vice versa, and in this way they make particular input more easily interpretable.

In turn, teacher (and peer) input which is easier to interpret is probably more available for processing at different levels of expected optimal relevance than the input that is more opaque.

In Chapter 5 the notion of the above mentioned levels of expected optimal relevance in L2 classroom input will be illustrated with interactional discourse samples derived from a corpus of L2 classroom data recorded in L2 English classrooms in Polish secondary schools.

However, before Relevance Theory applied to interpret L2 classroom input is presented in Chapter 5, the next two chapters (Chapters 2 and 3) will give an overview of two other perspectives on the role of teacher (and peer) input in its traditional sense of raw (primary) L2 data: an L2 teaching perspective and the classroom discourse perspective.

Notes

1. In the noticing-function the learner notices differences between his/her language and the target language, in the hypothesis-testing function he/she applies his/her underlying language rules to language production, and in the metalinguistic function he/she has an opportunity to reflect on the produced language.
2. The Universal Grammar Hypothesis refers to Chomsky's view of a universal mental faculty underlying all natural languages and consisting of a set of general grammatical rules applying to language acquisition (see Cook, 1985).
3. In cognitive approaches, L2 learning is viewed as mental processes, in which learners create representations of the target language in their minds. The cognitive models of L2 learning/acquisition are concerned with how L2 is comprehended and stored in memory, as well as what are the processes and strategies in L2 production (see Dakowska, 2003).
4. Bialystok's (1978) and Bialystok and Sharwood-Smith's (1985) models distinguish between L2 knowledge and control over knowledge. L2 knowledge refers to mental representations of the L2 code, which can be more or less analysed in the minds. L2 learners can have greater or smaller control over the knowledge, which is reflected in their fluency.
5. The term interlanguage (Selinker, 1972) refers to the language of L2 learners. It is claimed that interlanguage is systematic and has some characteristic features, such as e.g. fossilisation, when some non-target-like features permanently stay in interlanguage.
6. The term recast refers to the teacher's corrective repetition of the student's preceding erroneous utterance. Recasts are also very common in child-directed speech, when adults on the basis of the context expand and 'correct' child utterances. In naturalistic discourse between native and non-native speakers

recasts are less common because it is usually considered impolite to correct interlocutors' errors.
7. Alertness is considered to be a 'general readiness to deal with incoming stimuli or data' (Robinson, 1995: 295). Orientation is claimed to be based on expectations of what the stimuli might refer to, and detection is a focus on a specific piece of information.
8. Swain and Lapkin (1998) studied the construction of a story by two learners, and Parks and Maquire (1999) observed how non-native nurses collaborated with their supervisors and co-workers, in consequence producing highly collaborative pieces of writing.
9. The term lexicalised sentence stems (Pawley & Syder, 1983) refers to fixed clauses and sentences, or their parts, memorised as whole language chunks by native and non-native speakers, e.g. It must have been ..., which help them in fluent language production. In the early stages of L2 learning/acquisition non-native speakers rely heavily on memorised language.
10. In the latest version of their theory (Wilson & Sperber, 2004), the authors claim that human cognition tends to be geared to the maximisation of relevance, and they call it the Cognitive Principle of Relevance.

Chapter 2
L2 Teaching Perspective on the Role of Instructional Input

The Changing Status of L2 Teaching Methods

Although L2 acquisition theorists and researchers, both those stressing the role of the innate factors (the Universal Grammar), as well as those believing in the fundamental role of comprehensible input for L2 acquisition, are not directly concerned with L2 teaching issues,[1] a serious debate on the validity of L2 classroom teaching procedures has recently been conducted by theorists and researchers working from the angle of cognitive L2 learning theory (Skehan, 1998; Robinson, 2001).

Although instructed L2 learners receive L2 input structured, presented and practised in different ways through what are still commonly called methods of L2 teaching (see Richards & Rogers, 1986), it seems that the status of L2 teaching methods is changing at present. The radical Communicative Approach, which has been widely adopted in L2 teaching (at least in L2 English teaching) to exclude previous L2 teaching methods (Grammar-Translation, Audio-Lingual or Cognitive Code-Learning Methods) is giving way to a more balanced approach.

L2 teaching practitioners are nowadays advised to draw on a number of methods and techniques that work in particular teaching contexts. Significantly, popular English L2 teaching training course books (see Ur, 1996) do not refer to L2 teaching methods at all but focus on developing L2 knowledge and skills in an eclectic way within a broad communicative framework.

Taking the above reservations into consideration, let me overview the role of instructional input from the L2 teaching perspective, in which the development of L2 communicative competence is the primary goal of L2 teaching. Let us first focus our attention on the communicators and the audience, in other words, on L2 teachers and their secondary school students.

Native and Non-native L2 Teachers

Medgyes (1994) compares native and non-native L2 teachers, first of all in foreign language contexts, and concludes that the best L2 teacher is a native target language speaker teacher with near-native competence in the L1 of his/her learners. However, even if such a situation is theoretically ideal for L2 instruction, in practice the majority of L2 teachers are either native target language speakers without or with only partial competence in the L1 of their learners or, more frequently, non-native target language teachers, sharing their native L1 competence with their L2 learners. Their L2 competence may be varied, from near-native (ideally) to fairly low, depending on the availability of L2 teachers and L2 teaching demand.

Native speaker teachers are obviously more common in second language contexts because of their availability in a given country or region. As far as foreign language contexts are concerned, in particular with reference to L2 English teachers, the demand for English L2 courses in Europe is so great that qualified native speaker teachers are most frequently employed by private educational institutions that can afford it. Some qualified native speaker teachers are, however, employed by state educational institutions if L2 teaching in those institutions is supported by special international projects, in particular aimed at L2 teacher education. For example, in Poland and other post-communist countries in the 1990s, native speaker English, German and French teachers and teacher trainers were employed in state L2 teacher training colleges to help substantially increase the number of L2 English, German and French teachers in state schools after L2 Russian ceased to be the obligatory L2 to be taught in those countries at all school levels (see Fisiak, 1994).

The popular belief that native speaker teachers are somehow *better* than non-native speaker teachers is connected with another popular opinion that second language contexts are *better* for L2 learning than foreign language contexts. A native speaker teacher in a foreign language context is treated as a substitute for the whole second language context in that he/she is an expert in L2 linguistic knowledge and L2 cultural knowledge, and is believed to be somehow able to transfer these two kinds of knowledge to L2 learners. This transfer is believed to occur by provision of accurate L2 input while engaging in classroom communicative activities.

Native speaker teachers, particularly those who do not speak their learners' L1 and whose native culture is very different from their learners' culture, usually experience considerable stress and language/culture shock themselves. Paradoxically, their status of knowledgeable experts may be diminished by their role of L2 teachers within foreign language context schools, which follow deeply ingrained patterns of classroom behaviour (see Duff, 1995).

Non-native speaker teachers in foreign language contexts and their L2 use are a special focus of this book. Although their L2 competence is not always near-native, they have what Medgyes (1994) considers the greatest advantage over native speaker teachers, they share their L1 with L2 learners. Consequently, non-native speaker teachers can more easily focus on L2 form in terms of differences and similarities between L1 and L2. In the case of non-native speaker teachers their focus on form can be very efficient in their use of code-switching to L1 to explain lexical or grammatical problems that are time-consuming to explain in L2. Obviously, classroom L1 use by non-native L2 teachers can also have detrimental effects.

Non-native speaker teachers also usually share L1 cultural patterns with their learners, particularly if the age and social background gap between the teachers and their learners is not very great. In consequence, they may play the role of mediators between L1 and L2 culture (see Kramsch, 1993). In the present tendency to integrate L1 and L2 culture in L2 teaching, the role of non-native teachers as cultural mediators seems to be of paramount importance (see Niżegorodcew, 1998b).

Moreover, non-native speaker teachers can provide ideal role models for their L2 learners as those who have succeeded in the target language learning. They are more aware of the grammatical structure of the target language and are able to teach the underlying grammatical rules explicitly. They are also more aware of L2 learning and communication strategies. Lastly, what seem to be more important for non-native teachers than their target language competence are their teaching skills and personality (Zawadzka, 2004: 117).

Secondary Instructed L2 Learners

Secondary L2 learners have been traditionally considered the most appropriate age and education level group to learn L2s. Such a traditional view has its reflection in school systems, which usually give teenagers a considerable load of L2 instruction. Learning outcomes, however, are varied, depending on a number of environmental and inner factors (see Brown, 1994). In addition, educationalists consider adolescents the most difficult classes to teach on the grounds of their mistrust of authority and disruptive behaviour (see Ur, 1996).

Research in Polish secondary schools indicates that secondary instructed L2 learners in foreign language contexts achieve overall a satisfactory level of L2 fluency and accuracy. Komorowska's (1978) research on successful and unsuccessful secondary L2 learners assumed that successful L2 learning equalled attaining communicative competence, admittedly within the range of the L2 material in a given L2 course. The results of the study carried out on the population of over 300 secondary school English L2 learners in a foreign language context indicated that their grammatical and communicative competence levels were comparable (and relatively high), although the teachers and teaching materials were mostly focused on the development of grammatical competence.

Siek-Piskozub (2002) compared Komorowska's results with the results of another study on the effectiveness of English L2 teaching in secondary schools (Korpaczewska, 2000) carried out 25 years later, when teaching is much more communicatively oriented. The results measured in terms of pronunciation, fluency, lexical knowledge and grammatical accuracy, have been similar in both studies except for pronunciation, where a marked improvement has been found.

Such a state of affairs may seem perplexing for the English language teaching profession considering all the efforts to improve the knowledge of L2 English in Central Europe since 1990. Considering the large increase in numbers of L2 teachers and learners, however, a relatively high level of secondary learners' L2 communicative competence gives credit to the profession for maintaining in general high standards of secondary L2 instruction, notwithstanding changing socio-economical conditions and methodological approaches.

Most instructed L2 classes, whether in second or in foreign language contexts are mixed ability. This rather misleading term has nevertheless been widely accepted by the L2 teaching profession. It not only makes reference to different levels of observed proficiency among learners at the same level of instruction or different levels of L2 learning aptitude, but also refers to a multitude of other factors, which have an impact on L2 learning outcomes. Among the most obvious of those are previous L2 learning opportunities and experiences, attitude to L2 and L2 speakers, sociocultural background, general intelligence and personality (see Niżegorodcew, 1980; Skehan, 1989).

Learner differences are usually disregarded in main theories of L2 learning/acquisition. Such an approach can be justified at the present state of development of L2 learning theory. However, it should be treated as a temporary simplification. Similarly, the L2 teaching profession, particularly in the case of English L2 teaching, are provided with uniform instruction techniques, materials and resources which ignore individual differences among learners. The lack of individual approaches can also be observed in L2 teacher education.[2]

In second language contexts, L2 learners are usually immigrants, who have to struggle for their new identities in the host country. Their L2 classroom confidence and identity is likely to be vulnerable as the classroom is part of a larger society in which they feel insecure (see Hoffman, 1989). In foreign language contexts, more mature L2 learners may also struggle to establish their identities other than those of L2 learners, whose personalities are reduced due to their limited L2 proficiency (see Harder, 1980). On the other hand, secondary school foreign learning contexts may stimulate L2 learners to adopt new, more liberated identities, in which L2 use enables them to express meanings they may be reluctant to express in their L1 (see McMahill in Norton, 1997; Przebinda, 2004).

Whether in second or in foreign language contexts, secondary L2 learners are identified and viewed through the context of their immediate learning environment, that is the L2 classroom. That is why L2 learners' identities can be also described through their participation in L2 classroom discourse patterns (see Breen, 2001; Majer, 2003). Discourse studies focused on L2 learners' participation in L2 classroom interaction reveal, for instance, that some learners are much more active than others (see Allwright, 1980; Niżegorodcew, 1993a; Seliger, 1977) and they can generate more teacher and peer input (see Chapter 3).

The Background of Communicative Language Teaching (CLT)

Communicative Language Teaching (CLT), or the Communicative Approach, has been widely used in European private and state L2 instruction settings for the last thirty years (see Brumfit & Johnson, 1979). Its official status as an approved L2 methodology has been confirmed by the Council of Europe (Komorowska, 2000). It has also gained popularity and official approval in North America and Australia. Other parts of the world, at least those where English is taught as a language of international communication (*lingua franca*), follow in the footsteps of the communicative methodology.

Other L2s for international communication or L2s taught in second or foreign language contexts (especially German, Spanish, Russian and French) have been under considerable influence from L2 English teaching methodology, and, consequently, have adopted to a great extent CLT principles and classroom teaching techniques (see Zawadzka, 2004).

It is significant that CLT did not have solid theoretical underpinnings in any psychological and/or linguistic theory. The Communicative Approach was proposed and introduced into L2 classrooms in the 1970s of the 20th century as an alternative to the previous L2 teaching methods, mainly in opposition to the Audio-Lingual Method, which was clearly based on behaviouristic psychology and structural linguistics.

The Audio-Lingual Method was criticised by the proponents of the Communicative Approach for its limited success in the development of spontaneous L2 use, since L2 taught in the classroom according to very strict prescriptions did not result in the development of L2 communicative competence in naturalistic conditions.

Communicative needs in the uniting Europe, North America and in other parts of the world are such that the ability to communicate has been given priority over an accurate modelling of the target language patterns. New notional and functional syllabuses (Wilkins, 1976) were instrumental in pushing the issue of a new approach to the level of course designs and the preparation of new communicative teaching materials (see Munby, 1978).

It is credible that the crucial paradigm shift in L2 teaching was the shift of focus from teaching a language code, that is, developing learners' knowledge and skills in L2, to communicating with other L2 speakers. One of main theorists of the Communicative Approach, the educationalist Henry Widdowson (1978), claimed that instead of teaching the language code, teachers should develop communicative skills. This postulate had its distinct roots in the sociolinguist Dell Hymes's (1972) idea of communicative competence, embracing Chomskyan notions of language competence and performance.

Its accepted modified version (see Canale, 1983; Canale & Swain, 1980) divided communicative competence into:

(a) grammatical competence
(b) sociolinguistic competence
(c) discourse competence
(d) strategic competence.

In Canale and Swain's (1980) model, communicative competence encompassed knowledge and skills which are substantiated in language use. The model integrated both competence (L2 knowledge) and using knowledge (skills) in an appropriate way in a social context. Thus, the scope of the L2 teacher's responsibilities has been considerably enlarged.

CLT had its heyday in Britain in the late 1970s. Its impact in Britain and North America was considerable throughout the 1980s (see Savignon, 1983). However, even in the 1980s, the first critical opinions were voiced among British educationalists (Swan, 1985a, 1985b). Teaching communication skills was criticised for being inadequate, particularly for more advanced and sophisticated L2 learners, who had already acquired those communicative skills through their L1 and who needed L2 knowledge rather than communication skills.

The situation on the sociopolitical scene in Central and Eastern Europe changed in the early 1990s. Sociopolitical changes brought about immediate dramatic changes in the educational policy of the new democracies (post-communist countries). Instead of the compulsory teaching of Russian to all school learners above the age of 11, Central and East European countries introduced mass teaching of English, and to a lesser extent German and French (see Fisiak, 1994; Komorowska, 1994).

Great educational projects were launched to educate thousands of teachers in the target languages. CLT was the L2 teaching method which seemed particularly appropriate in that context because it was supposed to develop, first and foremost, fluency in L2 use. However, also in those L2 teaching contexts in flux, in spite of the initial enthusiasm, critical remarks have been formulated on the basis of L2 classroom research and practical teaching experience (Niżegorodcew, 1993b; 1995).

Applying one approach to L2 teaching, notwithstanding contexts of L2 instruction, has resulted in many theoretical doubts as to the viability of CLT (O'Neill, 1991), as well as leading to practical modifications, the most prominent being the Task-Based Learning (TBL) Approach (see Long & Crookes, 1991; Nunan, 1989).

Communicative Practice in the L2 Classroom

In contemporary L2 classrooms, the currents of change (Rossner & Bolitho, 1990) brought about by the official adoption of CLT as the approved L2 teaching methodology, and a seepage of ideas from L2 acquisition/learning research of the SLA academic world through L2 teacher training institutions to practical L2 classroom teaching, made classroom oral communication the crucial concern of the teaching profession.

CLT theorists' focus on L2 listening comprehension practice and communicative speaking activities indicates the fundamental role of classroom communication for L2 development, understood similarly to the role of input and interaction for L2 learning/acquisition in SLA theoretical considerations.

According to CLT theorists 'the objective of listening comprehension practice in the classroom is that students should learn to function successfully in real-life listening situations' (Ur, 1996: 105). According to Ur, L2 classroom listening practice should be based on simulated real-life discourse and simulated real-life tasks. In real-life situations most of the language people listen to is informal and spontaneous. People listen to other people with some purpose in mind. They also approximately know what the interlocutors are going to talk about and they realise who their interlocutors are. The interlocutors take the listeners' response into account and they adapt their discourse accordingly.

Consequently, in accordance with the principle of simulated real-life behaviour in the L2 classroom, the learners should be provided with 'genuine improvised, spontaneous speech [...], a listening purpose should be provided by the definition of a pre-set task, which should involve some kind of clear visible or audible response, [...] learners should be encouraged to respond to the information they are looking for as they hear it' (Ur, 1996: 108).

In listening comprehension activities learners are supposed to extract the needed information from what their teachers or their peers say, and either to give short non-verbal responses (e.g. obeying actions, ticking off items) or short verbal responses based on identifying general topics of the listening tasks (skimming) or identifying some specific information (scanning).

Communicative speaking practice is also implemented through classroom activities which are supposed to resemble real-life communication. According to the proponents of early CLT (see Littlewood, 1981), only three conditions were sufficient to ensure classroom communication leading to L2 development:

(a) communicative purpose
(b) information gap
(c) language choice.

However, the above initial strong claims were later modified, on the one hand, under the influence of the theoretical focus-on-meaning and focus-on-form debate (see Long & Robinson, 1998), and on the other, under the influence of L2 classroom research and observation (see Lightbown, 2000).

The Task-Based Approach has brought back specific language focuses to communicative listening and speaking practice (see Skehan, 1998). In typical L2 communicative classrooms learners work in groups or pairs, in which they practise both listening and speaking, being at the same time focused on particular topics or set on particular tasks.

In opposition to topic-based activities, in which groups of learners are asked to talk for a limited period of time on one of the chosen subjects, where language use and participation patterns are loosely controlled, in task-based practice learners are supposed to reach a specific goal and perform something (e.g. find a common solution to a problem, write a report, etc.) in a controlled situation.

Although both task-based and topic-based speaking activities are recommended to be used in communicative L2 classrooms, the task-based format of communicative practice is claimed to be particularly conducive to L2 learning/acquisition (Ur, 1996). The TBL research has accumulated a wealth of data showing correlations between L2 use and some task characteristics (see Skehan, 1998). A framework for the implementation of TBL has been proposed by Willis (1996).

Skehan (1998) presents an extensive discussion on the existing theoretical models of task-based instruction and their practical application in L2 classroom teaching. He also gives a survey of research on various task modifications and their influence on L2 learning outcomes. He is very optimistic in his evaluation of task-based instruction in which 'it has been possible to propose methods of organizing communicatively oriented instruction which balances a concern for form and a concern for meaning' (Skehan, 1998: 152).

From the practical teaching perspective, though, communicative activities are not always very successful. Let me quote what I wrote a decade ago about their weaknesses in a foreign L2 English context:

> EFL [L2 English] learners are usually given more freedom and responsibility than they are able to take. Their FL [L2] proficiency is generally at a low level and they are not accustomed to taking an active part in learning. They are frequently divided into small groups or pairs in which they are supposed to work on a task, before they have been equipped with necessary linguistic and sociolinguistic resources. [...] Some learners are at a loss as to what they are supposed to do/say and give up their parts to more active and/or proficient friends, who assume the role of group leaders [...] and monopolize the floor. Some learners switch to their native language [L1], while others use incorrect and/or inappropriate language. [...] Teachers have been made to believe that learners themselves possess sufficient FL [L2] resources, which can be activated by merely engaging them in communicative activities. (Niżegorodcew, 1995: 276)

Fluency and Accuracy Practice in the L2 Classroom

Let me now turn to those areas of L2 teaching where there is perhaps the greatest tension between what was considered traditionally the focus of L2 instruction, that is, L2 teaching according to a linguistic description (pronunciation, morphosyntactic rules, lexicon) combined with an idealised native-like model of L2 use, and what CLT (even in its weak version) has considered its main focus, that is, L2 development through communication in classroom situations.

The terminology referring to L2 teaching and L2 development reflects a fundamental tension between a language-focused approach and a communication-focused approach. It seems that the distinction could also be described as accuracy versus fluency practice in the L2 classroom.

A definition of accuracy becomes problematic from a sociolinguistic point of view, where there exists the dilemma of which language model should be considered an accurate model. Particularly in the case of L2 English, taught as a language of international communication (*lingua franca*), the debate whose language should be modelled is very fierce (see Phillipson, 1992).

Such a debate turns into a socio-political debate, where L2 teaching is treated as imposing cultural behavioural norms upon local communities (see Canagarajah, 1999). The issue is especially delicate in post-colonial countries with persisting ambivalent attitudes towards the language of the former oppressors. This issue is also relevant in the context of teaching L2 English as a foreign language and as a *lingua franca* in European countries, where more and more people resist a global culture, associated to some extent with the English language.

In L2 classrooms, attempts to completely give up presenting (deductively or inductively) grammatical rules in favour of communicative practice have not been successful (see Newmark, 1966). In other words, it has been discovered that it is impossible to abandon accuracy practice in favour of fluency practice. Consequently, the L2 classroom makes allowances for presentations of model intonation patterns, structures or phrases combined with implicit or explicit teaching of rules. Under the heading *The Necessity for Presentation* Ur writes:

> It would seem fairly obvious that in order for our students to learn something new [...] they need to be first able to perceive and understand it. One of the teacher's jobs is to mediate such new material so that it appears in a form that is most accessible for initial learning. This kind of mediation may be called 'presentation'; the term is applied here not only to the kind of limited and controlled modelling of a target item that we do when we introduce a new word or grammatical structure, but also to the initial encounter with comprehensible input in the form of spoken or written texts, as well as various kinds of explanations, instructions and discussion of new language items and tasks. (Ur, 1996: 11)

As may be observed, the author of the above introduction to the discussion on effective presentation techniques for L2 teacher trainees has been under the influence of the Comprehensible Input model. However, as a teacher trainer she focuses on those aspects of the presentation stage in which it is the teacher's responsibility to draw learners' attention to the material to be learnt, to make sure that they perceive the material accurately, to explain grammatical rules or the meaning of unknown vocabulary items, to illustrate with examples and, if necessary, to repeat explanations. To check understanding of the presentation procedures teachers are advised to elicit feedback from the learners.

From the SLA perspective, the presentation stage of L2 instruction is focused on the accurate noticing and comprehension of the input. Ur calls this stage initial learning. Further pedagogical focus on accuracy is provided during communicative practice through teacher corrections and self-repairs. I focus on them in the next section.

The concept of fluency involves a much greater complexity of issues than accuracy. First of all, in L2 pedagogy fluency is a misleading term. When one describes an L2 learner's performance as fluent, it means that he/she is proficient in native-like L2 use. On the other hand, in the L2 teaching jargon, fluency practice means oral communicative practice, when interlocutors are focused on conveying meanings rather than on formal correctness. The most typical fluency practice techniques include discussions and role-plays. They belong to topic-based activities since their primary aim is to talk on a subject.

Task-based activities also provide some fluency practice (e.g. find out everybody's opinion), although spontaneous generation and expression of ideas characteristic of free communication is more limited by the more controlled nature of tasks.

In trying to define the concept of fluency in more psycholinguistic terms it seems that fluency refers to the extent to which an L2 learner is able to demonstrate his/her control over the knowledge he/she has acquired/learned. I claimed elsewhere that there is no one satisfactory definition of fluency (Niżegorodcew, 1989, 2001) and people involved in fluency assessment (e.g. in oral proficiency exams) apply questionable assessment criteria.

The degree of control over the acquired L2 knowledge (see Bialystok, 1978; Bialystok & Sharwood-Smith, 1985) does not refer to the content of the knowledge. What follows from this consideration is one of possible approaches to fluency: it is 'the ability to fill time with talk' (Fillmore, 1979: 93). Most L2 educationalists and applied linguists would intuitively reject such an extreme limitation of fluency, but the other extreme view does not seem suitable, either, because it is too broad. According to that definition of fluency it is 'the ability to have appropriate things to say in a wide range of contexts' (Fillmore, 1979: 93).

Problematic specifications of fluency assessment are disturbingly common in practical L2 teaching.[3]

Shohamy (1996) claims that models of fluency should be based on models of communicative competence (see Canale, 1983). Other models that are relevant in discussing fluency are models of language production (e.g. Levelt, 1989). They are particularly important as far as execution of planned speech is concerned. In those models, fluency can be conceptualised as the facility of the execution of mental plans. In this sense, fluency encompasses control of the acquired knowledge with broad respect for intended meanings.

In turn, Bachman's model of communicative language ability in communicative language use combines language knowledge with strategic competence. Strategic competence in the positive sense is the ability to compensate for the linguistic deficiencies in the achievement of the communicative goal, that is, conveying the intended meaning (Faerch & Kasper, 1983).

Positive strategic behaviour leads to the achievement of the communicative goal while the negative strategic behaviour means avoiding difficulties or transferring the responsibility to the interlocutor. The use of achievement communication strategies is also correlated with the proficiency level. Learners that are more proficient use more achievement strategies. Other factors correlated with positive strategic behaviour are personality, task type, gender, and learner's L1.

Training in the use of strategy use may result in a higher fluency level, but there are still few studies providing evidence for significant gains using such procedures (see Solarczyk, 2004). My own research indicates that positive strategic behaviour can slightly increase low proficiency L2 learners' communicative competence assessed in a picture description task, but the most significant factor influencing communicative competence of the learners is their linguistic competence, that is, L2 proficiency level (Niżegorodcew, 1991, 1993a).

Finally, one more aspect of fluency should be mentioned. Fluency, that is, the ability to retrieve from memory the learned/acquired knowledge must take the pace of the retrieval process into account. Aptitude research indicates that so-called ideational ability, that is, the ability to quickly retrieve words with specific semantic and syntactic features is positively correlated with L2 learning success (Niżegorodcew, 1980; Skehan, 1989).

As I have tried to show, L2 classroom fluency development is an extremely complex issue since both teacher trainers and teachers are not certain what fluency is, and, consequently, how to assess it. Research in L2 learning/acquisition has not been very helpful in answering these questions.

Feedback and Error Correction in the L2 Classroom

Although the radical CLT approach claimed, in common with the more extreme positions of SLA Input and Interaction models, that fluency practice will suffice to ensure L2 development, L2 teacher trainers admit that L2 teachers may, and sometimes should correct learners' errors. Let me quote Ur:

> The recommendation not to correct a learner during fluent speech is in principle a valid one, but perhaps an over-simplification. There can be places where to refrain from providing an acceptable form where the speaker is obviously uneasy or 'floundering' can actually be demoralizing, and gentle, supportive intervention can help. Conversely, where the emphasis is on getting the language right, we may not always correct: in a grammar example, if the learner has contributed an interesting and personal piece of information that does not happen to use the target form; also, when they have got most of the item right we may prefer not to draw attention to a relatively trivial mistake. (Ur, 1996: 247)

As can be noted in the above remark, the author puts stress on two crucial things present in human communication: cooperation and focus on meaning. What is meant by cooperation in the communicative L2 classroom is a general interactional discourse principle, especially clearly seen in all those exchanges where a more competent person interlocutor is helping a less competent one.

Such a cooperative approach can be seen in the caregiver talk addressing children (Snow & Ferguson, 1977) and foreigner talk addressing non-native speakers (Ferguson, 1971). On the part of all those more competent interlocutors feedback is usually provided as unobtrusive scaffolding (see Chapter 1), also called vertical structures (see Hatch, 1978; Scollon, 1976), whose goal is to facilitate communication in L1 or L2. The focus is entirely on the meanings that the less competent speaker wants to get across. Such facilitative steps are also referred to as repairs in conversation (see Schegloff *et al.*, 1977).

But even in naturalistic interaction, more competent target language users are not always cooperative (it is not a rule as it seems to be assumed in SLA research) and their unobtrusive discourse building cooperation does not always follow Goffman's (1959) face-saving principle not to hurt their less competent interlocutors' feelings.

Gaies's (1977) study on teachers' input to L2 learners indicated that teachers use strategies similar to those observed in caregiver talk and foreigner talk, such as repetitions of questions, expanding and recasting learners' answers (providing corrected forms of learners' interlanguage answers) and prompting the right answers. All these strategies could be described as supportive interventions, obviously if done in a tactful way.

However, not all (perhaps only a minority) of L2 teacher corrective feedback strategies have traditionally been cooperative. Teacher/student cooperation is a relatively new concept in L2 teaching. The traditional L2 teacher's role, particularly emphasised in the Audio-Lingual Approach, involved outright correction of erroneous forms to prevent their fossilisation. It was believed that corrections helped to eradicate erroneous forms. Thus, the face-saving principle did not hold for the classroom discourse, and teachers were expected to explicitly correct errors.

Whether corrections in fact help in eradicating errors is still an open question. On the basis of an extensive L2 classroom research, Havranek and Cesnik claim that:

> Corrective feedback leads to improved performance both for those corrected and their peers, but its success depends on a number of variables which do not operate in isolation and are difficult or impossible to control in a classroom context. These variables concern the type of correction, the type of error and the learner's personal characteristics. Of all the corrections, those elicited successfully from the learners are the most successful. (Havranek & Cesnik, 2001)[4]

Since the CLT approach does not give L2 teachers very clear guidelines, first of all whether to correct learners' errors or to leave them uncorrected, and secondly, how to correct learners' errors, L2 teachers are frequently left to follow their intuitions, personal communicative styles and personal teaching theories (see Musiał, 2004).

L2 learners, also those in the communicative L2 classroom, as has been said, usually expect teachers to correct their errors. Consequently, if a teacher fails to correct an error which is noticed by other learners, they believe that the teacher is negligent or he/she favours the student who has made the error (Zawadzka, 2004). In turn, teachers' refraining from error correction in fluency practice may be responsible for students' negligent performance, a kind of recklessness in speaking (see Witalisz, 2004), where anything goes as long as the learners say something.

Thus, providing corrective feedback seems to be one of those aspects of L2 teaching where the traditional principle of error correction has collided with a communicative principle of refraining from error correction. In consequence, some inexperienced L2 teachers may misinterpret their role in the L2 classroom. I will discuss this problem at length in Chapter 5.

L1 Use in the Monolingual L2 Classroom

Monolingual L2 classrooms, in particular L2 classrooms in foreign language contexts, create special challenges for CLT. The Communicative Approach was first introduced in multilingual L2 classrooms in second language contexts, where L2 instructors were native speakers of the target language who did not know the L1s of their students. Such a sociolinguistic bias has had natural consequences for the rationale of CLT since classroom communication in a multilingual setting is possible only in the common target language.

CLT practice has been introduced into monolingual foreign language contexts without taking into account that both non-native teachers and learners share L1, which is for them the most natural medium of communication. What followed can be described as a whole gamut of classroom interaction patterns involving different proportions of L1 and L2 (both native-like and interlanguage). Classroom interaction patterns including L1 patterns are further discussed in Chapter 3.

Majer (2003) gives an extensive treatment of L1-based teacher talk and L1-based learners' communication strategies. He also quotes Atkinson (1993), who claims that 'too much use of L1 is probably the single biggest danger in any monolingual class' (Majer, 2003: 398).

Excessive use of L1 by non-native L2 teachers, as documented by Majer (2003), is dangerous because it turns a seemingly communicative L2 classroom into a content classroom, in which all authentic classroom communication, that is, talking about L2 learning tasks, administrative and discipline matters, as well as anything else that happens during the lessons and elicits comments on the part of the teacher or the learners, is done in L1. L2 is used exclusively as a subject-matter to be explicitly taught, commented on and assessed.[5] I will discuss this problem at length in Chapter 5.

On the other hand, there are studies of L2 classroom language use in monolingual contexts, where a judicious use of L1 by the L2 teacher and his/her tolerance for a limited L2 use by the learners seems to have positive effects for L2 development (see Eldridge, 1996; Harbord, 1992; Niżegorodcew, 1997), first of all, as a supportive medium of classroom communication and teacher/student rapport, but also as a factor providing in Vygotsky's terms 'the right kind of cognitive support' (Mercer, 1995: 92). Non-native L2 teachers in monolingual settings provide such support if they code-switch to L1 in order to facilitate comprehension of lexical items.

An interesting classroom research study was focused on teaching L2 English vocabulary in two adult student groups, with or without providing L1 translation equivalents of L2 lexical items (Stone, 1999). After a six-month course, both groups did not differ in the listening comprehension scores obtained in the final test. However, the group in which L1 equivalents were provided by the teacher had a more positive attitude toward L2 learning and higher self-evaluation scores in listening comprehension than the group in which only L2 was used. The experiment resulted in the author's rejection of her hypothesis that L1 use in L2 classrooms has a negative effect on learning outcomes. Although the discovered positive outcomes were mostly affective ones, the author concluded that L1 should be used in L2 teaching in monolingual settings.

Notes

1. Both theoretical approaches question the validity of L2 teaching methods indirectly by questioning the inherent value of classroom instruction in L2 acquisition.
2. According to Skehan (1998: 261) 'the teacher is usually equipped to be a pawn within a larger structure, rather than a mediator between materials, syllabuses, and the learners themselves'.
3. The following specifications of L2 English fluency assessment at a high proficiency level have been developed by a representative group of L2 English teacher educators in a foreign language context:

    5 (the highest score) – ability to converse at length with fluency in all situations, both abstract and everyday; hesitation only due to organizing thoughts;
    4 – as above; hesitation occurs occasionally when searching for suitable language;
    3 – ability to converse is not specified; hesitation occurs but does not adversely affect communication;
    2 – general hesitation which obstructs communication;
    1 – unacceptable hesitation even in everyday contexts; speech very disconnected. (Niżegorodcew, 2001: 190)

    Without entering into more detailed criticism, one can easily observe that the above specifications seem to combine both of the questionable definitions, that is, a highly fluent L2 speaker is supposed to talk without hesitation and to make appropriate remarks in a wide range of contexts. Thus, a fluent speaker is equated with a knowledgeable and skilful chatterbox.
4. Similarly, in a study on the effectiveness of elicited self-corrections and teacher error corrections, Czekajewska (1999) found out that about 75% of all corrected L2 learners' errors have been corrected by their teachers and only 25% were elicited self-corrections. Yet, out of those self-corrections, over 90% were remembered after the lessons during which corrections occurred. In the case of teacher corrections, students remembered only over 60% corrected forms (see Chapter 4). The question remains whether remembering corrected forms after lessons (in Czekajewska's study) or after a few days (in Havranek and Cesnik's study) can be considered as L2 learning success.
5. For instance, instead of taking advantage of real communicative situations in the classroom and use L2 to comment on classroom incidents, and elicit L2 comments from their learners, the L2 teachers treat the incidents as breaks in subject-matter teaching, which gives them a chance to indulge in small talk in L1, eliciting the same kind of small talk from the learners (see Majer, 2003).

Chapter 3
L2 Classroom Discourse Perspective on the Role of Instructional Input

L2 Classroom Discourse

L2 classroom discourse has been thoroughly analysed for at least four decades in terms of its structure, its functions and its role in L2 learning/acquisition. A number of authors have tried to systematise L2 classroom discourse according to different research approaches (see Allwright, 1980; Bellack *et al.*, 1966; Fanselow, 1977; Flanders, 1970; Jarvis, 1968; Moskovitz, 1971; Sinclair & Coulthard, 1975).[1]

From the perspective of this book the most interesting approaches to L2 classroom interactional discourse analysis are those that focus on the sociolinguistic and psycholinguistic aspects of the observed phenomena, and those that can have implications for SLA theory. They involve both the structural and functional aspects of classroom discourse. Among the issues analysed in those approaches that seem most relevant for the study of the instructional input are:

(a) Differences between naturalistic and L2 classroom discourse.
(b) Functions of L2 classroom discourse.
(c) Patterns of participation in L2 classroom discourse.
(d) Teacher talk and peer talk in L2 classroom discourse.
(e) L2 classroom discourse modifications.

Below I give a brief overview of these fields.

L2 Naturalistic and Classroom Discourse

Studies on the differences between L2 naturalistic and classroom discourse have been motivated by the existing studies on the naturalistic native speaker (NS)/non-native speaker (NNS) discourse (see Ellis, 1994), and their impact on SLA theory, in particular on the Interaction Hypothesis (Long, 1983).

In order to have a broader perspective on the role of instructional input in L2 development, it seems necessary, to outline fundamental differences between naturalistic and L2 classroom discourse in what is essentially different for these settings: communication in the former, and L2 teaching/learning in the latter. Even if, as in Communicative Language Teaching, L2 classroom activities simulate to some extent naturalistic communication, their primary aim is to teach language. Thus, characteristic features of L2 classroom discourse as opposed to L2 naturalistic discourse can be described as follows:

(a) The L2 teacher is the manager of classroom discourse.
(b) The L2 teacher is the main provider of L2 input, admittedly, assisted by teaching materials.
(c) Communicative intentions of L2 teachers and L2 learners are embedded in a complex framework of institutional, curriculum and task demands.

While managing discourse is not only classroom discourse domain, because more competent participants in naturalistic L2 discourse also frequently try to manage interactional discourse while talking to less competent speakers, managing behaviours in naturalistic discourse are mostly focused on negotiation of meanings in moment-to-moment interaction. On the other hand, L2 teachers manage classroom discourse not only, or even not primarily, to negotiate meanings (see Johnson, 1995; Majer, 2003).

The role of the teacher as the manager of classroom discourse has been extensively analysed from the point of view of such features as: the amount of teacher talk, repetitions, modifications in the use of syntactic patterns, vocabulary and phonological features, rate of speech, pausing, and, in the case of non-native teachers teaching monolingual classes, teachers' use of L1 (see Ellis, 1994; Majer, 2003).

The teacher's managerial role is particularly clearly seen in his/her dominance in the amount of classroom talk and unequal patterns of participation. Teachers have been found to talk much more than students (at least in teacher-fronted classrooms) and to exercise the right to interrupt learner talk by corrections and comments (Ellis, 1994; Majer, 2003). Their managerial role is reflected in the three-phase or four-phase structure of typical classroom discourse: teacher initiates, learner responds, teacher gives feedback and/or evaluation, and optionally learner repeats the correction (see Sinclair & Coulthard, 1975).

These features, though, are not characteristic only of L2 classroom discourse. They can also be observed in content classroom discourse. In fact, communicative classrooms have partly relinquished teachers' dominant position to learners, in particular due to the emphasis CLT puts on group work activities, in which the teacher's role is that of an organiser and monitor. In such contexts, the teachers' managerial role is weakened, which, in turn, may have negative consequences on the learners' interpretation of teachers' behaviour and may result in discipline problems (see Zawadzka, 2004).

Another crucial difference between L2 classroom discourse and naturalistic L2 discourse is the L2 teacher's role as the provider of planned L2 input. Input in naturalistic interaction is generated spontaneously in response to the speakers' communicative needs, while in the L2 classroom it is pre-designed by the syllabus, the authors of the teaching materials, and L2 teachers themselves as they plan their lessons. In fact, inexperienced L2 teachers perceive their role as limited to the accurate implementation of pre-planned activities (see Musiał, 2004). Thus, L2 classroom discourse is much more planned than naturalistic discourse (see Ellis, 1994).

In this respect, communicative activities, at least to some extent, bridge the gap between planned and spontaneously generated discourse/input. However, it should also be added that letting students participate in spontaneous classroom discourse provides inaccurate interlanguage-talk input for other learners, and, in the case of monolingual contexts, L2 input is often limited to the content of teaching, and all real class communication is done in L1 (see Majer, 2003). This issue will be subject of my considerations in Chapter 5.

The third difference between L2 naturalistic discourse and classroom discourse lies in communicative intentions of the speakers. Instead of having real life communicative intentions, as is the case in naturalistic discourse, L2 classroom discourse may have what McTear calls *pseudo-communicative* intentions (McTear, 1975, in Ellis, 1985), when teacher and learners' interaction is focused on communication embedded in the framework of the school, the L2 teaching curriculum and particular L2 learning tasks. Additionally, the peculiarity of L2 classroom discourse lies in its being at the same time the content and the medium of instruction. This aspect of L2 classroom communication will be also further discussed below and in Chapter 5.

Functions of L2 Classroom Discourse

As has been said before, L2 classroom discourse analysts have proposed different frameworks of analysis, which stemmed both from more sociolinguistically oriented conversational analysis (e.g. Sachs *et al.*, 1974) and from more pedagogically oriented interactional analysis (e.g. Allwright, 1980). One of the most influential systems for classroom discourse analysis was proposed by Sinclair and Coulthard (1975), who identified a hierarchical structure of content classroom discourse: lesson/transaction/exchange/move/act.

Such a hierarchical system enables researchers to analyse discourse in terms of its functions which are reflected in its structure. For instance, McTear (1975) claims that the three-phase structure of classroom discourse (initiating/responding/giving feedback) changes into the four-phase structure in L2 classroom discourse (initiating/responding/giving feedback/repeating). This four-phase structure is characteristic of discourse focused on language practice:

T = teacher, S = student
(1) **T:** What do you do every day?   initiating
(2) **S:** I do my homework.   responding
(3) **T:** Yes, you do your homework every day. giving feedback
(4) **S:** I do my homework every day.   repeating

It seems, though, that either three- or four-phase classroom discourse structure may change into the two-phase structure, more common in naturalistic communication when classroom discourse resembles real communication. It happens, e.g. when the teacher asks about something he/she does not know rather than about something they know (see *display-questions*, Long & Sato, 1983) and the only purpose of the question is checking students' knowledge (Niżegorodcew, 1991).

As has been said before, attempts at grasping the multi-layered nature of L2 classroom discourse in its potential for L2 learning/acquisition have been made since the 1970s. Some authors are expressly pessimistic as far as L2 development through classroom discourse is concerned, viewing such discourse as a distorted interaction (Gremmo *et al.*, 1978, in Ellis, 1984). Others, including Ellis, believe that L2 classroom discourse has a hidden potential for L2 learning/acquisition (Ellis, 1984). According to Ellis L2 classroom discourse reflects three goals:

(a) core goals, relating to the explicit purpose of teaching
(b) framework goals, relating to the general organizational management of lessons
(c) social goals, relating to more personal purposes, such as e.g. disciplining or praising particular students. (Ellis, 1984: 101)

According to Ellis, L2 classroom discourse is more similar to naturalistic discourse if it is focused on the framework and social goals. However, the author concedes that it is L1 rather than L2 that may be used in the accomplishment of framework and social goals in foreign language contexts (Ellis, 1984). This issue will be also further discussed in Chapter 5.

Edmondson (1985) outlined different classroom discourse worlds fulfilling different communicative functions in the L2 classroom. His idea of interactional speech acts (Edmondson & House, 1981) draws on Austin's (1962) and Searle's (1969, 1976) Speech Acts Theory. Speech acts at their illocutionary level refer to the speakers' intentions.[2] In interactional discourse, speakers' intentions are subordinated to the general interaction principles appertaining to a particular discourse type.

According to Edmondson (1985), the nature of the global communicative event, involving interactional discourse predetermines the speech acts to be performed in this discourse. Edmondson and House (1981) introduce three classes of interactional speech acts: informative, attitudinal and ritual. Attitudinal speech acts make references to the interlocutor's speech acts, while informative speech acts do not take them into account. In the L2 classroom, it is the teacher who is responsible for performing all attitudinal speech acts (e.g. accepting, apologising, promising), while the learners' role is limited only to informative speech acts, such as stating facts, giving opinions or expressing feelings.

Among other authors who focused on L2 classroom discourse, some notice the hidden potential of L2 classroom interaction for L2 learning/acquisition but they do not amplify on their ideas (see Breen, 1985, 2001; Faerch, 1985; Kramsch, 1985, 1993; Selinker & Douglas, 1985).

An elaboration of the idea that L2 classroom discourse has at least two levels has been proposed by Willis (1992), drawing on Sinclair and Brazil (1982). Willis used the terms inner and outer structure of L2 classroom discourse. The outer structure corresponds to the framework goals in Ellis's taxonomy, and the inner structure to the core goals, that is, the content of L2 teaching. Another broad framework for analysing L2 classroom interaction was proposed by Van Lier (1988). It is based on the teacher's control of the topic and/or of the classroom activity.

Notwithstanding the ongoing debate on the similarities and differences between L2 classroom discourse and naturalistic discourse, and the difficulties in specifying discourse units in those frameworks, what seems crucial in the debate is the role of particular types of interaction for L2 learning/acquisition. In fact, attempting to answer the question about the relative significance of classroom discourse goals, types or levels, we are trying to answer the question about what types of classroom interaction are conducive to L2 learning/acquisition.

It should be added at this point that the socioculturally oriented studies of L2 learning/acquisition and the sociolinguistic criticism of SLA research for ignoring social context (see Chapter 1) have made some SLA theorists and researchers more aware of the context of L2, yet, what is still lacking is common understanding of the basic assumptions about what is involved in L2 classroom discourse. It seems that studying L2 classroom discourse differently structured and allocated in different language functions may provide such a common ground.

Patterns of Participation in L2 Classroom Discourse

Studies on participation patterns in L2 classroom discourse have largely drawn on studies on ritualised conversation patterns in naturalistic communication, including telephone conversations (see Richards & Schmidt, 1983). Sachs *et al.* (1974), the pioneers in the field, treat a turn as the unit of conversational analysis. Two subsequent turns (e.g. in a telephone conversation) constitute an adjacency pair. The first part of an adjacency pair enforces the second part, e.g. if somebody is asked a question, they should reply. If they do not provide any answer, it is treated as a deliberate refusal to participate in the conversation. Sequences of adjacency pairs build up a topic. A conversational topic is nominated by one interlocutor, then it is taken up (ratified) by the other to be elaborated and commented upon by the topic initiator (Richards & Schmidt, 1983).

Such a three-phase structure of topic sequences in conversations resembles a three-phase structure of classroom exchanges, and enables comparison of these two discourse patterns. Studies of L2 classroom discourse patterns have accumulated a wealth of information on how the participants of L2 classroom interaction, that is teachers and learners structure their talk (see Chaudron, 1988; Ellis, 1994; Majer, 2003). The most frequently studied aspects of L2 classroom discourse have been teachers' questions and teachers' corrective feedback (see Kasper, 1985; Long & Sato, 1983), that is, the first and the third move in the three-phase sequence.

The question arises as to whether characteristic question types, e.g. display questions versus referential (real) questions, or various corrective strategies, e.g. explicit corrective feedback versus recasts, are inherently linked with instructional discourse, or whether they are discourse features dependent on the sociolinguistic and methodological context of L2 teaching, the age and maturity of the learners, the teachers' professional preparation, teachers' L1, classroom layout, or methods and techniques of L2 teaching.

It is unquestionable that some of the above variables have a direct bearing on discourse patterns. Display questions are more characteristic of traditional L2 classrooms, whereas referential questions occur more frequently in communicative activities in group work. Explicit corrective strategies are used in teaching adolescents and adults but not children since young learners are not able to grasp metalinguistic explanations (see Moon & Nikolov, 2000). Other variables, though, may influence L2 classroom discourse patterns only indirectly, e.g. some unqualified native speaker teachers are less likely to correct learners' errors, but their refraining from correction may rather be related to their lack of professional qualifications and experience than to their native speaker status.

It seems that participation patterns in the L2 classroom discourse, as in all educational settings, are first and foremost affected by the unequal distribution of power (see Celce-Murcia & Olshtain, 2000; Kramsch, 1993; Larsen-Freeman, 1980; Pica, 1987) and by the roles played by L2 teachers and learners (Zawadzka, 2004). Thus, the participation patterns of classroom discourse are clearly different from conversation patterns.

L2 teachers' authority seems to be naturally linked with their roles as experts and educators in their subject matter, classroom managers, and assessors of their learners' L2 proficiency. Such roles have traditionally been played by teachers. Firstly, teachers nominate students who they want to display their knowledge and skills in language performance. In turn, learners are expected to answer display questions as if they were real questions.

Secondly, teachers are granted unlimited participation rights, they can interrupt learners' turns, comment on them and correct formal errors. In fact, learners expect to be corrected in their use of L2 forms. Also learners are not expected to initiate classroom discourse since it is the teachers' role to nominate topics and to be responsible for the whole structure of the teaching cycles (lessons, courses). Finally, and perhaps most importantly, teachers have powerful tools to discipline learners if they happen not to follow the above unwritten rules of L2 classroom discourse, that is, they have the right (and the duty) to assess learners' performance.

In the last decades of the 20th century, though, these teachers' roles have been supplemented by new responsibilities. Teachers as L2 experts and educators are not only supposed to develop learners' linguistic but also their communicative competence (see Chapter 2). As has been said in Chapter 2, L2 teachers are supposed to assess not only accuracy but also students' fluency.

Additional roles have been imposed upon L2 teachers by CLT, those of adviser and conversational partner, and in the case of teaching L2s as languages for international communication, that of cultural mediator (see Kramsch, 1993; Richards & Nunan, 1990; Zawadzka, 2004). These are frequently incompatible with the traditional ones, and with the teachers' social identities, for instance, teachers face problematic situations concerning how to reconcile assessor and conversational partner roles, or how to develop pragmatic competence in a language that is also foreign for them.

Additionally, the impact of the Comprehensible Input Hypothesis, the Interaction Hypothesis and cognitive approaches to language learning on L2 teacher education, has resulted in increasing doubts regarding nearly all traditional teacher roles. Paradoxically, while radical hypotheses have been weakened by their proponents (see Chapter 1), their backwash effects persist in L2 teacher training institutions and in numerous L2 classrooms, where some teachers sacrifice accuracy for the sake of fluency practice. I will discuss this issue further in Chapter 5.

Learners' participation in L2 classroom discourse used to be severely limited in traditional L2 classrooms. Learners were in the position of inferior participants, who were supposed to answer teachers' questions and display their L2 knowledge and skills when nominated. They were not supposed to initiate classroom exchanges.

On the contrary, during communicative activities and oral tasks learners are stimulated to participate actively in discussions, role-plays and other oral (and written) activities. However, they may be reluctant to exercise these participation rights, particularly when their L2 proficiency is low. In teacher-fronted class activities or interactions with a more competent interlocutor, they have been observed to use avoidance communication strategies or passive repetitions of previous teacher's moves (Niżegorodcew, 1991, 1993a). What can change learners' participation patterns is the type of task in group work, where learners interact with one another, in particular when one of them has the information the others do not possess. On the whole, learners take more initiative and talk more in group work, while some of them, usually more proficient ones, may then play teachers' roles and assume their participation rights (see Majer, 2003).

Consequently, what can be observed in L2 classroom discourse, particularly in L2 English classrooms, as far as patterns of participation are concerned, is a mixture of traditional L2 classroom discourse patterns, such as three- or four-phase discourse structure, display questions and corrective feedback, and naturalistic conversational patterns (see Fryc, 2000; Majer, 2003; Przebinda, 2004). Teachers nominate speakers and initiate exchanges, but frequently they do not provide any corrective feedback and do not acknowledge the answers. They may interrupt communicative activities and correct errors in an unsystematic way. Finally, they seem to assess learners for staying on task rather than for accomplishing the task. Such participation patterns on the part of L2 teachers, as documented in the available data (see Chapters 4 and 5), seem to indicate a transitional state between superficially approved of methodologies and teachers' ingrained beliefs about how they should teach (see Fryc, 2000; Karavas-Doukas, 1996; Musiał, 2004).

L2 Teacher Talk and Peer Talk

Research on characteristic features of L2 teacher talk have been carried out following extensive research on features of foreigner talk (FT) (see Wesche,

1994). Consequently, L2 teacher talk, that is, the language used by teachers while addressing their students, has been compared to the language used by native speakers while addressing non-native speakers (see Ellis, 1994).

The feature which is most characteristic in foreigner talk, as well as in caregiver talk, that is, the language used in addressing young children, is its focus on communication with a less proficient and less experienced language user (see Snow & Ferguson, 1977). Such a focus results in NS simplifications at all language levels: segmental and suprasegmental phonology, morphology, syntax and semantics, in the slower pace of speech, as well as in modifications of discourse structure. Syntactic and semantic simplification may also entail elaboration if, for example, a given vocabulary item is paraphrased (see Wesche, 1994).

Although simplifications and adjustments to NNS level of comprehensibility have been discovered in numerous studies, their amount, range and type vary and depend on NSs' experience in communicating with NNSs, their attitude towards NNSs, and their motivation to engage in successful communicative exchanges (Wesche, 1994).

One of sociocultural SLA theories, Giles's Accommodation Theory (Giles, 1977) taps an important aspect of variability in L2 use. The theory tries to account for the variability of L2 use by the perceived sociocultural distance between the learner's own group (ingroup) and the target language community (outgroup) (see Ellis, 1985). NNSs who are positively predisposed towards the target language community subconsciously follow the target language forms used by their NS interlocutors, while those who wish to mark their own identity and have negative attitudes towards the target language community tend to preserve (fossilise) interlanguage forms. The same pattern of converging to or diverging from the interlocutor's speech can be also perceived in NS input to NNS. NSs who are positively predisposed to NNSs accommodate their speech to ungrammatical NNS interlanguage talk, whereas those with negative attitudes stick to the target language forms, even if they fail to communicate successfully their meanings to NNSs.

Target language communities are not directly available in foreign language contexts, yet the variability of L2 use as an important factor in L2 classroom communication is also characteristic of L2 teacher talk. It is variable in the degree to which teachers focus on form and/or on meaning (see Johnson, 1995). Such a variable focus is connected with the function of L2 teacher talk, which first and foremost, as opposed to FT, is L2 teaching. In consequence, it is supposed not only to provide the learners with grammatical L2 input, to help them understand L2 input, but also, simultaneously, to manage L2 classroom L2 learning (Majer & Majer, 1996, in Majer, 2003).

L2 teachers' talk focused on L2 learning, which is intimately linked with L2 classroom language use, can also be called metatalk (Faerch, 1985). The primary aim of L2 teacher metatalk is to focus the learners' attention on some aspects of L2 phonology, morphology, syntax, or semantics, as specified in a lesson plan, teaching material or occurring in classroom communication, in order to make them salient for the students to learn. In addition, one of the characteristic features of L2 teacher talk is the use of non-verbal support of the meanings that teachers are communicating by means of gestures and visual aids. The use of such teaching aids is part and parcel of L2 teaching pedagogy, in particular L2 teaching which does not refer to translation into L1.

However, in NNS L2 teacher talk in a monolingual foreign language context translation into L1 is a frequent teaching technique. Moreover, in such contexts, teacher talk focused on L2 learning is frequently switched to L1. The reason why NNS L2 teachers talk in L1 about L2 grammar and vocabulary may be justified by the perceived discrepancy between learners' proficiency level and complexity of the language to be explained. The usefulness of L1 commentaries for L2 comprehension (and eventual acquisition) is not yet known. It seems that some types of metatalk, both in L1 and L2, may be more useful than others (see Król, 2004). On the other hand, metatalk commentaries may be inaccurate, complicated and demotivating for the learners (see Majer, 2003). L1 use in the L2 classroom will be further discussed in Chapter 5.

L2 teaching, as has been said above, involves two functions of teacher talk: providing L2 linguistic data (input) in such a way as to make it salient for the students to learn, and, at the same time, managing the teaching/learning process. In the first function L2 teacher talk combines the characteristic features of content classroom teacher talk studied in the classroom discourse analytic approach with some characteristic features of foreigner talk (FT). This particular register was first studied by Henzl (1973, 1979) and Gaies (1977) as a separate register. Later, however, a growing interest in the role of interactional discourse modifications for L2 acquisition (Long, 1983), shifted the research focus from linguistic features of L2 teacher talk to features of L2 interactional discourse, first of all, in naturalistic NS/NNS contexts.

One of the characteristic features of L2 teacher talk as described by Henzl (1973, 1979) is its grammatical well-formedness, as opposed to ungrammatical FT. This finding corresponds with the L2 classroom language teaching focus. Another characteristic feature of L2 teacher talk, according to Gaies (1977) (see Chapter 2), are special teaching strategies used by L2 teachers, such as repeating one's own questions, repeating and expanding learners' answers (recasts), as well as prompting answers. All these strategies could be considered as both facilitative for learners' L2 comprehension and production, and conducive to classroom management.

However, other features of L2 teacher talk discovered in classroom research studies (see Mehan, 1979) seem to be more conducive to classroom management than to L2 learning. As mentioned before, those features involve pausing phenomena: wait time and use of fillers, the amount of teacher-talking time in comparison with student-talking time, rate of speech, use of metatalk, and modifications and simplifications (or elaborations) in the use of syntactic patterns, vocabulary and phonological features. In the case of non-native teachers in monolingual classes, one of the most characteristic features of their talk is the frequent use of L1. Some teachers were observed not to give students enough wait time, to monopolise classroom talking time, to speak, even at higher proficiency levels, at an unnaturally slow rate, to simplify phonetics and prosody, and to use formal hypercorrect language (see Chaudron, 1988; Ellis, 1994; Majer, 2003; Wesche & Ready, 1985).

The latter observations can be also linked to interlanguage features in L2 teacher talk. In teaching L2 English, Majer (2003) distinguishes between TESLese and TEFLese, the former being the language of NS teachers in second language context multilingual classrooms, and the latter the language of NNS teachers in foreign language context monolingual classrooms. Majer claims that some TEFL teachers provide their students with target-like interlanguage rather than L2 (probably due to their own lack of L2 proficiency) but others may subconsciously lower (accommodate) their L2 proficiency level to their low-proficiency students out of solidarity (see Giles's Accommodation Theory). The observed phenomenon refers most importantly to phonological features.

Other interlanguage features in L2 teachers' language involve the use of non-target conversational routines. It seems that if they occur in classroom interaction, they may be due to a subconscious process of accommodation to learners' interlanguage, yet they may also indicate a fossilised stage in the teachers' backsliding from the target language to interlanguage due to classroom communication with low-proficiency interlocutors. There is no doubt that L2 teacher interlanguage talk merits further research.[3]

Peer talk in its own right as a source of L2 input for classroom learners has merited much less interest than teacher talk. Flanigan (1991) analysed tutor talk (peer talk) in the elementary L2 classroom from the point of view of linguistic and interactional modifications. She discovered that while talking to less proficient L2 learners, higher proficiency L2 learners did not simplify their talk either lexically or grammatically although they modified it interactionally.

Similar conclusions were reached by Majer (2003) on the basis of his classroom interaction data. It seems that children and adolescents are not yet able to adjust the level of their language to the proficiency level of their peers. They are, however, able to introduce discourse modifications, such as repetitions and comprehension checks, to help less proficient peers complete their tasks. On the other hand, L2 peer talk interactions in which higher proficiency learners guide their less proficient peers how to complete classroom tasks are rare in monolingual classrooms. What can be observed in such classrooms is immediate switching to L1 whenever misunderstandings occur. This particular issue will be discussed in detail in Chapter 5.

Communicative activities and task-based learning involve letting students talk in small groups or pairs. Thus, peer talk has been accepted as an inherent part of fluency development practice. The question arises of whether large quantities of interlanguage peer talk are a constraining factor in instructed learners' L2 development, in particular those learning in a foreign language context and having very limited access to NS input.

Porter (1983 in Wesche, 1994) claims that NNSs interacting with other NNSs do not make more language errors than while interacting with NSs. According to Wesche (1994), very little is known about the relative significance of interlanguage peer talk input in comparison with native or near-native teacher talk input. Some evidence from Canadian immersion projects indicates that although grammatical and lexical errors seem to be quite persistent, older learners show slow progress towards NS norms.

In a foreign language teaching context, where NS norms are indisputably beyond learners' reach, the possible limitations of peer talk input in terms of its negative effect on target-like L2 development seem to be outweighed by the positive pedagogical effects of pair and group work in terms of better classroom atmosphere. However, as Wesche (1994: 238) writes 'the long-term effects of frequent interlanguage input from such activities [learner-learner interactions], particularly when there is a shared L1, are not known'.

L2 Classroom Discourse Modifications

L2 discourse modifications in NS/NNS interactions in naturalistic situations, due to Long's Interaction Hypothesis (Long, 1983, 1985) have become perhaps the most closely studied research area in input and interaction studies in the last two decades. Hatch's taxonomy of interactional moves (Hatch, 1978) has been elaborated by Long, and later Pica and her colleagues (Wesche, 1994). According to Long, discourse modifications, such as confirmation checks, comprehension checks, clarification requests, expansions, self-repetitions and other-repetitions, occur much more frequently in NS/NNS than in NS/NS interactions.

As has been said in Chapter 1, these modifications according to the original version of the Interaction Hypothesis, were hypothesised to be indirect causal factors for L2 development. However, more recently Long modified the Interaction Hypothesis (Long, 1996), claiming that the discourse modifications could be just one of the factors facilitating L2 development in some of its aspects.

In L2 classroom discourse, not all of the modifications occurring in naturalistic NS/NNS interaction have been observed (Long & Sato, 1983). L2 teachers frequently use comprehension checks, but confirmation checks and clarification requests are much less common. L2 teachers check whether students have understood what the teachers have said but they hardly ever ask for students' confirmation whether their utterances have been understood by the teachers.

Such an imbalance in the use of discourse modifications by the teachers and learners is a reflection of the dominant role of the teacher in classroom interaction. Teachers frequently ask display questions where the answers are well-known to them. Consequently, they do not need any clarification of the answers. On the other hand, learners do not ask for confirmation and clarification of meanings because they do not usually feel responsible for classroom interaction. I have found (Niżegorodcew, 1993a) that low-proficiency L2 learners overuse other-repetitions and appeals for the interlocutor's help. I called them, respectively, passive and active communication strategies.

It seems that L2 classroom discourse modifications *per se* cannot be considered crucial factors in L2 learning/acquisition (see Ellis, 1994). Firstly, because they are limited and distorted in comparison with natural L2 discourse modifications. Secondly, because in monolingual L2 classrooms most of the negotiation work between teachers and learners is carried out in L1. And finally, because clarification requests, repetitions and other L2 discourse modifications, even if they occur in the L2 classroom, refer to the meaning of lexical items. Thus, they may affect lexical learning rather than what is considered the core of L2 acquisition, that is, acquisition of the L2 grammatical system.

Notes

1. However, as Majer (2003) writes:

    Finding common ground for evaluating different approaches to classroom discourse analysis does not seem an easy task. This is because the works [...] pursue diverse goals and draw from various types of research design. Thus, whilst some [...] derive from the linguistic tradition of conversational analysis and ethnomethodology, others predominantly answer practical needs of [...] teacher education and [...] teacher development. Next, beside primarily descriptive works [...] we are also dealing with those that aspire to account for the socio- or psycholinguistic nature of the studied phenomena [...]. Furthermore, there are studies with implications for second language acquisition theory as well as those that focus on language teaching rather than learning. Finally, while certain works can be classified as quantitative, psychometric research studies [...], others rely solely on ethnographic qualitative data analysis. (Majer, 2003: 37)

2. Speech Acts Theory distinguishes between locutionary, illocutionary and perlocutionary acts, referring, respectively, to the meaning, function and result of an utterance.
3. The issue of NNS teacher interlanguage is of fundamental significance for classroom L2 learning/acquisition theory. According to the Input Hypothesis, NNS teacher L2 classroom input is insufficient for the learners to reach the target language norm because it is not roughly tuned, at least not for more than average proficiency-level students. In Universal Grammar terms, such input is not varied enough and, even if it is grammatical, it is not provided in sufficient amounts as to result in the successful restructuring of learners' interlanguage.

Chapter 4
Evidence from L2 Classroom Discourse Research Projects

Jagiellonian University English Department Projects on Teachers' Input in L2 English Classroom Interaction (1984-2004)

Research projects: An outline of two decades of research

I started supervising MA research projects in applied linguistics in the English Department of the Jagiellonian University (Kraków, Poland) in the 1980s. Since then seven projects have explored qualitative and quantitative aspects of L2 English classroom interaction and teacher talk input in Polish secondary school settings. They were the following:

Ewa Kusibab (1984) 'The contribution of classroom interaction to the development of communicative competence'

Anna Kosiarz (1985) 'Teachers' questions at two levels of foreign language proficiency'

Dorota Puchała (1993) 'EFL classroom uses of Polish (L1) and English (L2) by non-native teachers of English'

Agnieszka Czekajewska (1999) 'The effectiveness of spoken error correction in secondary school L2 classes'

Joanna Mazur (2000) 'Bilingual education at the secondary school level in Kraków'

Anna Fryc (2000) 'Using communicative activities in Polish secondary schools'

Anna Przebinda (2004) 'Discussion or role-play? Helping secondary school learners develop their speaking skills'

It should be added that the first two projects (Kusibab, 1984; Kosiarz, 1985) had been completed before the socio-political and educational changes that occurred in Poland after 1989, and the remaining ones while the changes were already in progress. As far as the teaching context of the former projects is concerned, the teachers selected for the research were fully qualified and experienced non-native teachers. L2 English was taught at that time to a limited number of secondary school learners, however, some extended courses, including those selected for the research, involved more contact hours of English per week than other ordinary courses (usually six hours in the extended courses versus three hours in the ordinary ones).

The changes after 1989 involved both a dramatic increase in the number of English language learners and teachers and a growth in popularity of the Communicative Approach (see Fisiak, 1994; Komorowska, 1994). L2 English teaching in the Polish school setting has acquired some characteristic features of formal classroom teaching in a monolingual context combined with some features of the Communicative Approach in second language learning contexts (see Chapter 2). When the projects were commenced (in the 1980s) my general aim in guiding MA student authors to undertake their research was to explore the potential of the L2 classroom input and interaction in a monolingual context for the development of communicative competence in L2 English. Later (in the 1990s and continuing to the present time), we have tried to discover those characteristic features of a monolingual L2 classroom context that constitute its strengths as well as weaknesses.

Before, the L2 classroom input and interaction data are reinterpreted in Chapter 5 in the light of relevance theory as having different levels of expected optimal relevance, I present the aims of the student authors, their research methodology and subjects, as well as the main findings of the research projects.

Aims

The first research project combining L2 classroom interactional discourse with the assessment of communicative competence of secondary school learners of L2 English was carried out by Kusibab (1984). The author wrote:

> The aim of the empirical part of this dissertation is to answer the question if the class under observation was being prepared to real communication in English and what kinds of the teacher–learner interaction were involved in foreign language teaching. (Kusibab, 1984: 36)

In the following year, in another case study project, Kosiarz (1985) tried to discover patterns of communicative (with an information gap) and non-communicative (without an information gap) teacher questions in L2 English classrooms at two levels of L2 proficiency. Kosiarz hypothesised, based on Long and Sato's (1983) research, that at a lower level of L2 proficiency teachers would ask more questions that were non-communicative.

As has been said before, in the 1990s, MA research projects concerning teachers' input in L2 English classroom interaction focused on the exploration of various aspects of L2 English teachers' language in classroom discourse, such as the use of L1 by L2 teachers, teachers' correcting moves, characteristic features of L2 subject-matter teaching, and the use of communicative activities.

Thus, Puchała's (1993) research question concerned non-native L2 teachers' use of L1 in L2 teaching. She assumed that they would be using more Polish (L1) than English (L2) in grammar lessons, and more English (L2) than Polish (L1) in non-grammar lessons. She adopted Ellis's taxonomy of classroom goals into core, framework and social goals (Ellis, 1984), and she analysed the language used by four teachers in grammar and non-grammar lessons.

Czekajewska's (1999) project was concerned with L2 teacher correction of learners' spoken errors. Drawing on Slimani's (1987) PhD dissertation, Czekajewska (1999) put forward the following hypotheses:

(1) Learners remember the correct forms better if the forms were elicited from them than in the cases when the correct forms were provided by the teacher.
(2) When the focus of the activity is on form, learners remember the correct forms better than in meaning-oriented activities.
(3) Learners' remembering of the correct forms provided by the teacher is better if they repeat the correct form after the teacher provides it. (Czekajewska, 1999: 38)

An exploratory study by Mazur (2000) investigated partial bilingual content-based instruction in two secondary schools in Kraków (Poland). The researcher was interested in the relationship between subject-matter instruction and L2 (English) teaching, and classroom use of L1 (Polish) and L2 (English) in content-based instruction.

Two other MA projects focused on exploring how communicative language teaching was implemented in L2 English classroom activities a decade after its introduction into L2 teacher training in Poland. Fryc (2000) compared non-native English teachers' attitudes towards the Communicative Approach with the implementation of its principles in L2 classroom communicative activities. She hypothesised that the teachers did not implement communicative principles in their teaching practice.

In the most recent project, Przebinda (2004) hypothesised that role-plays were more conducive than discussions to the development of L2 students' speaking skills. Specifically, she claimed that during role-plays students spoke more and used less L1 than during discussions.

Methodology and research subjects

The described MA research projects were integral parts of the MA theses written by their authors. The students had limited access to L2 classrooms and no financial and organisational support that would enable them to conduct larger projects in language learning and teaching. Therefore, all the projects under consideration were case studies. The authors tried to find evidence for their hypotheses either by multiplying the number of teachers and classrooms participating in the research or by observing a selected teacher and an L2 classroom for a longer period of time. Examples of the former approach are Fryc (2000), who observed communicative activities implemented by twenty teachers in 20 different classrooms, and Kosiarz (1985), who analysed questions asked by four teachers in eight classrooms (32 lessons in total), whereas the latter was effected by Kusibab (1984), who observed classroom discourse during 30 lessons, taught by one teacher, and Przebinda (2004), who carried out her observations in five classrooms, in each of them during six communicative activities, half of them being role-plays and the other half discussions.

The most common research methodology in the described projects was focused or semi-focused classroom observation. The identified classroom discourse samples were analysed and interpreted in the light of the project hypotheses. The observation systems used in the projects were based on the COLT scheme (Allen et al., 1984) and other observation schemes designed for teachers (Wajnryb, 1992) (Fryc), as well as on observing whole discourse units (lessons or activities), and analysing instances of language use relevant for the projects (interactional patterns: Kusibab; teachers' questions: Kosiarz; teachers' L1 use: Puchała; teachers' corrections: Czekajewska; L2/L1 use and input modifications in content classrooms: Mazur; L1 use, pausing and willingness to talk during role plays and discussions: Przebinda).

The analysis of the above features of L2 classroom discourse was either purely qualitative (Kusibab, Mazur) or qualitative and quantitative (Kosiarz, Puchała, Czekajewska, Fryc, Przebinda). In the quantitative analysis, the authors used descriptive statistical techniques. The most important findings of the described research studies are presented below.

Findings

General findings

Each of the above authors carried out her research individually. In the following survey of their research findings, however, I present them as a body of research with common aims, research subjects and methodologies, set in a common L2 teaching/learning context. I believe I am justified in doing so because I was responsible for choosing the fields and methodologies of my MA students' research, and guiding them in their research focuses, as well as monitoring their progress throughout the research stages towards the completion of their MA theses.

What is particularly interesting from our present perspective are MA students' attempts to assess monolingual learners' L2 communicative competence as a classroom process rather than as a global product of teaching and learning. Consequently, the student researchers did not try to test learners' L2 proficiency in large cross-sectional research designs, but they focused on individual classrooms and teachers in their daily interactions, mostly in longitudinal case studies.

When the first author (Kusibab) conducted her research in 1984, the development of communicative competence in the L2 English classroom had already been advocated in Poland on theoretical grounds (Komorowska, 1978), but the focus on the development of linguistic competence was so predominant that Kusibab did not expect any real L2 communication to take place in a classroom setting. What she discovered, however, was contrary to her expectations: the observed teacher was able to use nearly exclusively L2, and she managed to engage her learners in real communication. A detailed description of Kusibab's findings is given below.

After the socio-political and educational changes of 1989/1990, a dramatic quantitative increase in L2 English teaching and learning (see Chapter 2) became a challenge for L2 classroom research. What was needed were the 'state of affairs' studies, in particular those in which the approved communicative L2 teaching principles could be confronted with the observed classroom practice. Among the MA project authors, Fryc carried out the widest observational research on communicative activities in the monolingual setting. She discovered that communicative activities have taken roots in Polish secondary L2 classrooms, but she also found that both teachers and learners were first of all focused on performing what they considered to be communicative tasks rather than on real communication. A detailed description of Fryc's findings is given below.

Other MA studies explored specific features of monolingual L2 classroom discourse. Their authors discovered a number of non-communicative features, such as teachers' asking display questions (Kosiarz), teachers' code-switching to L1 (Puchała), teachers' corrections (Czekajewska) and subordination of L2 practice to subject-matter teaching (Mazur).

In the most recent project (Przebinda, 2004), the author, herself a graduate of a teachers' college and a classroom teacher, has demonstrated a high level of determination to make classroom communicative practice resemble real communication. She has found that role-plays are better communicative activities than general discussions.

Classroom interaction and the development of communicative competence (Kusibab, 1984)

As has been said above, Kusibab did not expect her subjects (a non-native teacher of English and her secondary school learners) to engage in real classroom communication in L2. However, to her surprise, she found out that such communication did take place. In real communicative exchanges about current classroom matters, the teacher made her students speak L2.

Excerpts 1–7 come from Kusibab (1984):

(1) T (addressing students who are late for class): Isn't it too late?
    S: My byliśmy na obiedzie. /We have had our lunch/.
    T: In English, please.
    S: We are late because of dinner.

(*Dinner* and *lunch* are often confused by Polish students). (Kusibab, 1984: 60)

(2) T: Malgosia, next exercise, please.
    S: Ja nie mam. /I haven't got it/.
    T: In English, please.
    S: I have only exercise C. I haven't other exercises. (Kusibab, 1984: 60)

The teacher used classroom routines to elicit real communication in L2, and, consequently, in the majority of cases the learners communicated with the teacher in L2. In the following exchange, the students were supposed to prepare homework assignments based on the books they read:

(3) S (excuses herself): I've just started to read it so I can't tell anything else about it.
    T: But it's not the only book you've read in all your life.
    S: No, but I wanted to tell about the book I am just reading.
    T: Yes, but it's too little. What can you add?
    S: I'm reading this book very fast.
    T: So you enjoy it, don't you?
    S: Yes. If I like a book, I read it very fast. (Kusibab, 1984: 61)

If the students started classroom communication in L1, the teacher nearly always answered in L2:

(4) S: A co tam pisze? /What is written over there?/.
    T: If you cannot see, you can change the place. (Kusibab, 1984: 44)

The most characteristic feature of the classroom interactions was their focus on the tasks. The tasks involved grammar and vocabulary practice or oral presentations based on home readings.

(5) (In the following excerpt the teacher asked for some examples of conditional clauses).
S: If she had eaten the mushrooms, she would have been ill.
T: Does it mean that she has eaten the mushrooms or she hasn't?
S: She hasn't.
T: Yes, of course. (Kusibab, 1984: 42)

(6) (In the following exchange the learner asked for a vocabulary item she could not remember).
S: What 'tyre' is?
T: Oh, it's nothing new for you. You have already had this word. You must have remembered it. (Kusibab, 1984: 53)

(7) (The teacher asked the student to comment on another student's presentation).
T: Do you like Bogdan's monologue, Iwona?
L: Yes, I do.
T: Why?
L: It was long. He didn't make mistakes. It was very interesting. (Kusibab, 1984: 56)

Classroom interaction samples collected by Kusibab provided her with evidence that real communication took place in the observed classroom. Although it was limited to classroom matters and language learning tasks, and most frequently initiated by the teacher, it referred to various areas of the students' lives and their interests. The teacher asked real questions and seemed to be genuinely interested in the answers. The students were given ample opportunities to express their opinions. The teacher did not monopolise the floor. Kusibab also observed the teacher's attitude towards errors. The teacher did not interrupt learners' presentations to correct language errors, but she pointed them out afterwards.

Consequently, Kusibab concluded that communicative competence was developed in the observed classroom through elements of real communicative exchanges. It was possible to develop communicative competence in that particular group, according to Kusibab, due to the high level of students' motivation to learn L2. They studied regularly at home and they took active part in class activities. Moreover, the group was not very numerous (19 students) and they had six 45-minute classes of L2 per week.

Among the limitations of the observed techniques used to develop communicative competence, Kusibab noted that the teacher did not differentiate learners' roles by introducing role-play activities, neither did she pay much attention to L2 social formulas and degrees of formality in the target language.

Teachers' questions (Kosiarz, 1985)

A further attempt at assessing communicative L2 teaching at the secondary school level carried out in the 1980s by Kosiarz (1985) was interpreted by the author as disconfirming her hypothesis that L2 English teachers asked more questions with an information gap at a higher level of L2 proficiency than at a lower level. The number of display questions (without an information gap), which the author called non-communicative questions, and those with an information gap was approximately equal at lower and higher levels of proficiency (out of 728 questions collected and analysed in the data). On the basis of the quantitative analysis of her data, Kosiarz drew the conclusion that the observed four teachers were focused on the development of linguistic competence rather than communicative competence.

Another non-communicative aspect of the analysed questions was their primary function of checking students' knowledge and/or practising L2 skills, which was reflected in the structure of interaction. The observed classroom discourse provided numerous examples of teachers' display questions followed by students' answers, and teachers' assessing comments, frequently expanding students' answers.

The following excerpts of classroom discourse come from Kosiarz (1985):

(8) T: Is there a lift in the building where you learn?
    S: No.
    T: No, there is no lift in our school. (Kosiarz, 1985: 84)

(9) T: What does a stunt man do?
    S: He does dangerous things.
    T: Yes, he does dangerous things for other people. (Kosiarz, 1985: 79)

(10) T: How would you paraphrase 'the devoted family man'?
     S: A man loving his family.
     T: Yes, a family loving man. (Kosiarz, 1985: 80)

(11) T: What is the point of reference of this sentence? Past, present or future?
     S: Past.
     T: Yes, this sentence refers to the past. (Kosiarz, 1985: 81)

However, such a structure was not the rule. In the case of the questions with an information gap, instead of evaluating the answer the teachers asked other communicative questions.

(12) T: Is there a lift in your house?
     S: Yes.

T: On which floor do you live?
S: I live on the third floor.
T: Do you prefer to use the lift or walk up the stairs?
S: I prefer using the lift. (Kosiarz, 1985: 84)

(13) T: Susan, what have you never done?
S: I have never spoken to Ronald Reagan.
T: Do you hope to speak to him one day?
S: Yes, I do. (Kosiarz, 1985: 77)

Although the provided data does not include many instances of the above communicative sequences, the average number of communicative questions per class, amounting to 44.1% at the lower level, and to 48.65% at the higher level, indicates that the observed teachers involved their students in real communication, admittedly, subordinated to language practice and strictly controlled by the teachers. There were also some differences in teachers' questions at the lower and higher level of proficiency: repeated questions at the lower (examples 14 and 15) and probing questions at the higher level (examples 16 and 17).

(14) T: Can you dance well? Can you dance well?
S: No, I dance very badly.
T: So you are a rotten dancer, aren't you? (Kosiarz, 1985: 73)

(15) T: Is he witty? Czy jest dowcipny? /Is he witty? /Is he witty?
S: Yes, he is.
T: Yes, he is. (Kosiarz, 1985: 72)

In (15) the teacher provides an L1 translation equivalent of the L2 question and repeats the question once again. As has been discovered by discourse researchers (see Chapter 3), repeated (and translated) questions are common in caregiver speech to young children and in foreigner and teacher talk. They are claimed to help less proficient speakers in L2 comprehension. However, it should be remembered that the questioning techniques in L2 teaching do not aim exclusively at making questions comprehensible. They primarily focus on the elicitation of accurate answers.

Probing questions are communicative open questions, which let L2 learners provide extended answers. Kosiarz (1985) observed such questions only in more proficient classes.

(16) T: How did you spend your winter holidays? Barbara.
S: I was in Koninki.
T: Can you say something more about your holidays?

S: I was skiing there, playing cards, reading books and doing other things.
T: (accepts the answer in a non-verbal way). (Kosiarz, 1985: 83)

Interestingly, the teacher in (16) does not correct interlanguage verb forms used by the learner.

(17) T: What are some reasons for travelling?
S: People want to see the world, to meet friends, sometimes on business.
T: That's right. (Kosiarz, 1985: 80)

Kosiarz (1985) concludes her research study saying that the observed teachers' questions differed considerably from questions asked in naturalistic communicative exchanges, firstly, because a large proportion of them were non-communicative (without the information gap), secondly, due to the occurrence of teachers' assessing comments, and finally, because of the teachers' dominance in classroom interaction. The observed students were very passive and they initiated only very few exchanges. The researcher recommends group work, pair work and role play as useful techniques that could make students more active in class (see Fryc, 2000; Przebinda, 2004).

Teachers' use of L1 Polish in L2 English classrooms (Puchała, 1993)

L1 use in L2 class seems to be one of the most conspicuous phenomena distinguishing monolingual L2 classrooms from multilingual ones (see Niżegorodcew, 1997). One of the first MA classroom research projects completed in the 1990s (Puchała, 1993) tried to explore the existing state of affairs in non-native teachers' L1 use in L2 classrooms. Such a research focus was also partly due to the impact of communication strategies research, including my own research on communication strategies in L2 classroom discourse at a low level of proficiency (Niżegorodcew, 1991, 1993a).

As has been said before, Puchała observed all instances of L1 (Polish) use in L2 (English) classrooms during eight lessons of English conducted by four experienced teachers of English at an intermediate level of proficiency (in the third grade of the secondary school). The researcher observed each of the teachers during one lesson focused on a grammar point (a grammar lesson) and during the other lesson focused on developing language skills (a non-grammar lesson). Puchała recorded the lessons and transcribed the recordings (360 minutes of recorded material).

The quantitative analysis focused on the percentage of L1, L2 and mixed (L1 and L2) turns in the teacher talk, as well as the percentage of total time taken by these turns. The research hypothesis that the observed teachers would use relatively more L1 than L2 during grammar lessons was confirmed. On the whole, there were approximately 90% of teacher L2 turns in non-grammar lessons, corresponding to approximately 90% of teacher talking time, and approximately 58% of L2 turns in grammar lessons, corresponding to approximately 26% of teacher talking time.

On the other hand, the researcher recorded approximately 4% of teacher L1 turns and 6% of mixed turns in non-grammar lessons, corresponding, respectively, to approximately 3% and 7% of teacher talking time, and approximately 22% of teacher L1 turns and 20% of mixed turns in grammar lessons, corresponding, respectively, to approximately 52% and 22% of teacher talking time.

The interpretation provided by Puchała for the discrepancy between the number of L2 and L1 turns, and the time taken by those turns in grammar lessons is highly speculative but of some interest for this book perspective. The author suggests that once L1 was used by the teachers in grammar lessons for the explicit teaching of L2 grammar, they entered into the L1 mode and seemed to be unable to switch to L2, even after they stopped explaining grammatical rules. I will discuss this interpretation in Chapter 5.

Another difference between grammar lessons and non-grammar lessons as far as the total teacher talking time is concerned, is the teachers' dominance in the classroom discourse in grammar lessons (over 50% of class time), in comparison with about one third of class time taken up by the teachers in non-grammar lessons. On the other hand, there were considerable individual differences between the four teachers in their use of L1, L2 and mixed turns, particularly in grammar lessons.

The qualitative analysis of the classroom discourse data aimed at distinguishing patterns of L1 and L2 use in different language functions. The main categories were based on Ellis's division of classroom discourse goals into core, framework and social goals. Puchała also tried to subdivide those categories into different language functions (see Allwright, 1988), such as, modelling, correcting, eliciting student self-correction, etc. (core goal); giving instructions to elicit desired actions, introduction of new topics and activities (framework goal), and disciplining, management and small talk (social goal). Over 100 samples of classroom L1, L2 and mixed exchanges exemplify those language functions. One of the conclusions that can be drawn from examining them is that clear-cut patterns of teachers' use of L1 and L2 are difficult to find in the data. The author speculated that the subjects were not even aware of their use of L1 in many instances, and she suggested further research on teachers' awareness of their L1 use.

The following excerpts come from Puchała (1993).

Grammar lessons

At the moment when the teacher starts explaining L2 grammar, he switches to L1:

(18) T: Some kind of competition is going to be organized [...]. All right. Grammar, grammar! Proszę państwa, chcę wrócić do tego ostatniego zdania, które nam zrobiło problemy. /Ladies and gentlemen, I would like to come back to the last sentence that was a problem for us/. (Puchała, 1993: 31)

It is interesting to note that the teacher uses the phrase 'ladies and gentlemen' to address school learners. Since this addressing phrase is used many times in the data of that particular teacher, it seems to be his idiosyncrasy.

The teacher translates her request into L1 and insists on an answer in L1:

(19) T: Now tell me why we use this tense in this first exercise. Proszę mi powiedzieć, dlaczego używamy tego czasu w pierwszym ćwiczeniu. Proszę po polsku. /Tell me, please, why we use this tense in the first exercise. Please, tell me in Polish/. (Puchała, 1993: 31)

Another interesting feature of providing translation equivalents of one's requests is a different level of formality and politeness. While speaking in L1, the teacher is polite and rather formal *proszę mi powiedzieć* /could you please tell me/, whereas in L2 the teacher sounds very direct and rather impolite.

The teacher corrects errors:

(20) S: We have been in theatre ten times in this year.
T: Bez 'in'. Mówiłam, że przyimki czasu nie dotyczą jakich słówek? Proszę powtórzyć. /Without 'in'. Haven't I told you that prepositions referring to time are not used with which words? Repeat, please/. (Puchala, 1993: 37)

It should be noted that only one error has been corrected (and possibly noticed) by the teacher, and that the teacher's awkward question structure seems to result from her sudden decision not to provide the answer, but to make the learners revise grammar by themselves.

The teacher comments on the form of the students' utterances:

(21) S: Did you see the ...
T: O, dobrze. /Oh, good/.
S: Did you see the film?
T: Yeah. Did you see this film yesterday? (Puchała, 1993: 48)

The teacher's interrupting praise comes even before the learner was able to finish her utterance. Obviously, the teacher was utterly preoccupied with the form and not with the meaning.

The teacher explains L2 forms:

(22) T: [...] 'In' albo 'at'. 'Come to' but 'arrive in' or 'at'. Kiedy 'in'? Kiedy myślimy o mieście całym: 'to arrive in Cracow'. A jeżeli mówimy 'to arrive at' to mówimy o punkcie w mieście. Na przykład: 'to arrive at the station, at the airport' [...]. / 'In' or 'at. 'Come to' but 'arrive in' or 'at'. When 'in'? When we think of a whole town: 'to arrive in Cracow'. And when we say, 'to arrive at' we talk about a place in the town. For example 'to arrive at the station', 'at the airport'/.

It seems that the teacher moves to the L1 mode of speaking gradually. First, she uses L2 words in her comment (*but* and *or*), later she code-switches to L1 completely.

Non-grammar lessons
The teacher corrects errors:

(23) S: She normally gets up at about seven o'clock but that day she can stay in bed for another half an hour.
T: Are you talking about a particular day?
S: Yes.
T: Yes. So you must say 'on that day she could'. Right? 'She could stay in bed'. (Puchała, 1993: 36)

It is more common for the teachers in non-grammar lessons, even if they focus on L2 forms, as in (23), to use L2 in their comments.

The teacher elicits student self-corrections:

(24) S: I should have written 'War and Peace'.
T: Written 'War and Peace'? Are you Leo Tolstoy?
S: Sorry, read. (Puchała, 1993: 38)

Yet, even in the non-grammar lessons the teachers code-switch to L1:

(25) S: Father one of the children.
T: English, please. Ojciec jednego dziecka ... /The father of one child/.
S: Father of one child said ... (Puchała, 1993: 39)

The first remark seems to mean *say it in correct English*, but the immediate code-switching to L1 and providing a translation equivalent of the required

L2 phrase may indicate the teacher's impatience and irritation. Probably, as noted by Puchała, the teacher's translation into L1 did not help the learner.

The teacher comments on a passage in the teaching material:

(26) S: The food they were eating was bad. They didn't like it.
      T: They didn't like it, yes, the girls. But did the nuns complain?
      S: No, they didn't. They just were used to this.
      T: Yes. For them it was 'nothing short of doom'. All right now. The girls made some suppositions. You know, they were trying to imagine Imelda's past. Right? Her four years in Dublin. What did they imagine? Do you remember? What could have happened? What kind of life she had? Katarzyna? What did they imagine? (Puchala, 1993: 51)

The teacher tries to elicit an account of the story from the learners. She asks many questions, not leaving any time for the learners to answer them. Apparently, her questions serve as a lead-in to an account the teacher expects to hear from the nominated learner. The language of the exchange is L2, which as Puchała notes, is used in the classroom discourse during the whole lesson.

Talking about organisational matters, disciplining the learners and chatting with them were, according to Puchała, the language functions most frequently rendered in L2. Yet, the data present many instances of L1 use in the same functions. As the researcher states, it is difficult to find an underlying pattern of L2 or L1 use.

(27) T: All right now. You have the text and I'm going to read it. If there are any words you don't understand, underline them.
      S: Can we take them with us?
      T: Yes, yes. O.K. You can take the copies ... (Puchala, 1993: 56)

(28) T: Could you distribute these pages – one per desk. Now open your copy books on our last lesson. Proszę otworzyć zeszyty na naszej ostatniej lekcji. Nie ma wystarczającej ilości? /Please, open your copy books at our previous lesson. Aren't there enough copies?/. (Puchala, 1993: 59)

The researcher does not see any explanation for the above sudden code-switch to L1 and providing a translation equivalent of a comprehensible L2 utterance. Elsewhere she claims that the teachers may have translated into L1 to make their instructions as clear as possible.

The teacher comments on the learners' suggestion to talk about a funeral:

(29) T: This obsession with death you ladies cherish is going to kill me one day. Proszę coś zaśpiewać natychmiast. Dość mam śmierci. /Please, sing something immediately. I've had enough of deaths/.
Ss: (give the title of a song)
T: Ready, steady, go! (Puchała, 1993: 69)

In the above exchange the teacher, apparently emotionally moved, switches from a personal comment in L2 to a nearly hysterical demand in L1, to finally code-switch again with an L2 set phrase used in a wrong context. We can only speculate about the reason of such behaviour.

The teacher disciplines a disruptive learner:

(30) T: Krzysiu, mam się zobaczyć z Twoim tatusiem albo mamusią? /Krzyś, do you want me to see your dad or mum?/
S: Nie. /No/
T: Na wywiadówce. /At the parents'meeting/.
S: Nie. /No/.
T: Exercise number seven. (Puchała, 1993: 74)

The above switch to L1, according to Puchała, is a perfect illustration of natural and harmonious co-existence of the two languages in an L2 classroom in a monolingual context. In Chapter 5 I will try to re-interpret such instances of co-existence of L1 and L2.

Teachers' feedback (Czekajewska, 1999)

Czekajewska's project, completed in 1999, that is, nearly a decade after the Communicative Approach was introduced in Poland as an approved method in L2 teacher training institutions, was another case study focused on discovering patterns of L2 teachers' oral feedback at the secondary school level.

Czekajewska recorded errors and their corrections during 20 L2 English lessons conducted by four teachers (five lessons per teacher). Altogether, the researcher collected 116 cases of corrected errors. The majority of them concerned erroneous uses of grammatical structures. Others were phonological and lexical errors. The observed groups of learners were at different levels of proficiency, from the pre-intermediate to the advanced level. The research design, modelled on Slimani's (1987) PhD dissertation involved asking the learners who had made the errors if they remembered the corrected forms.

The researcher, who was a teacher at the same school, had assumed before the research that corrections in form-focused activities would be better remembered than corrections in meaning-oriented activities. The research findings did not corroborate that hypothesis. Czekajewska found out that in both types of class activities immediately after a lesson the learners who made the errors remembered approximately 70% of the forms corrected during that lesson.

As far as teacher-correction or self-correction is concerned, the number of all errors corrected by the teachers amounted to 75% and the number of those self-corrected by the students to 25%. However, out of all self-corrected errors, over 90% were remembered after the lessons. In the case of the errors corrected by the teachers, the students remembered over 60% of teacher-corrections.

Finally, the researcher discovered that the students who had made the errors repeated the corrected forms after the teachers in over 70% of the corrections, and remembered about 50% of the repeated corrections. On the other hand, in the case of the forms corrected by the teachers but not repeated by the students who had made the errors (which amounted to nearly 30% of the cases), the students remembered about 10% of the corrections.

The quantitative analysis of the study results enabled the author to draw some tentative conclusions about the effectiveness of error correction. She concluded that the type of activity in which a correction was made did not matter for the noticing and storing processes, admittedly for a short period of time. The author further concluded that in the observed meaning-focused communicative tasks learners did not focus only on the meanings to be expressed but also on the formal correctness of their utterances. That is why they probably paid equal attention to the corrections made by the teachers in both types of activities.

On the other hand, the author concluded that the self-corrected forms were remembered better than the forms corrected by the teacher, because of the learners' effort involved in reflection and self-correction of the erroneous forms. Finally, Czekajewska arrived at the conclusion that a repetition of the corrected forms following a teacher correction had a positive effect on remembering the corrected forms by the learners.

The qualitative analysis of Czekajewska's classroom discourse data provides interesting examples of self-correction and teachers' corrections and provides some support for the quantitative results, which, however, cannot be generalised because of the limited scope of the research.

The following excerpts come from Czekajewska (1999).

The errors from (31) to (38) were self-corrected after the teacher's feedback (a prompt, providing an L1 translation equivalent or an explicit rule). The corrections (31–34) were made in grammar-focused exercises, and were remembered after the lessons by the students who had corrected their erroneous forms after the teachers' feedback comments. Both L1 (31, 32) and L2 (33, 34) were used by the teachers to provide feedback:

(31) S: We have been sitting here since an hour.
T: Pewnyś? Jaka jest różnica między 'since' i 'for'? 'Since' od jakiegoś czasu, 'for' przez jakiś okres czasu. /Are you sure? What is the difference between 'since' and 'for'? 'Since' from a given time, 'for' during a period of time/.
S: We have been sitting here for an hour. (Czekajewska, 1999: 68)

(32) S: She wished she had had enough money.
T: (shakes his head)
S: (does not answer)
T: Żałowała, że nie ma wtedy, w tym samym momencie, kiedy o tym mówiła, nie wcześnie! Słuchajcie! Tu następstwo czasów nie obowiązuje! /She wished she had it then, at the moment when she spoke about it, not earlier! Listen! The sequence of tenses does not apply here!/.
S: Aha! She wished she had enough money! (Czekajewska, 1999: 70)

(33) S: She asked me if I am hungry.
T: But it was in the past!
S: If I was hungry. (Czekajewska, 1999: 67)

(34) S: I wish I had passed the competition.
T: Passed? You don't say 'to pass a competition'. What do you say?
S: Win! I wish I had won the competition. (Czekajewska, 1999: 70)

The corrections (35–38) were made during meaning-focused activities, and were also remembered by the students who had corrected their errors following the teachers' feedback. The teachers elicited student corrections either in L2 (35, 36) or in L1 (37, 38):

(35) S: I would like to see the other culture.
T: The other?
S: (hesitates)
T: The other? Are you sure? Does it mean there are only two cultures?
S: I would like to see another culture. (Czekajewska, 1999: 72)

(36) S: I'm more better than her.
T: More better? There is too much of something.
S: I'm better than her. (Czekajewska, 1999: 73)

(37) **S:** I also like thrillers like *The Silence of the Sheeps*.
T: Ja Ci dam 'sheeps'! 'Owca' po angielsku ma taka samą liczbę mnogą jak pojedynczą! /Come on! 'Sheep' in English has the same plural as singular/.
S: Aha! Sheep. (Czekajewska, 1999: 71)

(38) **S:** I think she has twenty.
T: I think ...
S: (does not answer)
T: No, jak powiemy 'Ma dwadzieścia lat'? /How do we say 'She is twenty'?/.
S: I think she is twenty. (Czekajewska, 1999: 72)

Finally, the following errors (39–42) were corrected by the teachers, and were remembered by the students who had made them. Errors (39) and (40) were made during form-focused activities, and errors (41) and (42) in meaning-oriented tasks:

(39) **S:** He decided change his job.
T: To change his job.
S: To change his job. (Czekajewska, 1999: 75)

(40) **S:** I saw her yesterday in the bus.
T: On the bus.
S: Tak? Dziwnie. /Is it so? Strange/. (Czekajewska, 1999: 82)

(41) **S:** He has given some money.
T: He hasn't given anything! He was given!
S: He was given some money. (Czekajewska, 1999: 83)

(42) **S:** There is information about closing museums.
T: So the tourists wouldn't come!
S: No, do której są czynne muzea. /Well, how long museums are open/.
T: Ah! About the closing times of the museums.
S: Yes. About the closing times of the museums. (Czekajewska, 1999: 89)

L2 instruction in the content classrooms (Mazur, 2000)

In an exploratory case study of classroom interaction in L2 (English) content classrooms Mazur (2000) observed 15 lessons conducted by 10 teachers in two secondary schools in a Polish city. In the schools under observation, selected subjects were taught in L2 (English). According to

Fishman and Love's classification (Cohen, 1985: 173) the described programme can be called a partial bilingual approach. Mazur recorded and analyzed about 120 instances of teacher L2 and L1 input and classroom interaction.

The schools under observation had run L2 subject-matter programmes since 1993 (in school A) and since 1994 (in school B). In the school year 1997/1998, when the observations were made, the programmes included four school subjects in school A and six school subjects in school B. The observations were carried out in grades 0, 1, 2 and 3. Grade 0 was an additional year of intensive instruction in L2 (before the other four years) to enable the learners to follow L2 instruction in school subjects in the subsequent years, since some students started the programme from the beginner level. Thus, 0 grade learners had three to four lesson periods of L2 (English) instruction (two to three hours) per day. Additionally, English was taught in content classes, where L2 terminology was introduced to be later expanded in grade 1. The following lessons were taught in the observed classes: history (grade 0, 1, 3), geography (grade 0, 2), biology (grade 1), chemistry (grade 0), physics (grade 1, 2, 3), mathematics (grade 0, 1) and computer science (grade 0).

One of the observed teachers was a native speaker; the remaining teachers were university MA graduates in particular school subjects. Additionally, most of them had formal TEFL (Teaching English as a Foreign Language) qualifications, or at least a good command of the target language. The physics lessons in grades 1 and 3 were taught by the native speaker teacher.

In her study results Mazur (2000) notes that the analysed bilingual programmes in both schools were not properly co-ordinated in language progress and content. Neither were they equipped with an adequate number of appropriate teaching materials. Although the teachers were fully qualified in their subjects, they did not have enough expertise in L2 teaching techniques, such as, for instance, practising newly introduced language in group tasks.

Mazur (2000) further notes that in the classes under observation the non-native teachers most frequently used L2 at word or phrase level to teach the target lexicon. The most popular technique of teaching was translation into L1. Although some teachers made efforts to use L2 in presenting their subject-matter, others spoke predominantly in L1, and code-switched to L2 only to provide the learners with subject-matter terminology. Such language use was understandable in grade 0, when the students were at a very low level of proficiency, but it seemed to undermine the idea of L2 content instruction in higher grades. The data show that the teachers' language of class management and organisation, as well as language of social interaction was mainly L1 (Polish), whereas L2 (English) was used only for formal teaching (lecturing, explaining).

The following excerpts come from Mazur (2000). The first examples of teacher classroom language (43–51) derive from grade 0. The following ones (52–65) come from grades 1, 2 and 3. The last examples (66–75) are taken from the native speaker's lessons. In each case the grade level and the subject is marked:

Geography, grade 0

(43)   **T:**   OK. Today we'll watch a film that is similar to 'Twister'. I'd like to answer some questions before we start. Where are the most violent volcanoes located?
       S: What is 'violent'?
       T: Proszę? W tym przypadku 'gwałtowny'. /Pardon? In this case 'violent'/.

(44)   **T:**   Where is the tornado alley located?
       S: Co to jest 'alley'? /What is it 'alley'?/.

(45)   **T:**   Why are tornadoes unpredictable?
       S: Unpredictable?
       T: Nieobliczalne. /Unpredictable/. (Mazur, 2000: 89)

Mathematics, grade 0

(46)   **T:**   In mathematics the definition of distance must be strict, unambiguous. (T writes the word 'unambiguous' on the board). Co to znaczy? /What does it mean?/.
       S: Jednoznaczna. /Unambiguous/.
       T: Unambiguous.
       S: (copying the word 'unambiguous' from the board). Co tam jest? /What is it there?/.

(47)   **T:**   I proszę zadania. (And now homework questions). Check if there exist such points ABC that (...).

(48)   **T:**   Proszę wykonać dany rysunek w zeszycie używając cyrkla. /Please, make a given drawing in your copy-books using compasses/. (Mazur, 2000: 91)

History, grade 0

(49)   **T:**   Czym dzisiaj się zajmiemy, proszę państwa? Pomału się będziemy rozstawać z Republiką. To proszę państwa nasza przedostatnia lekcja przed klasyfikacją. /Ladies and gentlemen, what shall

we do today? We'll be slowly leaving the Republic. Ladies and gentlemen, this is our last but one class before the end of the term /.

(50) T: W drugiej sferze, którą się zajmowaliśmy był political system. /In the second area we dealt with there was a political system/. We'll do so: name vocabulary concerned with it, for example, 'patrician' – a member of the upper class, and 'plebeian' – a member of the lower class.

(51) T: A senatorial resolution, what's that? Po polsku 'rezolucja', czyli? /In Polish 'resolution', so?/.
S: Uchwała? /Resolution?/.
T: Bardzo słusznie, uchwała, stanowisko podejmowane przez większość głosów. /That's right, a resolution, a decision taken by the majority of the votes/. Senatorial resolution. Jak to przełożymy? /How shall we translate it?/.
S: Uchwała Senatu. /A senatorial resolution/.
T: Tak jest, uchwała Senatu. /That's right, a senatorial resolution/.
(Mazur, 2000: 98–99)

History, grade 3

(52) T: Kontynuacja lekcji poprzedniej. Proszę o rozdanie atlasów i tekścików. 'Unification of Germany'. Dobrze. Zostawiliśmy Niemcy w roku 1849. Oddolna próba [zjednoczenia] przez społeczeństwo, która się nie udała. /Continuation of the previous lesson. Please, distribute atlases and reading passages. 'Unification of Germany'. All right. We left Germany in 1849. The society made an attempt [to unify Germany], which failed/.

(53) T: Zanim przeczytamy dalej, chciałbym, aby Państwo zaznajomili się z tym słownictwem. /Before we read on, I would like you, ladies and gentlemen, to get acquainted with the vocabulary/. (T writes on the board: 'duchy', 'principality', 'provisions', 'universal suffrage'). 'Duchy', 'principality' – 'księstwo' w języku angielskim jest. /They mean in English 'duchy'/. 'Provisions' – 'warunki pokoju'. /Provisions of peace/. 'What are the provisions of the peace treaty?' Co to znaczy 'suffrage'? Czy mamy jakiś synonim? /What does 'suffrage' mean? Do we have a synonym?/.
S: Franchise.
T: Co w takim razie będzie znaczyło 'universal suffrage'? /What does 'universal suffrage' mean then?/.
S: Głosowanie powszechne. /General election/.

(54) T: Tak, dobra. Ale zobaczymy jak Bismarck doszedł do swego celu, do zjednoczenia Niemiec. Następny akapit tekstu, proszę bardzo go przeczytać. /Yes, OK. But let's see how Bismarck achieved his goal unifying Germany. Next paragraph, could you please read it/.
(Ss read the text).
T: So, in short. How Bismarck achieved his goal?
S: By force.
T: By force. We know it, yes? There are three steps mentioned here. Yes, X? (T nominates a student).
S: He waged a war against Denmark and allied with Austria, and surrendered both principalities. (Mazur, 2000: 86–87)

Physics, grade 2

(55) T: Dzień dobry. Co się stało z waszym dziennikiem? (...) Czy ja Państwu w końcu zadałam te zadania? /Good morning. What has happened to your register book? Have I finally assigned you those questions?/. OK. So last time we talked about hydrostatic pressure. So, hydrostatic pressure. Let's revise the formula.

(56) T: OK. Today we've got the continuation of what we had on the previous lesson – Pascal's Principle. Czyli co to będzie? Twierdzenie Pascala. /So, what is it? Pascal's Principle/. Do you remember? Było w klasie 7. /You had it in grade 7/. (A student gives the definition in L1)
T: No to teraz proszę po angielsku. Pan X, proszę. /Now then, please give the definition in English. Mr. X, would you?/.
S: Pascal's principle: 'Any change in pressure applied to fluid is transmitted equally throughout the fluid.'
T: If we've got the term 'fluid', what does it refer to?
S: Gas or liquid.
T: Gas or liquid. If we've got a balloon filled with air, the additional pressure will be transmitted equally throughout, and the similar situation is if we have a ball filled with liquid. (...) Pascal's Principle is used in very many situations, for example, we've got hydraulic brakes in a car (...).

(57) T: What happens if we press the brake, Kasia?
S: Car stops.
T: OK. So, what's the situation? There is a hydraulic system in a car. The hydraulic system works in this way: if we have a car and its four wheels, (T draws a car on the board). This force should be greater than the force that we use. We've got pistons. Po naszemu, to co się rusza. /In our mother tongue 'that part which moves'/.

Tłoki. /Pistons/. We've got two pistons and two cylinders, we imagine we apply our force here and due to Pascal's Principle ... (T writes the equation on the board) So this is the proposition: The ratio of F1 and F2 is equal to the ratio of S1 and S2. Wyprodukuje większą siłę, gdy przyłożone do większej powierzchni. (...) Wykorzystujemy to w prasach, podnośnikach hydraulicznych wszelkiego rodzaju, bez wkładania dodatkowej energii my uzyskujemy duży efekt. /A greater force will be produced if applied to a greater surface. This is used in hydraulic presses, lifts of all sorts; without putting additional effort, a great effect is achieved/. (Mazur, 2000: 96–98)

Geography, grade 2

(58) **T:** Chciałem jedną osobę zapytać. Proszę bardzo. /I would like to ask one person. Please, volunteer/. What are the conditions of forming deserts? Any volunteers? X jest? Jest. Z zeszycikiem proszę. /Is X present? Present. Please, come here with your little copy-book/. Speak up.

(59) **T:** Z czasem, poprzez działalność (fal), tę attrition, bo te kamienie się ścierają, tworzy się plaża. /Gradually, due to the activity (of the waves), due to attrition, because those stones get worn down, a beach is formed/.
S: How do we say 'attrition' in Polish?
T: Atrycja. /Attrition/. (Mazur, 2000: 90)

Mathematics, grade 1

(60) **T:** Niestety nie przyniosłam wam sprawdzianów. Za tydzień w poniedziałek postawię wam oceny. Tylko proszę o ciszę. Ostatnio mamy funkcje liniowe, tak? Dzisiaj dalej będziemy robili sobie zadania, ale słownictwa angielskiego było niewiele i powiemy sobie dalej ... Może nam ktoś przypomni. /I am afraid I haven't brought your tests. In a week, next Monday I will give you your grades. Please, be silent. Recently we have had linear functions, haven't we? Today we'll be solving more problems, but there were few (new) English terms, and we will say more ... Can somebody remember?/. (T asks a volunteer). Napisz wzór funkcji liniowej. /Write the formula for the linear function/. How would you call it in English?

(61) **S:** X intersect when the function have got.
T: Has got.
S: Has got nieskończoną liczbę. /An infinite number/. Endless, infinite number (...).

(62) **T:** Piszemy drugie zadanie. /Let's write the second problem/. Find equation of a straight line.
   L: Find the equation?
   T: Find the equation. Thank you X. (Mazur, 2000: 102)

Mathematics, grade 1

(63) **T:** Pozostałe kąty to są kąty wypukłe. /The remaining angles are convex angles/. Convex angles. (T writes L1 and L2 terms on the board).

(64) **T:** Adjacent angles.
   S: Po polsku? /In Polish?/.
   T: Kąty przyległe. /Adjacent angles/. Their sum equals 180 degrees. (T draws on the board).

(65) **T:** Alternate – naprzemianległe /alternate/. (T writes L1 and L2 terms on the board). We have two pairs of alternate angles:
   (a) Interior: because they lie inside two parallel lines,
   (b) Exterior: because they lie outside two parallel lines.
   Who can show where they are? (Mazur, 2000: 92)

Physics, grade 1

(66) **T:** And what we are going to look at: two ways to change the temperature of something. Two ways to increase and decrease the temperature of something. Increase. I place an object with something hotter to perform work on the object. (T demonstrates). How can you increase the temperature? (T demonstrates).
   S: Rub them.
   T: Yea, rub them together. This is the way to increase the temperature.

(67) **T:** What's the force when you ... (T demonstrates).
   S: From our muscle.
   T: No, when you press your hands together ... (T demonstrates).
   S: Friction.
   T: Friction.

(68) **T:** Now a bicycle pump. Let me draw a pump for you. OK. (T draws on the board). I'll introduce some names for you which are going to be important: a cylinder – this is it? (T points to the picture). Cylinder, piston, the rocker arm. (T writes the terms on the board). Inside the cylinder something goes up and down, this is a piston. When the piston goes up, air comes into the pump. Basically, this is the rocker arm, this is your handle, up and down.

Evidence from L2 Classroom Discourse Research Projects

(69) **T:** What if we do this, close that so? (T demonstrates). What happens to the air?
S: First of all it condenses.
T: Compresses.
S: And it becomes warmer.
T: Why it becomes warmer? Because ...
S: You do work on it.
T: So when you compress the air, the temperature of the air goes up, and why? Because the piston does work on the air by pushing down on it some force. And that's what makes the temperature of the air go up. Any questions?
S: No.

(70) **T:** What if you do this, what if you quit pushing up? (T demonstrates). The temperature of the air goes down.
S: Because the air pressures it.
T: Because the air pushes it up. The air has done work. There was work done by the air. Your bicycle, a bicycle pump. Do you have any questions? This is what I want you to know. I want you to know the difference between the work being done by the air and on the air, compressing it or allowing the air to go up.

(71) **T:** There are two things which are different here from your bicycle pump (...) and the other thing is the spark plug.
S: Spark?
T: Yes, spark. You know what a spark is?
S: Yes.
T: So the spark burns gas. Spark plug. It's not air, here it's gas.

(72) **T:** Converting heat to work. Let's think about this. A heat engine is anything which converts heat to work. Are you a heat engine?
S: Yes.
T: Sure you are! We are heat engines. We produce heat in form of calories (and we convert it) into work. We eat, we breathe, we move, think. (Mazur, 2000: 92–95)

Physics, grade 3

(73) **T:** OK, this is what I want to get into you today. Subject: Three ways waves change direction: one – reflection, two – refraction, three – diffraction. (T writes the terms on the board). [...] three – a change of direction when a wave strikes or hits an obstacle.
S: Strikes an ... ?

T: Yes, in a medium. I can step outside into the hallway and you cannot ever see me but you can hear me.

(74) T: What is the Law of Reflection?
S: Q1 = Q1′
T: Hey! How many of you have played billiards?
S: What? Pool!
T: Yes, pool. If it strikes head on, the angle of incidence is 0. That is the term we use in English. Simple enough?
Ss: Yea.

(75) T: The Law of Refraction is this. (T writes the formula on the board). OK, so what determines what a K is like? Only the two media determine what the constant is.
S: Density, for example, different type of glass has different density.
T: When the light goes through the water it refracts. Hey, how about this? Twinkling stars, they do not turn on and turn off. (Mazur, 2000: 95–96)

Communicative activities I (Fryc, 2000)

Fryc's (2000) project entitled 'Using communicative activities in Polish secondary schools' focused on classroom communication and explored the implementation of the Communicative Approach in the monolingual L2 teaching context at the secondary school level. The project combined direct class observation with a survey of teachers' attitudes towards various aspects of the Communicative Approach. The researcher observed communicative activities conducted by 20 non-native English teachers in 20 different secondary classes at the intermediate level of L2 proficiency. All the observed teachers had full qualifications to teach English as a foreign language, although their teaching experience varied.

Fryc's findings provide valuable information on the state of affairs in communicative teaching in the monolingual class setting, although, admittedly, the author observed L2 classrooms in only four secondary schools and treated her research as a case study. However, even such a limited study shows, mostly in qualitative but also in quantitative terms, some characteristic patterns of non-native teachers' behaviour in the L2 classroom. It has also enabled the researcher to compare the observed communicative activities with the teachers' opinions on the Communicative Approach.

As has been said before, the observation scheme was based on Allen et al.'s (1984) COLT and Wajnryb's (1992) Observation Tasks. The observations took into consideration the following aspects of the communicative activities:

- type of activity
- number of students and duration of the activity
- materials used in the activity
- participant organisation and seating arrangements
- teacher and student roles
- focus on accuracy and error correction
- teachers' and students' use of L1 and L2.

One half of the observed activities were whole-class discussions, and the other half consisted in pair and group-work. The number of students varied, from 10 to 20; the average duration of the activities amounted to 12 minutes. The observed teachers, except one person, did not use any other materials beside their course books. In the majority of cases the seating arrangements were traditional, in pair-work activities students who were sitting together were made conversational partners.

Most of the observed teachers presented the activities to the students, and controlled their progress during the activities and in the follow-up stage. Some teachers monitored pair-work activities, while others did not participate in that stage at all. Fryc observed that in most cases instead of talking freely, the students were preparing for the follow-up presentations required by the teachers. They even made notes and tried to memorise dialogues. In the follow-up stage, the teachers usually chose some pairs to perform the activities once again and then the teachers made comments on the form and content of the performance. During the discussions, it was usually the teacher who nominated the speakers and controlled the progress of the discussion. Most of the discussions did not have a follow-up stage.

However, some teachers let the students behave more naturally, they did not control them very strictly, they monitored group performance without obtrusive interference, and they let the students make their own comments in the follow-up. The most interesting aspects of the observations from the perspective of this book are the last two: teachers' focus on accuracy, and L2 and L1 use.

The researcher concluded her observations claiming that the majority of the teachers focused on formal accuracy and corrected nearly all students' errors, frequently during the activities. However, a careful analysis of the recorded samples indicates that the teachers varied in their attitude towards errors, from explicitly explaining during the interaction why particular forms were wrong, through unobtrusive elicitations of correct forms from the students, to disregarding formal inaccuracies in student language. Obviously, the recorded samples do not sometimes include any teacher language, as was the case when the researcher recorded unmonitored exchanges. The variations in teacher error correction are most clearly seen in general discussions.

The teachers' use of L2 and L1 during the observed communicative activities varied considerably as well. Approximately, half of the teachers used L1 while correcting errors, providing grammatical and lexical explanations or managing the activities. In such a way, the researcher concluded, they communicated to the students that the language of real classroom communication was L1. This conclusion is particularly interesting in the light of the following discussion (see Chapter 5).

In the observed communicative activities, according to Fryc, the students focused first of all on the completion of the tasks, and their communicative purpose was of little importance to them. This was particularly clearly seen in the preparation of the dialogues the students were supposed to present later to the teacher. In such cases, the students switched to L1 in real communicative exchanges, where they discussed both the content and the form of the planned presentations.

In contrast to group and pair-work, general discussions seemed to involve the students more into meaningful communication in L2, and L1 was used only sporadically. The researcher came to the conclusion that the students were not prepared to work in groups. This claim will be further discussed from the RT perspective in Chapter 5.

As far as the information-gap principle and the language choice principle are concerned (see Chapter 2), Fryc notes that the students frequently knew what they would say in L2, since they had prepared their presentations beforehand or they knew each other very well. On the other hand, they often lacked appropriate ideas, because they did not identify with the roles they were supposed to play or the contexts of the roles were unfamiliar to them. The choice of the language was also only partly free, due to a very close adherence to the activity instructions in the course books. The above methodological considerations, in particular the optimal type of communicative activities to promote speaking skills, became the focus of interest of Przebinda's (2004) project.

The other research method in Fryc's (2000) MA project – the attitude scale, modelled on Karavas-Doukas (1996), was developed to provide information on the observed teachers' attitudes towards the Communicative Approach. The attitude survey included 18 statements the teachers were to agree or disagree with (on a five-point scale). The statements concerned group work, the role of grammar teaching, error correction, and the role of the teacher and the students in the L2 classroom.

The result scores in the attitude scale show that the majority of the teachers had positive attitudes towards the Communicative Approach, but that some of their answers were inconsistent. However, the inconsistencies may have resulted from the unclear form of the statements, and not from inconsistent attitudes. For example, the statement: 'Direct instruction in the rules and terminology of grammar is indispensable if the students are to learn to communicate effectively', does not say that direct grammar instruction should replace communicative activities. The teachers who agreed with the above statement and also with the seemingly opposite statement: 'For most students language is acquired most effectively when it is used as a vehicle for doing something else and not when it is studied in a direct or explicit way', could have understood the above statements as referring to the dichotomy between learning and acquisition, where the former statement referred to accurate and the latter to fluent communication. In fact, the term 'effectively' may mean both aspects of communication.

Such an interpretation of the inconsistencies observed in the teachers' answers has been mentioned by the researcher, although she favours another interpretation, that the survey results express the teachers' doubts about the implementation of the Communicative Approach. It is a pity that Fryc (2000) did not try to compare the findings from the attitude survey with direct observation of particular teachers. Such an attempt will be made in Chapter 6 in the discussion on the methodological implications of the projects findings.

The following excerpts of L2 classroom discourse during role-plays and general discussions come from Fryc (2000). The first examples (76–80) illustrate teacher approaches to learner errors, ranging from explicit explanations in L1, through elicitation of correct forms from the learners, to disregarding erroneous forms.

The whole class discussion about the Zodiac signs of the students' family and friends. The teacher monitors the activity and corrects students' errors in an explicit way.

(76) S: My mother and father is a libra. And they are real libras. For example: mother never quarrel with father and they are ...
T: Aniu, trzecia osoba nie 'quarrel' tylko 'quarrels'/ the third person not 'quarrel' but 'quarrels'/.
S: Mother never quarrels with father and they also can't decide because typical libras are not ... zdecydowani /undecided/.
(Fryc, 2000: 103)

The whole class discussion about problems illustrated in the pictures. The teacher monitors the activity, and in the majority of cases, she recasts erroneous utterances. A learner presents her opinions:

(77) **T:** Could you present your opinion?
S: I think that animals should live free and they can't be keeping in cages.
T: Should be free and they can't be kept in cages, OK?
S: They can't be kept in cages. I also think it's also stupid teaching monkeys to be like human beings. It's not natural.
T: Powinnaś powiedzieć /you should say/: it's stupid to teach monkeys to behave like human beings.
S: They should live in ...
T: Wilderness.
S: Teach them to cook, speak is making harm to them.
T: Doing harm to them.
S: The second picture I think relates to the problem of cripple.
T: Is related to the problem of the disabled. 'Cripple' to jest trochę nieładne słowo. / ... is not a very nice word/.
S: I think it is good to learn disabled to make varied things.
T: Nie 'learn' ale 'teach' disabled to do various things. Coś jeszcze? /Not 'to learn' but 'to teach' [...]. Anything else?/.
L: No. (Fryc, 2000: 115)

The improvised task involves talking about a party. The teacher monitors the activity, and tries to elicit corrections from the learners:

(78) **S1:** How did you like the party?
T: Enjoy the party?
S1: Yes, enjoy the party.
S2: Very much, there were my friends which I didn't see for a long time and I can talk to them again.
T: Friends who ... it's a person, right?
S2: Oh yes. There were friends who I didn't see (Fryc, 2000: 107)

The whole class discussion is focused on national stereotypes. The teacher monitors the activity. She asks clarification questions focused on the meaning and elicits corrections from the students:

(79) **T:** OK. Now let's think about Poles. [...]
S: They are hostile.
T: Could you explain what you mean?
S: They like people when they come to them.
T: You mean they like having guests. They are not hostile, but ...

S: Oh yes, hospitable. Zawsze to mylę. /I always mix them up/. (Fryc, 2000: 113)

The whole class discussion is based on a reading passage. The teacher manages the activity, but does not correct any errors.

(80) T: OK. We've read the text about Eton college, what do you think about going to such a school?
S1: I think that it is very positive to go to schools like Eton, because it's good quality teaching.
S2: But it's not a nice company there.
S1: Company?
S2: No the friends. /There are no friends there/. People who go there are snobs. They think they are the best.
T: What do the others think?
S3: I think you can go to other places to meet friends, not in school.
S4: Ciekawe gdzie? /I wonder where?/.
S5: Yes, it's not easy. School is best for knowing friends.
S1: But what with job? You can get better job if you go to Eton.
T: How about boys? What do you think about it?
S6: I wouldn't mind. The school may be cool.
S7: And the prospects of career are better.
S4: Yeah, you later earn more money. And you are best professional in your ... dziedzina? /discipline/.
S8: Field.
T: Yeah. Now, what do you think about our school in comparison with Eton?
S1: Our is nicer. It's not stiff.
S2: We have better direct relation with teachers.
S6: It's not hard. (Fryc, 2000: 119)

The next examples (81–83) show instances when the teachers use L1 to explicitly teach L2 or to manage the activities.

A student characterises his friend in a whole class discussion. The teacher explicitly teaches L2 while monitoring the activity:

(81) S: He organize people well.
T: He organizes. Ale zazwyczaj czasownik 'organize' nie używa się do osób. Można organizować coś, a nie ludzi. Tak jak po polsku zresztą. Możesz powiedzieć 'He is a good organizer'. /But usually the verb 'organize' is not used with people. You can organize something, not people. The same is in Polish. You can say ... /.
S: He is a good organizer. (Fryc, 2000: 103)

The students enact a role play. One of them is a surgeon and the other a news reporter. They are provided with role cards in which the situation and the communicative goals are specified.

While monitoring the activity, the teacher manages the activity, explicitly teaches L2 and recasts erroneous utterances:

(82) T: O czym rozmawiacie? /What are you talking about?/.
   S1: O przeszczepie wątroby. /About liver transplantation/.
   T: OK. Proszę kontynuujcie. /Please, continue/.
   S2: This will be a progress in medicine.
   T: This will bring some progress.
   S2: Yes.
   S1: Już wszystko. /That's all/.
   T: Na pewno? Spróbujcie wymyślić jakieś dodatkowe pytania. /Are you sure? Try to think of some additional questions/.
   S1: How much it costed?
   T: Nie 'it costed', ale 'did it cost'. Pamiętaj o operatorze. /Not 'it costed' but 'did it cost'. Remember about the operator/.
   S1: How much did it cost?
   S2: Quite a lot of money. (Fryc, 2000: 121)

The students enact a role play. One of them is a newcomer in London and the other knows the city quite well. The situation and the communicative goals are specified. The teacher monitors and manages the activity:

(83) T: No, na czym skończyliście? Proszę kontynuować. /Where have you finished?   Please, continue/.
   S: Teraz mówimy o poczcie. /Now we are talking about the post office/.
   T: No, to dalej. /Carry on, please/.
   S: High Street Post Office. Opening hours: Monday, Tuesday, Thursday and Friday from 9 to 5:30, Wednesday and Saturday from 9 to 1:00 [...].
   T: No dobra, idźcie dalej. /OK, carry on/. (Fryc, 2000: 100)

The students focus first of all on the completion of the tasks according to the role play cards, which is their real goal, while the communicative goal of the activities is of little importance to them.

The following examples (84–85) show how the students code-switch to L1 in pair and group work tasks.

A group of three students prepare a dialogue between a complaining woman, her noisy neighbour and a policeman. They manage the activity by themselves. The teacher does not interfere:

(84) **S1:** They play loud music at night. I can't fall to sleep. And my husband also. And he is ill.
S2: You can't play so loud music after 10:00. This is law. You live with... mieszkańcy /inhabitants/ (neighbours).
S3: You know this is a crazy woman. We are not playing loud. She is crazy skrzypaczka /violinist/. She will listen even no, ten szept, jak jest szept? /She will even hear... whispering, how do we say whispering?/.
S1: No co ja mam mówić dalej? /What shall I say next?/.
S2: No mów byle co, że masz męża chorego. /Say whatever you want. Say that your husband is ill/.
S1: No dobra. /OK/ But my husband is very ill. It's not me. He can't sleep.
S2: And do you often play the violin?
S1: No, only on day, not at night.
S3: Trele morele! /Rubbish!/. She plays all the day and in morning also. I can't sleep in morning.
S2: No dobra, koniec. /OK. The end/.
S1: No, ale musisz powiedzieć co mamy zrobić. /But you must tell us what we are supposed to do/.
S3: No mów, bo ona na pewno nas weźmie. /Say something, because it's sure she (the teacher) will ask us/.
S2: No dobra. To obydwie musicie sobie zapłacić karę. /OK. You will pay each other a fine/. (Fryc, 2000: 101)

The students are engaged in an information-gap pair work activity. Two students are supposed to discuss on the basis of the provided questions whether they are optimists or pessimists. The questions refer to their future lives and to the future of the world. (The activity including the original questions is also discussed in Chapter 5: 153.) The teacher does not interfere:

(85) **S1:** Co masz w pierwszym? /What do you have in the first question?/.
S2: Yes. A ty? /And you?/.
S1: C. A standard of living?
S2: (Will) stay the same.
S1: Ja też, a w trzecim? /Me too, and in the third one?/.
S2: Co to znaczy 'to live to work' i 'work to live'? /What does it mean [...] and [...] ?/.
S1: To drugie chyba, że praca cię tylko utrzymuje, ale tak właściwie to jej nie lubisz.

/I think in the second one that your job just gives you a living, but you don't like it/.
S2: A pierwsze odwrotnie, tak? /And the first one is the opposite, right?/.
S1: Nie wiem. /I don't know/.
S2: No dobra. /OK/ My children will have more dangerous childhood. A twoje? /And yours?/.
S1: More comfortable. No, a co z tą pracą? /And what about that job?/.
S2: Ostatnie. A ty? /The last one. And you?/.
S1: B.
S2: About the world teraz /now/. Do you think that as we learn more, we are becoming more tolerant of people of different nationalities, religions, czy /or/ colours?
S1: Żadne z tych. Tolerancja się nie zmieni. /None of them. Tolerance won't change/. (...)
S1: To trzecie to jest już całkiem głupie. /The third one is completely stupid/.
S2: No ja mam 'safe', bo może nie będą szkodzić środowisku. /I have 'safe' (sources of energy), because perhaps they won't do harm to the environment/.
S1: No to ja też mam 'safe'. /So I also have 'safe'/.
S2: Ostatnie – 'more materialistic' /The last one ... /.
S1: No i jeszcze 'more selfish'. /And another one ... /. (Fryc, 2000: 111)

Communicative activities II (Przebinda, 2004)

Przebinda (2004) compared two most common types of communicative activities: role-plays and discussions. She tried to find out whether role-plays were more conducive than discussions to the development of L2 students' speaking skills. She claimed that during role-plays students would speak more and they would use less L1 than during discussions. The researcher observed 30 communicative activities focused on the same topics, half of them being role-plays and the other half discussions. The observations were made in five secondary L2 classes at different levels of proficiency, from pre-intermediate to upper-intermediate.

The crucial difference between Fryc's (2000) and Przebinda's (2004) observational research studies was that in the latter study, the researcher herself planned the entire lessons including the speaking activities. While Fryc's study was principally exploratory, Przebinda had a clear L2 teaching hypothesis in mind. She had chosen three topics: reality shows, education and computers, as topics of common interest, and she had planned six lessons, two lessons for each topic, one of them including a role-play, and the other a group discussion. The speaking activities (role-plays and discussions) in each lesson were introduced as follow-up activities to the reading tasks. The three teachers who taught the observed groups followed the design of the lessons, and in each of the lessons the researcher recorded one group of three students during the speaking activity, so as to obtain recorded speaking samples of role-plays and discussions from the same students.

The recorded samples of the role-plays and discussions have been analysed in terms of the number of turns taken by the participants, the number of L1 and L2 turns, and the number of unfilled pauses. The results of the analysis indicate that the students spoke more and made fewer pauses during role-plays than in group discussions. They also used less L1 during role-plays.

Another research method was a survey for all the students who took part in the observed lessons (52 students) and for their three teachers. The researcher wanted to find out their attitudes towards role-plays and discussions, in particular in terms of their relative facilitating effect on the development of speaking skills, expressing opinions, usefulness in language practice, authenticity and personal preferences.

The students found role-plays more conducive to speaking, more useful in language practice and generally a preferable communicative activity. On the other hand, the majority of them admitted that discussions were more facilitative in expressing opinions and they were closer to real-life conversations. The teachers noted the advantages of both methods, but they also underlined the facilitative aspects of role-plays in developing speaking skills. All three teachers stated that in their classes they used role-plays as frequently as discussions.

Przebinda concluded her research with the claim that role-plays were more conducive than discussions to the development of speaking skills. Nevertheless, she admitted that since some students preferred the latter technique, and since it had some advantages, it should have its place in the L2 classroom.

It is interesting to view the above mentioned beneficial aspects of role-plays in the context of accuracy (form-oriented) and fluency (meaning-oriented) practice, as well as from the perspective of L2 classroom real and simulated communication. I will try to reinterpret Przebinda's findings in Chapter 5.

The following four excerpts are taken from Przebinda (2004). They focus on education (one of the three topics of the speaking activities). In order to better appreciate them, they are presented without abbreviations. The samples come from two groups (out of five). The order of presentation follows the sequence of the lessons during the research (the first lesson involved a group discussion, and the following one – a role-play). The groups are marked with the letters A and B. The students' age in both groups is 17 years. The students in group A are females, while in group B they are males. Group A comes from an academic type secondary school (*liceum*), the students attend a class with an extended programme in Spanish. They have been described by the researcher as the most diligent group among the five groups. Group A students are at the upper-intermediate level of proficiency. Group B comes from a technical type secondary school (*technikum*). Group B students are at the pre-intermediate level of L2 proficiency. The type of activity is indicated in each case.

Comparing education in South Korea and in Poland (on the basis of a reading passage about the South Korean educational system). The students' task is to discuss advantages and disadvantages of the two educational systems, and to compare their effectiveness in terms of future opportunities and the quality of life.

Group discussion

(86) Group A (students 1, 2 and 3)
 S1: (reads the questions provided by the teacher)
 S2: *What do you think? Which system is better?*
 S3: OK, so let's talk about the Korean one. Probably they are more educated.
 S2: They get better job, opportunity to study later at university and ... I don't know ...
 S1: How long?
 S3: Probably the same. (It is not clear from the transcript what the students mean.)
 S2: 17 hours [of studying per day]. It's stupid. Naprawdę jakiś beznadziejny system. /It must be an awful system/.
  (pause)
 S1: So they have seven hours to have a shower, sleep, eat breakfast and ... 17 hours ... so they sleep almost 5 hours. This is the disadvantage.
 S2: It's stupid, you can't relax, talk to your parents ... they have no private time. I don't like it.
 S1: And they are more intelligent in the classes but their life ... They don't know how to live.
 S3: I agree.
  (pause)
 S2: *OK, so which system is more effective?*
 S1: I think this system have more advantages and disadvantages and Polish system have advantages and disadvantages so we must put them ... together ... choose ... I think that ... that the

Korean system ... with this system you could receive better job but the problems you will be ... have ... I mean in ... I think that in Korean system you get a better job so better life, but it's not so good life if you don't have the ...
S3: Private life.
S1: Private life and ... and ...
S2: You don't know how to ...
S3: How to behave, how to act.
S2: Yes, so I think that our system is better.
S3: It's not better but it's more for people as to say. /= it's more humane, so to speak/.
(pause)
S2: No one is the best but I think our is better than the Korean system.
S1: So that's all?
S2: That's all.
S3: The end. Koniec. /The end/. (Przebinda, 2004: 121)

(87) Group B (students 4, 5 and 6)
S4: Dobra, no to zaczynamy. /OK, let's start/.
S5: (reads out one of the questions) *What are the advantages of the Polish system?*
S4: Polish system is better. We don't have to stay in school for 17 hours a day. And we don't have to study so much.
S5: Yes. In Korea people must study too much ... But they know more things when they finish school.
S4: But they are so tired ... they can't do nothing. They don't have time for playing sport or something like this. All the time they study. It's stupid ...
(pause)
S5: No, to w ogóle jest bez sensu. /It's total nonsense./
S6: (reads out a question) *But which one is better?*
S4: Polish is better. We are not tired ... We have more time.
(pause)
S5: A praca? Oni mają szansę dostać lepszą pracę i kasę. /And work? They have a chance to get a better job and more dough/.
S6: No tak, ale przecież na nic nie majączasu. To nienormalne. /That's right, but they have no time for anything. It's not normal/.
S5: In Korea you can get a good job.
S6: A w Polsce nawet jak dużo umiesz, to nie możesz dostać dobrej pracy. /And in Poland even if you know a lot, you cannot get a good job/.
(laughter)

S5:	(reads out a question) *Which system gives you better opportunity to get a better job?*
S6:	No to ten w Korei. /The Korean one/.
S5:	*Better life?*
S4:	I think Polish.
S6:	We have more time ... and we have time for fun.
S5:	Tak, i na imprezki. /Yes, and for little parties/. (laughter) (pause)
S6:	No to co? Wszystko już? /So what now? Is that it?/.
S4:	Dobra, koniec. /OK, the end/. (Przebinda, 2004: 123)

An interview with two candidates for one place at the best language school. Each candidate has to persuade the head teacher to choose him/her. The head teacher has to choose the better candidate. Students receive role cards with a description of the situation and goals of the role-play (their identities, motivations and background).

Role play

(88) Group A (students 1, 2 and 3)

S3:	Good morning and welcome to the language school.
S2:	Good morning.
S1:	Hello.
S3:	I'd like you to tell me something about you because we have only one place left in one of the groups, so one of you will have to leave ... so ... just tell me something about you and then we will decide. So maybe you can start?
S2:	OK ... so my name is Barbara Brown and ... I've learned English for six years and I know also French and Latin very well.
S3:	Why do you want to learn English?
S2:	My boyfriend is English and I want to communicate with him.
S3:	OK, I have a question for you – could you tell me why do you want to study at our school?
S2:	Just like I said. I've learned English for six years and I still don't speak it very well. We're going to England next year and my girlfriend ... boyfriend (laughs), and we will work there, so I want to study hard.
S3:	OK, thank you. Now, what about you Ms J.J. Small?
S1:	My name is J. Small and I want to study at your school because I want to be an English teacher.

S3: Yes ... and what about your experience with learning languages? Do you have any experience?
S1: I've studied in many language schools and it was ... it was not good. They were not good schools and now I'd like to study at your school because it's the best school of English and I think that it could be a good chance for me.
S2: And I want to say that I'd like to study English for one year and I want to speak English very well and my communication must be also very well.
S1: So I think I'm a better person because I already speak English so ...
S2: I speak English too. And I've studied English for six years and I want to ...
S3: OK, but let's talk about other languages now. Do you think that you have ... when you study other languages, do you think that you learn them easy? Or is it quite difficult to learn them?
S1: For me it's easy. I speak also German and Spanish and ... I think that's all I can really say ...
S2: For me too. I like learning languages and it's easy for me. (pause)
S1: I think that studying other languages is very important because we have to communicate with people from other countries and it's very important. So because of it I study German and I can speak German very well and a little bit in Spanish.
S3: OK ... well ... do you have anything to add?
S1: I think that my person is really good for this place and I think you should choose me.
S3: OK, thank you very much for coming. And I guess I will be back in five minutes and then I will decide who gets the place.
S2: OK, thank you.
S1: Thank you and see you later. (Przebinda, 2004: 125)

(89) Group B (students 4, 5 and 6)
S4: Good morning. I wanna join this best English school. I have learnt English for 6 years.
S5: Yes, OK. And you?
S6: I also want to learn in this school. I want to learn English because it's so good here.
S5: All right. Tell me something more. My problem is that I must choose you. I have one place in my school so try to ... well ... tell me something more.

S6: I have learnt English for 4 years and I know German also and Spanish very well.
S5: Oh, that's good. That's very interesting. Do you like German?
S6: Yes, yes. I love German. But I think English is more easy.
S5: Yes, it's true. And what about you? Do you know any languages?
S4: I know French basic and Latin also. I am really the best person for this place.
S5: But why do you think so?
S4: I want to learn English because I am going to England ...
S6: And I ... I also want to go to this school. I will be a teacher in the future.
S4: I can pay for this place. I can pay big money. 4000 pounds. (pause)
S5: Why do you want to come to my school? There are other schools too.
S4: Because this school is really the best. I heard it in television. It's the best in the country.
S6: But you are not the best candidate in this country. Remember it.
S5: Have you learnt any other languages?
S6: Yes, I know German and Spanish. I said this.
S5: Why do you need our school? Show me that you are the better candidate.
S6: Because this school will give me a dyplom /certificate/ and I need it because it will help me to get a better job.
S4: And I need it because I must communicate with my girlfriend. And when I go to England I must get a good job there.
S5: Yes, I get it. But how can I choose? I don't know who is better. I think I will take you all because you are great and you are the best. And I will make a big group for this year.
S6: OK, thank you very much, Mr Headteacher.
S4: Thank you very much. And see you on the lesson. Good bye.
(Przebinda, 2004: 127)

Chapter 5
Classroom Discourse Data Interpreted in the Light of RT: Levels of Expected Optimal Relevance of L2 Classroom Input

L2 classrooms in monolingual L1 settings can be described as full of inherent conflicts, first of all, between a focus on fluency and a focus on accuracy, second, between real and simulated communication, and finally between L2 and L1 use. Let us try to account for those communicative and educational tensions in the light of Relevance Theory. The research data, which was presented in Chapter 4 according to their authors' aims, will be interpreted in this chapter from the perspective of Relevance Theory (RT) as levels of expected optimal relevance of L2 classroom input connected with explicit and implicit language teaching.

Instructional Input in the RT Perspective

In accordance with RT, the learners in L2 classroom discourse have to choose a context of existing assumptions which are brought to bear on the interpretation of teachers' utterances: whether the teacher's input should be interpreted as explicit or implicit teaching of the target language (L2), in other words, whether the language is used by the teacher in order to give them opportunities to hear a model utterance and to practise it, or to provide them with opportunities to communicate in L2.

According to my definition of instructional input, in other words, of the language intentionally presented by the teacher to facilitate the process of L2 learning, it does not follow from it that either of the above interpretations is more facilitative. The teacher may use language to communicate meanings or to model and practise forms with the same intention of facilitating L2 learning.

For the sake of simplicity in our discussion, let us assume, as teachers usually assume, that although the process of language learning is not fully understood yet, certain types of teacher input are better than others in facilitating language learning. I do not wish to enter here into methodological considerations of classroom teaching techniques, neither do I want to discuss models of language acquisition, although later in this chapter, a brief theoretical proposal of the interpretation of instructional input for L2 learning/acquisition is given. I would like to focus on a functional interpretation of linguistic input.

RT distinguishes two layers of intention in ostensive-inferential communication: the informative and the communicative one (see Chapter 1). On the basis of our classroom data evidence, one can come to the conclusion that ostensive-inferential communication refers to two modes of instructional input. First, the teacher wishes to communicate to the learners her informative intention of teaching them the target language (L2) explicitly by focusing on the accuracy of linguistic forms. Second, she wishes to communicate to them her informative intention of teaching them the target language implicitly by focusing on fluent expression of meanings. The first intention is realised in L2 classroom discourse in metalinguistic utterances either in explicit presentation of the linguistic data to the learners, or in explicit or implicit corrections of learners' language. The other intention is realised in focusing on the content of the lessons or in classroom communication, which can be either real or simulated.

Obviously, at first, the language input must be decoded at the level of phonology, morphology, syntax and semantics. The teachers usually facilitate the task of input decoding by identifying learning tasks in such a way as to initially focus the learners on a particular language problem in what is called accuracy practice. The language which is practised then by the teacher as well as by the learners is the linguistic content of language learning. That is what SLA theorists call forms-focused instruction or focus-on-forms (FonFs) approach (see Long & Robinson, 1998). Such language use is of little interest to me, because it does not involve any fluency practice and L2 communication, although, obviously it has its place in L2 classroom practice (e.g. in traditional language drills).

However, in contemporary L2 classroom language use, pure accuracy practice has mostly given way to fluency practice, or fluency practice combined with accuracy practice, in what is generally called Communicative Language Teaching (see Chapter 2). The question arises about the problems involved in the interface between explicit and implicit language teaching in fluency practice combined with accuracy practice.

In the light of RT, focusing on fluency or on accuracy can be interpreted as an automatic process of searching for optimal relevance. In the process, however, as has been said before, the intended meanings of L2 forms may be easily misinterpreted due to the primary automatic search for meaning in partly or wrongly decoded language. Such an incomplete knowledge of the L2 code can be found at any level of L2 learning, but it is particularly characteristic of lower levels of L2 proficiency. The Communicative Approach with its stress on quick and superficial understanding processes (listening and reading for gist, skimming), has made contemporary L2 classrooms especially prone to misunderstanding and misinterpretation.[1]

I would like to propose the claim that L2 teachers' instructional input can change the level of expected optimal relevance from an automatic search for meaning to momentarily focusing on the code and adjusting one's interpretation to the original meaning of the message. Such an interpretation is in line with what Doughty (2001: 249), calls 'small cognitive windows of opportunity' through which teachers can intervene by focusing on form in otherwise meaning-focused activities (see Chapter 1). As has been said before, Doughty claims that teachers' repetitions with corrections (recasts) of learners' erroneous or incomplete forms, following immediately those forms, are most useful for the internalisation of the target forms at the level of cognitive macroprocessing.[2]

In the following L2 classroom discourse excerpts, teachers' utterances can be treated as input facilitating learners' momentary focus on the code in otherwise meaning-oriented interactions. One of the most common facilitating techniques is asking questions and more or less explicit elicitation of self-corrections from the students. Otherwise, the teacher can correct erroneous forms herself. We can also call them input-driven shifts of the level of expected optimal relevance requiring more or less effort to arrive at contextual assumptions. In other words, learners are made momentarily aware that what they have said is formally wrong, even if understood by the audience.

(90) T: What was the weather yesterday?
 S: Yesterday it was bad weather because it was cold and it rained.
 T: All the day?
 S: No, with breaks. It rained in the morning from six a.m. o'clock.
 T: If you use *a.m.*, do not use *o'clock*. (Kusibab, 1984: 125)

The above classroom excerpt is a fragment of L2 classroom communication which by the Communicative Approach standards might be called artificial, since the teacher knows what the weather was like the day before, and the aim of her question is to elicit a correct (and full) answer from the learner. Similarly, the question can be called a display-question (Long & Sato, 1983), since the teacher wants the student to display her L2 knowledge.

However, the learner's answer (*Yesterday it was bad weather because it was cold and it rained*) is treated by the teacher as if it had been totally correct and appropriate, since the teacher does not recast it. The teacher seems automatically to be focused on the utterance meaning. According to RT, it is the meaning of the learner's answer that is optimally relevant for the teacher at that given moment, because it produces enough contextual effect for the least processing effort. Continuing this train of thought, we can claim that in the next turn (*All the day?*) the teacher does not care so much for a display of the student's knowledge as for real communication, which, in turn, elicits more target like answer (*No, with breaks*).

What happens in last two turns in the discourse excerpt is an example of the above mentioned momentary focus on the code in otherwise meaning-focused communication. The learner produces an erroneous form (*from six a.m. o'clock*), which becomes optimally relevant for the teacher in the context of her role of an educator. In her comment the teacher focuses on the code (*If you use a.m., do not use o'clock*). What can the learner infer from this comment according to RT? I believe that the teacher communicates to the learner her intention to teach her the target language explicitly, in other words, that the level of expected optimal relevance has been shifted from focusing on meaning only to focusing on meaning and the code.

Carroll (1995) claims that input focused on formal correction is irrelevant in language learning (see Chapter 1), and that the native speaker's answer in her anecdote is a metalinguistic comment which is clearly irrelevant to the objectives of the ongoing conversation (Carroll, 1995). She further adds that it must be irrelevant to be understood as metalinguistic correction, and that such an understanding is possible only when no other interpretation is possible.

However, non-native speakers usually expect to be treated as foreigners, which involves their expectation that what they say (or attempt to say) in L2 will be interpreted not only at the level of communicating meanings, but also at the level of the code itself, its correctness, appropriateness, etc. As has been argued before, a semantic interpretation of an L2 utterance may be postponed and its formal features can come to the fore. It could be claimed then that the native speaker's comment was not irrelevant to the non-native speaker and that he quickly understood the correction. He could have even practised the corrected version of his question on another native customer.

Coming back to example (90), the teacher's metalinguistic remark does not remind the learner of a general rule irrelevant for the ongoing discourse. Conversely, her remark can become relevant for the learner in the context of L2 classroom discourse, which is primarily language teaching discourse, where explicit instructional input focused on the language code is part and parcel of L2 use (see Chapter 3). The exchange ends with the teacher's comment, but we can easily imagine the next step, in which the learner interprets the teacher's metalinguistic remark as an elicitation of a self-correction, and she corrects herself following the teacher's comment. Her possible next turn could have been: *It rained in the morning from six a.m.*[3]

On the other hand, Carroll (1995) seems to be right when she claims that the most explicit corrections are most effective in terms of learners' interpretation of the corrective role of the teachers. Let us compare the two following excerpts. The teacher and the students are engaged in a communicative activity in a general L2 classroom debate whether lying can be excused.

(91) T: [...] Do you agree?
 S: No, I think you shouldn't lie under no condition.
 T: Under any condition.
 S: Yes.

(92) T: Ewa, would you lie to your parents?
 S: Yes, if I want go out and they did not let me to go.
 T: They don't let you go. You can't say 'to go' after 'let'. You should use 'to go' after 'want'. Repeat, please.
 S: If I want to go out and they didn't let me go.
 T: Don't let me. (Fryc, 2000: 102)

In (91) the teacher's recast (*under any condition*) may have passed unnoticed by the learner, her implicit corrective intention may not have been identified, whereas in (92) the explicitness of the teacher's metalinguistic comment and her insistence on learner repetition of the corrected form makes the learner momentarily focus on the code, which results in at least short-term remembering of the corrected form. According to RT, if the learners pay attention to the input, it becomes relevant to them. In (92) there is evidence that the learner has paid attention to the teacher's comment, because she has self-corrected her answer after the teacher's elicitation. We do not have such evidence in (91), where the learner's agreement (*yes*) is ambiguous. She either confirms her previous statement (*I think you shouldn't lie*) or she agrees with the teacher's correction. Only in the latter case has she paid attention to the formal features of the utterance.

Examples of implicit corrections are provided in the excerpts coming from content lessons conducted by a native speaker teacher (Mazur, 2000). The focus in the following classroom discourse is on the content, and the teacher's implicit corrections of wrongly used lexical items may pass unnoticed.

(93) (see 69)
    T: What happens to the air?
    S: First of all, it condenses.
    T: Compresses.
    S: And it becomes warmer.
    T: Why it becomes warmer? Because...
    S: You do work on it.
    T: So when you compress the air, the temperature of the air goes up and why? Because the piston does work on the air by pushing down on it some force. And that's what makes the temperature of the air go up. Any questions?
    S: No.
    T: What if you do this? What if you quit pushing up? (demonstrates). The temperature of the air goes down.
    S: Because the air pressures it.
    T: Because the air pushes it up. The air has done work. There was work done by the air. Your bicycle, a bicycle pump. Do you have any questions? This is what I want you to know. I want you to know the difference between the work being done by the air and on the air, compressing it or allowing the air to go up. (Mazur, 2000: 94)

In (93) the learners do not ask clarification questions about the meaning of difficult items if they understand the processes being described by the teacher, although in the case of a native speaker teacher such clarification questions could have been expected.

In the following excerpt (94), the learner's clarification question (*spark?*) seems to be misinterpreted by the teacher as a request for repetition rather than for an explanation of the lexical item. The teacher's comprehension check (*You know what a spark is?*) implies an affirmative answer, which is given by the learners. It seems that they do not want to acknowledge their ignorance to save face. It remains to be seen if all of them understand the meaning of the word, in spite of the teacher's repetition of it. Probably a non-native teacher in a monolingual class could have been more successful in clarifying the meaning by providing a translation equivalent in L1 (*świeca* /spark plug/).

(94) (see 71)
    T: There are two things which are different here from your bicycle pump [...] and the other thing is the spark plug.
    S: Spark?
    T: Yes, spark. You know what a spark is?
    S: Yes.
    T: So the spark burns gas. Spark plug. It's not air, here it's gas. (Mazur, 2000: 94)

A similar misinterpretation of the learner's question can be traced in another lesson conducted by the same teacher.

(95) (see 73)
    T: (explains what has been written on the board) [...] three: a change of direction when a wave strikes or hits an obstacle.
    S: Strikes an ...?
    T: Yea, in a medium. I can step outside into the hallway and you cannot ever see me but you can hear me. (Mazur, 2000: 96)

The learner most probably did not hear or understand the lexical item (*obstacle*). However, the native teacher's interpretation of the learner's question refers to the meaning of the described process of diffraction and not to the form and meaning of a particular lexical item. We could say in line with RT that the learner's incomplete knowledge of the L2 code (here: of a lexical item) and/or difficulties at the level of processing of the L2 spoken by a native speaker interfere with immediate comprehension of the teacher's explanation. What becomes automatically relevant for the learner is the form of the lexical item (*obstacle*). Had the learner explicitly asked for the explanation and/or repetition of the item, the teacher could have provided such a clarification. However, an implicit clarification request (*strikes an ...?*) is not interpreted by the native speaker teacher as a request to focus on the code, and he carries on his explanation of the diffraction process.[4]

Let us come back to other examples of explicit corrective input in otherwise meaning-oriented exchanges.

The teacher is asking learners how they would organise a house-warming party for different groups of people:

(96) T: What would you buy for old people, Marek?
    S: Cake, juice, cassette with serious music.
    T: Could you use the words: *some, any* in front of each item?
    S: Some cake, some juice, a few cassettes. (Fryc, 2000: 109)

Learners are discussing national stereotypes (see 79):

(97) T: Now let's think about Poles.
    [...].
    S: They are hostile.
    T: Could you explain what you mean?
    S: They like people when they come to them.
    T: You mean they like having guests, they are not hostile, but ...
    S: Oh, yes, hospitable, zawsze to mylę / I always mix ithem up/. (Fryc, 2000: 113)

Learners present their opinions concerning scenes in the pictures (see 77):

(98) T: Could you present your opinion?
      S: I think that animals should live free and they can't be keeping in cages.
      T: Should be free and they can't be kept in cages, OK?
      S: They can't be kept in cages.
      [...]
      S: The second picture, I think relates to the problem of cripple.
      T: Is related to the problem of the disabled. *Cripple* to jest trochę nieładne słowo /is not a very nice word/.
      S: I think it's good to learn disabled to make varied things.
      T: Nie *learn*, ale *teach* disabled to do various things. /Not *to learn* but *to teach*/. (Fryc, 2000: 115)

As can be noted in (98), if incorrect forms are numerous, the teacher's attention is automatically shifted towards accuracy focus, even if she has initiated a communicative activity, and she corrects nearly every second lexical item. It seems that the learners in (98) have not practised the required forms in more controlled activities, and they are not able to express their meanings fluently enough in a communicative activity.

Examples (99–106) illustrate teachers' and peers' input provided either to correct erroneous forms or to supply unknown items. The metalinguistic input is frequently elicited by pausing or explicit requests. The excerpts come from classroom communicative activities: general and group discussions and pair work role-plays:

(99) S: I think heating should be ... I don't know how to say it.
      T: You mean radiators should be protected. (Fryc, 2000: 98)

(100) S: Doctors should lie to patients, deadly ill.
      T: You mean patients suffering from incurable diseases. (Fryc, 2000: 102)

We could wonder if the provision of the necessary lexical items in (99) or the recasting of inaccurate lexical items in (100)[5] was explicit enough to be noticed by the learners. As has been said before, implicit input may not be the best input to focus learners on form. Yet, it seems a better solution than leaving errors uncorrected, or recasting only one error, as in (101), which does not give learners much information about their inaccuracy.

(101) T: Now, what do you think about euthanasia? In Polish *eutanazja* [...] Ewa? Łukasz? OK, Łukasz, please.
      S1: Yes, because people must have right to choose death if they don't want to live no more.

	T:	Any more.
	S2:	And what do you say if somebody from your family dies. Will you agree with him and you want him to die?
	S1:	If he wants.
	T:	And (addresses S3) what do you think?
	S3:	I agree with S2. You can't decide about death. Only God can.
	T:	Hm, OK. (Fryc, 2000: 105)

We can only presume that the communicative impact of the topic made the teacher reluctant to provide more corrective input focused on inaccurate forms.

(102)	S:	But sometimes patient is weak and he will ... zalamie się /break down/.
	T:	Break down. (Fryc, 2000: 106)
(103)	S:	There were my friends which I didn't see for a long time [...]
	T:	Friends who ... it's a person, right?
	S:	Oh yes. There were friends who I didn't see[6] (Fryc, 2000: 107)

In the following excerpts the teacher has withdrawn, leaving the floor to the learners engaged in communicative activities. As can be noted, one of the learners, probably the one at a higher L2 proficiency level, assumes the role of the teacher, and provides necessary input.

(104)	S1:	I think it's awful when people show their feelings like this. And it's ... poniżający /humiliating/.
	S2:	Humiliating?
	S3:	Yes.
	S1:	OK, so it's humiliating. (Przebinda, 2004: 111)
(105)	S1:	The general idea of reality shows is ... is ... jak jest 'zarobić pieniądze'? /How do we say 'earn money'?/.
	S2:	To earn big money.
	S1:	Wow! And it's a good business. (turns to the teacher) Jak jest reklama? Bo po niemiecku to jest 'Werbung'. /How do we say 'advertisement'? In German it is ... /.
	T:	Advertisement.
	S2:	Advertisement. OK.
		[...]
	S1:	No a jak powiedzieć, że jest dużo przemocy i seksu? /How should we say that there is a lot of violence and sex?/.
	S2:	There is a lot of violence and sex. (Przebinda, 2004: 113)

It is worth noting that in (105) it is S2 who repeats the word *advertisement* and who seems to be paying more attention to corrective input than S1, who asks questions about the unknown lexical items, but later does not repeat the provided items (*earn money, advertisement, violence, sex*).

In (106) the learners enact a role play, which is believed to involve them in speaking in L2 to a greater extent than a discussion (see Przebinda, 2004). Yet, even during a role play activity one learner corrects the other when she notices her search for an appropriate lexical item.

(106) S1: I'm absolutely against.
       S2: You are so ... so hard, really ...
       S1: Strict.
       S2: Yes, strict. You are very strict, Mummy. (Przebinda, 2004: 117)

Instructional Input: Explicit Teaching

Explicit presentation of the linguistic data to the learners

One of the most common teaching techniques of explicit presentation of the linguistic data to the learners is asking them direct questions about the target language system. In our database, such questions have been collected by Kosiarz (1985). They primarily focus on the elicitation of accurate answers. The first examples (107–110) illustrate how teachers elicit the L1 translation equivalents of the L2 lexical items.

(107) T: Do you know what the word *excursion* is?
       S: Wycieczka /excursion/.
       T: Yes. (Kosiarz, 1985: 68)

(108) T: Co to jest *recipe*? /What does *recipe* mean?/
       S: Przepis /recipe/.
       T: Good, przepis /recipe/. A jak jest *recepta*?[7] /And how shall we say p*rescription*?/.
       S: (no answer).
       T: A prescription, a prescription. (Kosiarz, 1985: 71)

(109) T: What is *pneumonia*? Anyone?
       S: (no answer).
       T: Zapalenie płuc /pneumonia/. Zapiszcie to sobie. /Write it down, please/. (Kosiarz, 1985: 75)

(110) T: What does it mean *to do research*?
       S: Prowadzić badania. /To do research/.
       T: Right. (Kosiarz, 1985: 80)

In the above excerpts the learners have to interpret the teacher's input as either giving them an opportunity to hear the correct translation equivalent of a given lexical item, or to provide them with an opportunity to communicate in L2. If the teacher asks her question in L1, as in (108), there is no doubt that the former is the case. However, if the teachers, as in (107), (109) and (110) ask their questions in L2, they also communicate to the learners that they provide an opportunity to communicate in the target language, to negotiate the meanings. Thus, the choice of the language of classroom communication shifts the learners' attention from a total focus on an isolated L2 lexical item to a focus on a lexical item embedded in real communication. The observed teachers used either L1 or L2 to ask the above questions, and there are no grounds to claim that there was a consistent pattern of L1 or L2 questions. They seem to have been randomly distributed in the samples.

According to RT, we can say that although the language used by the teachers communicated to the learners the level of expected optimal relevance of classroom discourse, higher in the case of communication in L2, the learners automatically focused on the meaning of lexical items to be translated, without paying attention to the remaining part of the questions, because they understood their function (asking about L1 translation equivalents), and that was optimally relevant at the moment.

There are not very many examples in the collected discourse samples of the explicit presentation of the grammatical data to the learners. The few (111–112) which can be found in the excerpts follow the learners' incorrect use of verb forms and serve as elicited recall of grammatical forms:

(111) T: What is the past participle of the verb *say*?
       S: Said.
       T: Yes, good, continue, please. (Kosiarz, 1985: 81)

(112) T: Jakie są formy czasownika *spend*? /What are the forms of the verb *spend*?/.
       S: Spend, spent, spent.
       T: That's right. (Kosiarz, 1995: 84)

An example of explicit modelling of L2 by the teacher comes from Puchała (1993). The example was given as a teacher metalinguistic comment during accuracy practice:

(113) S: Are you going to do some sightseeing?
       T: 'Are you going to do some sightseeing'? albo /or/ 'Are you going to do any sightseeing'? (Puchala, 1993: 35)

As has been said in Chapter 4, the observations made by Puchala (1993) distinguish between lessons focused on teaching grammar and lessons focused on developing skills. The following explicit metalinguistic remark in a non-grammar lesson was made in L2:

(114) S: A może być 'I don't want you to argue with me'? /Can we say...?/.
T: It is 'I want you not to do this'. Witek, it is the same situation as we had with 'I would rather'. 'I would rather go', right? 'I would rather not go'. 'I would prefer to go'. 'I would prefer not to go'. When asking questions we can use 'Would you rather be a teacher'? You have this in a question. [...] And this is the negative of this sentence. Can you understand? Would you like me to write it on the blackboard? (Puchala, 1993: 52)

The learners' attention is focused on the structure presented by the teacher, which is the content of explicit teaching, but since the teacher uses L2 for classroom communication, after a while, particularly because of the length of the teacher's comment, the learners may also focus their attention on some formal features of L2 discourse, especially on the structure of the final question (*Would you like me to write it on the blackboard?*), which is identical with the structure modelled by the teacher (*Would you rather be a teacher?*).[8]

However, most of the teachers' explicit metalinguistic remarks have been made in grammar lessons, where the explicit teacher input consisted mostly of L1 or mixed L1/L2 moves (115–116):

(115) T: Podmiot, a potem? Po podmiocie jaki ma być czas? /The subject, and then? After the subject which tense should be used?/.
S: Przeszły /the past tense/.
T: Do tyłu, tak jak w mowie zależnej, prawda? I pamiętamy jeszcze, że 'I wish' zawiera... /Back, as in reported speech, isn't it? And we remember that in 'I wish' there is ... /.
S: Przeczenie /a negation/. (Puchała, 1993: 54)

(116) (see 22)
T: 'In' albo 'at'. 'Come to' but 'arrive in' or 'at'. Kiedy 'in'? Kiedy myślimy o mieście całym: 'to arrive in Cracow'. A jeżeli mówimy 'to arrive at', to mówimy o punkcie w mieście. Na przykład, 'to arrive at the station', 'at the airport'. /'In or at' [...] When 'in'? When we think of a whole town:'to arrive in Cracow'. And when we say 'to arrive at', we talk about a place in the town. For example, 'to arrive at the station', 'at the airport'/. (Puchała, 1993: 53)

The L1 communication in (115) about the L2 grammatical system can serve as an example of classroom grammar talk, a kind of pedagogical grammar, in which the teacher uses her own simplifications and abbreviations while eliciting students' answers about the presented structure. From the RT point of view, through the use of L1 in metalinguistic comments the level of expected optimal relevance is firmly established on explicit language teaching.

In (116) we have a mini-lecture on the use of prepositions for locations, in which the teacher starts communicating in L1 (*in* albo /or/ *at*), then switches to L2 (*'Come to' but 'arrive in' or 'at'*), to code-switch back to L1 in the following question (*Kiedy 'in'?/When 'in'?/*) and to give a whole mini-lecture in L1, except for the L2 examples.

Why does the teacher start talking in L1, then switches to L2 and immediately comes back to L1? According to RT, it can be claimed that code-switching raises or lowers the level of expected optimal relevance of classroom communication. Code-switching to L2 raises the expected level of relevance, because the learners are expected to notice the teacher's communicative intention to focus them not only on the meanings but also on the formal features of the L2 code. However, as has been said before, an automatic search for meaning rather than focusing on the formal features may interfere with the process of accurate interpretation of the teacher's message. That is why perhaps the teacher, who had an intention of raising the level of expected relevance, having realized that the learners may find difficulty in an accurate interpretation of her comments on the basis of L2 communication, has again code-switched to L1.

Teacher corrections of learners' language

While the presentation of the linguistic data to the learners with the intention of focusing their attention on the L2 code is usually explicit, because otherwise, according to RT, our cognition would automatically focus on the meaning of the message, and not on its form, the corrective intention may be more or less explicit. Accordingly, as has been said before, the learners may focus their attention momentarily on the form while attending to meanings. It has also been said that the most explicit corrections seem to be the best for recognising the teacher's corrective intention.

In our data, Czekajewska's (1999) study provides findings that can be most easily interpreted in the light of RT. Her original hypothesis that teacher corrections in form-focused activities would be remembered better than corrections in meaning-oriented activities has not been corroborated. Elicited self-corrections in both types of activities were remembered better than teacher corrections. The finding may indicate that it is not the global type of classroom activity (meaning-oriented or form-oriented) but rather the local environment of contextual assumptions governed by the principle of relevance that make a particular utterance (here: correction) relevant for the learner. Let us see how some of the examples in Czekajewska's data provide evidence for the local environment of contextual assumptions, which make the learners focus their attention on the form.

Among the local aspects of classroom corrective communication that could be distinguished in the observed exchanges, meaning-oriented and form-oriented activities generated different elicitation patterns. While in form-focused activities elicitations of self-corrections presented the rules or indicated learners' error in more or less explicit ways, in meaning-oriented activities most of the teachers' corrections were less explicit. The teachers repeated parts of the learners' incorrect utterances and stopped just before the errors or they asked questions which could indicate that they had not heard or understood the preceding utterances.

All the following corrections were remembered after the lessons. In the following excerpts (117–122) the teachers elicited learner self-corrections in form-focused activities:

(117) S: She asked me if I had recently been eating apples.
T: (shakes his head) Where should 'recently' be put in your sentence?
S: She asked me if I had been eating apples recently? (Czekajewska, 1999: 67)

(118) S: She asked me if I'm hungry.
T: But it was in the past!
S: If I was hungry. (Czekajewska, 1999: 67)

(119) S: We have been sitting here since an hour.
T: Pewnyś? Jaka jest różnica między 'since' i 'for'? 'Since' od jakiegoś czasu, 'for' przez jakiś okres czasu. / Are you sure? What is the difference between 'since' and 'for'? 'Since' from a given time, 'for' during a period of time/.
S: We have been sitting here for an hour. (Czekajewska, 1999: 68)

(120) S: I think be able to drive is very important.
T: Lepiej byłoby użyć gerundu, tej formy z '-ing', bo to jest umiejętność jazdy, czyli po angielsku 'bycie zdolnym'. /It would be better to use the Gerund, the '-ing' form, because it is an ability to drive, i.e. in English 'being able'/.
S: Being able to drive. (Czekajewska, 1999: 69)

(121) S: It costed a lot.
T: What's the past form of the verb 'to cost'?
S: It cost a lot. (Czekajewska, 1999: 69)

(122) (see 34)
      S: I wish I had passed the competition.
      T: Passed? You don't say 'to pass a competition'. What do you say?
      S: Win! I wish I had won the competition. (Czekajewska, 1999: 70)

    The elicited corrections in form-focused activities more or less explicitly present the linguistic data to the learners. The choice of the language of presentation seems to depend on the expected L2 proficiency level of the learners. By explicitly presenting the rules, or explicitly indicating that what the learners said was incorrect, the teachers made their corrective intentions clear to the learners. The language of corrective communication does not seem to be as important as in the case of longer metalinguistic presentations. First of all, corrections are short and focused on particular errors. If the teachers support their corrections with longer presentations of grammatical rules, they usually code-switch to L1 (119–120). In the light of RT, as has been said before, they lower the level of expected optimal relevance of metalinguistic communication.

    In the meaning-oriented activities (123–127) the teachers elicited learner self-corrections less explicitly by asking questions or repeating learners' utterances up to the error:

(123) S: I'm not a person who don't eat meat at all.
      T: I'm not a person who ...
      S: ... doesn't eat meat. (Czekajewska, 1999: 71)

(124) S: What is she look like?
      T: What is she look like?!
      S: What does she look like? (Czekajewska, 1999: 71)

(125) S: I would swimming.
      T: What would you do?
      S: I would swim. (Czekajewska, 1999: 72)

(126) S: Many peoples want to go there.
      T: Many ...
      S: Many people. (Czekajewska, 1999: 72)

(127) (see 35)
      S: I would like to see the other culture.
      T: The other?
      S: (hesitates)
      T: Does it mean there are only two cultures?
      S: I would like to see another culture. (Czekajewska, 1999: 72)

    Teacher corrections in form-focused activities cannot be usually mistaken for classroom communication, so they are utterly explicit in their corrective function. They are usually short teacher turns, which are frequently followed by student repetitions of the corrected forms. The following excerpts (128–131) illustrate teacher corrections in form-focused activities. Some of them were remembered after the lessons, while others were not:

(128)   S: She looks at me angry.
        T: Angrily.
        S: Angrily.
        (not remembered). (Czekajewska, 1999: 75)

(129)   S: He decided change his job.
        T: To change his job.
        S: To change his job.
        (remembered). (Czekajewska, 1999: 75)

(130)   S: I've been here since three of May.
        T: Since the third of May.
        S: (does not repeat)
        (not remembered). (Czekajewska, 1999: 76)

(131)   S: She has been running in the park since two months.
        T: Once again.
        S: (does not answer)
        T: For two months!
        S: (does not repeat)
        (remembered). (Czekajewska, 1999: 78)

If we compare (128) and (129), what can distinguish the teacher correction in the latter is its saliency in the initial position versus lack of saliency in the final position in the former. The learner may not have noticed the teacher correction in (128) even if he repeated it. The two other examples (130) and (131) differ in the focus of teacher correction. In the latter the focus of the correction is the focus of the activity (*since* or *for*), while in the former it is a grammatical point not in focus in the current activity (*three* or *the third*).

From the RT perspective, meaning-oriented teacher corrections are more interesting than form-focused teacher corrections. As has been said before, they are much less explicit than form-focused corrections, and similar to elicited corrections. Consequently, the learners may misinterpret the teachers' corrective intention. Yet, such misinterpretation can be avoided if the teachers' input communicates its double purpose: real communication and corrective feedback. In the following example there is little chance of student misinterpretation of the teacher's correction:

(132) S: I don't know if I would get succeed.
       T: What do you mean?
       S: (hesitates)
       T: You mean you are not sure if you would succeed?
       S: Yes!
       (remembered). (Czekajewska, 1999: 89)

In the above example of teacher correction (recast) during a communicative activity (general discussion) the teacher's question (*What do you mean?*) may be treated either as an elicitation of student correction of an erroneous form/s or it may be a clarification request focused on the message the student intends to communicate. In fact, the two interpretations coincide, because the teacher's correction (*You mean you are not sure if you would succeed*) clarifies the intended student's meaning. The student acknowledges both the correction and the clarification (*Yes!*).

The problem arises as to whether teacher corrections are always interpreted as corrections, which from our perspective equals the question of whether they are relevant for the learners on the level of expected optimal L2 classroom discourse. If the classroom discourse requires the learners to focus both on fluency and accuracy, in other words, if the teacher elicits learner corrections and corrects learners' errors while focusing primarily on communicating meanings, then the corrective input will be relevant for the learners since they will automatically attend to it. However, if the classroom discourse is focused entirely on fluency, and learners' errors are recast by the teachers, then the corrections are not perceived as real corrections and they are not attended to, and consequently, they are not remembered and recalled by the learners.

The former situation can be demonstrated by some examples. Our data provides us with some evidence of temporary student focus on the formal side of the teachers' corrections in the learners' repetitions of those corrections and remembering them after the lessons. It seems that the deeply ingrained classroom habit of repeating teacher corrections may be treated as a useful device in turning the learners' attention to formal features of the language code. Numerous repetitions can be found in Czekajewska's data. All the following corrections (133–137) were remembered after the lessons:

(133) S: I'm also interested in group sports.
       T: Team sports.
       S: Team sports. (Czekajewska, 1999: 82)

(134) S: He has given some money.
       T: He hasn't given anything! He was given!
       S: He was given some money. (Czekajewska, 1999: 83)

(135) S: It doesn't do difference if you eat a lot or not.
T: It doesn't make difference.
S: It doesn't make difference. (Czekajewska, 1999: 84)

(136) S: I think the dinosaur is three hundred million years ago.
T: Once again!
S: (does not answer)
T: Three hundred million years old.
S: Three hundred million years old. (Czekajewska, 1999: 86)

(137) S: They couldn't give me so many informations.
T: So much information.
S: So much information. (Czekajewska, 1999: 87)

In the whole corpus of our classroom discourse data, there is one case of student correction of a teacher language error in a mathematics class:

(138) T: Find equation of a straight line.
S: Find the equation?
T: The equation. Thank you. (Mazur, 2000: 103)

Let us recall a non-native customer in Carroll's example expressing his gratitude to a native speaker after he has corrected his grammar, instead of supplying him with the required information. Similarly, in the above example the teacher acknowledges the learner's correction of her language error. She does not interpret the learner's question as inquiring about the content of the lesson, whether he is to find the equation or something else. Rather, she is immediately aware that she has made a language error, and she repeats the corrected part of her turn. In other words, she acts as a language learner, who repeats the corrected form, and momentarily focuses her attention on the form. In the light of RT we can say that the student has shifted the level of relevance from the meaning focus to the form focus, and that his intention was rightly interpreted, due to the teacher's language awareness and the knowledge she possessed about the learner who made the correction (his high proficiency level).

On the other hand, however, Fryc's (2000) corpus provides us with discourse data collected during communicative activities (139–141), which give some support to the irrelevance of corrective input for the ongoing classroom discourse, at least in the case of some classes. Teachers' corrections of learners' errors are not followed by learners' self-corrections, or, quite frequently, the teachers do not provide any corrective feedback. Both teachers and learners are focused on the completion of communicative tasks set by the teaching materials.

In the following excerpt, the students discuss some controversial statements about medical care based on a teaching material. The teacher monitors the activity. The relevant statement from the teaching material is given in italics:

(139) *The state should pay for all medical care. There should be no private medical care.*
    S1: I think it's not good that the state pay for all medical care. Anyway we will pay to ZUS (national insurance) and only we'll have no choice.
    T: You mean we would have to pay an insurance tax anyway.
    S1: Yes, the money will the same, but the quality of medical care not.
    T: The amount of money would be the same and only the quality of treatment would differ. What do the others think? Aniu?
    S2: I think it's good for poor. They could get medical care if state would pay, and if it is private they could not pozwolić sobie na to /afford it/.
    T: They wouldn't be able to afford it.
    S2: Yes, they would not be able to afford it. (Fryc, 2000: 105)

The teacher's recasts (*You mean we would have to pay an insurance tax anyway* and *The amount of money would be the same and only the quality of treatment would differ*) are not interpreted by S1 as corrections, and he does not self-correct or repeat the recasts. On the other hand, S2 uses an L1 phrase to communicate the meaning she was not able to express in L2. After the teacher's recast, she repeats the L2 utterance. Accordingly, the teacher's input seems to be optimally relevant on different levels of expected optimal relevance for different learners.

While S1 is focused on fluency practice only, and does not interpret the teacher's comments as accuracy-oriented corrective feedback, S2 focuses her attention on the code as well. Her L1 phrase (*pozwolić sobie na to* /afford it/) could have been a communication strategy – an appeal for help to the teacher (*How should I say it in English?*). After the teacher has provided the required phrase, the learner acknowledges the teacher's corrective move by repeating it.

However, the majority of the classroom data collected during communicative activities indicate that teachers' corrections are not, in fact, treated by the learners as the corrective feedback which requires focusing on the form and repeating the corrected utterance. We can interpret it as searching for meaning only and disregarding form. The expected optimal level of relevance is set at communicating meanings, and the code in which the meanings are communicated becomes unimportant. Consequently, in a monolingual context, the teachers do not seem to correct errors in L2 any longer, rather they provide L2 translation equivalents of the L1 utterances used by the learners.

In the following excerpt, the learners are involved in a general discussion on national stereotypes:

(140) T: Why did you say that the first picture represents an American?
S1: Because they are fat and they keep their legs on table.
S2: They also have such hats like cowboy.
T: What other stereotypes do you know?
S3: Russian, they drink very much alcohol.
T: Yes, and the French, do you know anything about their stereotype?
S1: They eat żaby /frogs/.
T: Frogs, yeah?
S4: Also French love. French are good lovers. 'Sztuka kochania'. /The art of loving/, it is from French, I think.
T: You mean that you associate the French with love?
S2: Yes, and they also drink wine.
S5: I think of Japanese as hard working and business people.
T: And the others? What comes to your mind when you think of Japanese?
S6: Cars, computers. (Fryc, 2000: 113)

The above classroom discourse excerpt shows the teacher's input during the activity focused on fluency practice which can hardly be called corrective. The teacher provides a translation equivalent of an L1 lexical item (*żaby* /frogs/), which is not repeated by the learner who uses the L1 word in the previous turn. Except for one case, the teacher does not correct errors in the use of articles, and in the case where she provides a rather elaborate recast (*You mean that you associate the French with love*), the corrected article use (*the French*) does not seem to be noticed by the learners.[9]

Why did the teacher not play her role of Corrector? On the one hand, an answer seems to be given in her opinions on language teaching (Fryc, 2000). The teacher strongly agrees with the statement that the teacher should correct only those errors that distort communication, and she disagrees with the statement that all errors should be corrected and that the teacher should correct erroneous forms herself (Fryc, 2000: 147). Thus, the teacher's beliefs about the right way of teaching find support in her classroom behaviour.

Yet, there is another layer of communication in the observed phenomena. If we interpret L2 classroom discourse in the light of RT, the teacher neglecting her role as the provider of more or less explicit corrective input and letting students carry on their communication without paying attention to incorrect forms, communicates to them her intention to focus entirely on the completion of the communicative task rather than on engaging in meaningful communication (*What other stereotypes do you know? Do you know anything about their stereotype? What comes to your mind when you think of...?*). Such questions can be interpreted as *Say anything in English which is somehow referring to our topic*. Paradoxically then, disregarding formal correctness may also mean disregarding factual appropriateness. What the teacher communicates to the learners and they infer is a very low level of classroom communication indeed, where *anything goes*. This aspect of communicative activities will be discussed in Chapter 6.

A similar pattern of beliefs on error correction in another teacher's answers corresponds with her behaviour during a role-play she monitors. The teacher corrects only two minor grammatical errors, and she does not pay attention to the students' interlanguage forms and pragmatic errors. What seems to matter for the teacher is the completion of the task, in other words, filling the time with talk.

Two students act out a telephone conversation with a friend who has been ill. The roles require one of them to end the conversation (*Say you have to go and give a reason. Your friend must respond appropriately and make arrangements to meet at another time.*)

(141) S1: Hello, Ania.
 S2: Hello, Susan.
 S1: Why haven't you been to the party?
 S2: Because I'm ill.
 S1: Oh, sorry. What problem do you have?
 S2: Grypa /flu/. Yes, I have flu.
 S1: Oh, and the party was great, I enjoy it.
 T: I enjoyed it.
 S2: Who was at the party?
 S1: Everybody oprócz /except/ you.
 T: Everybody but you.
 S2: What were you doing?
 S1: Dancing, talking, listening music.
 T: OK. Ask about some friend that you both know.
 S2: How was Marek?
 S1: Yes, he came at the party with his girlfriend.
 S2: Did you talk to him?
 S1: No, he was all the time with Ela. OK, I have to go. I have an appointment. So I'll visit you tomorrow.
 S2: OK. Bye.
 S1: Bye. (Fryc, 2000: 123)

The teacher's disregarding formal correctness (*OK* without recasting the previous student utterance *dancing, talking, listening music*) communicates to the students a low level of expected optimal relevance, where anything they produce is accepted by the teacher, as in the following exchange (Q: *How was Marek?* A: *Yes, he came at the party with his girlfriend*).

The teacher's behaviour cannot be accounted for by her lack of proficiency in English. She is an experienced secondary school teacher of English (eight years of teaching experience at the time of the above data collection). She had graduated from English Studies with an MA degree and EFL teaching qualifications. She was also aware that the lesson was observed and recorded. It seems that this teacher's and other teachers' classroom behaviour can be at least partly accounted for by a misinterpretation of the Communicative Approach (see Chapter 2).

Instructional Input: L2 Classroom Communication

Let us now consider instructional input from the perspective of RT in the L2 classroom communication. As has been said in Chapter 1, SLA theory draws on a rather oversimplified distinction between form-focused and meaning-focused instruction, while, as I have attempted to demonstrate in the previous sections, the form and the meaning in the L2 classroom discourse are very close indeed, and there is a constant attention shift between one and the other. Additionally, what sometimes seems to be meaning-oriented discourse, may be only focused on task completion, whereas what seems to be form-focused discourse, can be meaningful in the instructional context, e.g. in explicit L2 teaching.

Let us distinguish between two types of L2 classroom communicative language use: real communication and simulated communication. By real communicative language use, I understand talking about the matters which are authentic in the L2 classroom: the teaching/learning content or organisational and social matters.

Besides real communicative language use, L2 classroom communication involves a stage which in L2 teaching is traditionally called 'language production', and which involves simulated communication, in other words, fluency practice. In Communicative Language Teaching this type of activities, frequently conducted by groups of learners, and only monitored by the teacher, is considered particularly beneficial for language learning (see Chapter 2).

In the following sections of this chapter I will try to interpret real communication and simulated communication in the light of RT.

Real communication

Talking about the learning content

When L2 teachers ask questions about the L2 learning content, usually about the content of reading or listening passages, the underlying content does not only serve as a content basis for free communication, but also as a grammatically pre-structured and lexically adapted L2 samples, upon which patterned questions and answers can be practised. Let us see an example of such a teaching technique below (142):

The teacher first introduces the topic orally. She speaks all the time in L2. Then she reads the passage out, and the learners are supposed to listen in order to understand the gist of it. Later on, the learners are to read the passage carefully in order to understand more detailed information. Finally, the teacher asks some comprehension questions. The learners ask some questions about lexical items, but the teacher does not provide translation equivalents in L1. She tries to make the learner recall the lexical items and guess them from the context. She is also observant of the learners' behaviour, and she admonishes a misbehaving student. The teacher's verbal and non-verbal behaviour communicates to the learners that what she says is relevant on the level of classroom L2 communication combining meaning and form focus:

(142) T: Close your books. Now we are going to have listening comprehension. The title of the reading is *A Wonderful Place for a Swim*. I suggest that you write the explanations from the blackboard afterwards. Now, listen carefully. (The teacher reads the passage out.)
T: Now, read this to understand and you yourselves will answer questions. (The learners read the passage).
T: How are you sitting, Peter?
S1: What 'tyre' is?
T: Oh, it's nothing new for you. You have already had this word. You must have remembered it. (The learners have finished reading the passage).
T: Now, when you understand the text, I suggest that you answer some questions. What did they go to the river for?
S2: They went fishing and they wanted to have a rest.
T: What did they do before they started fishing?
S3: They had to pump up the tyres.
T: What did they order Mike to do?
[...]
(The teacher asks a couple of similar questions. The learners answer them on the basis of the text they have read).
T: Yes. It means that you understand the text. (Kusibab, 1984: 87)

As has been said before, according to the Communicative Approach, such language use has been called pre-communicative (see Littlewood, 1981), since the learners are not allowed to say whatever they want, but they have to follow a grammatical pattern and to use particular lexical items. In addition, the teacher is asking questions not to discover anything new for herself, but to check if the students have understood the reading passage.

However, it cannot be denied that the learners communicate meanings, and they are focused at least as much on meanings as on forms. The distinction between language use in the above activity and an activity in which the students would tell the teacher about their own trip, lies in the underlying learning content, in this case the reading passage. In the case of their own trip described in class, the learners would not have linguistic data (the passage) to refer to, and their only resources would be their non-verbalised memories. What would be missing then would be the facilitating input of the structures and lexical items, which can be readily used in the classroom account based on a reading passage. There is no need to add that an account without an underlying learning content would induce numerous L2 errors.

If the L2 classroom discourse, in particular, the teacher's classroom language is focused on the underlying learning content, then according to RT, it communicates to the learners its relevance in the role of the teaching discourse. The teacher's questions in (142) are perceived as optimally relevant on the level of real communication focused on the learning content.

Let us provide more examples of similar classroom communication. They are concerned with teaching grammatical structures, yet they also provide real communicative opportunities for the learners.

(143) T: Here we have a lot of things: a box of candy, a doll, a record, a book, a dictionary, a flower, a radio. You are going to visit your friend in London. He has his birthday. Come and choose what to give to your English friend for his birthday. Remember to use Conditional Sentences Type II.
 S1: If my friend had a birthday, I would buy him a book for a present.
 T: Why?
 S1: Because I think that the book is the best present.
 S2: If my friend had a birthday, I would give him a radio.
 T: Why?
 S2: Because he likes music and it's a very good radio.
 S3: If my friend had a birthday, I would give her a German dictionary.

T: Why?
S3: Because she learns German. (Kusibab, 1984: 88)

In the next example (144) the teacher's turns link classroom management with teaching grammatical structure. Using a repetitive pattern, she makes the grammatical point relevant to the learners, without losing sight of real communication:

(144) T: Could you open all the windows, please? It is warm in the class. Change your place, Witek, and sit down over there. Yes, Marcin, and now you will be a nice boy. Bożena, open the windows! What did I tell Bożena?
S1: You told Bożena to open the windows.
T: Witek, change your place. What did I tell Witek?
S2: You told Witek to change his place. (Kusibab, 1984: 99)

The learners interpret the above exchanges as relevant on the level of expected optimal relevance combining meaning-oriented with form-oriented practice. The reason why they perceive the teacher's turns as relevant seems to involve two aspects: the combined effect of the teacher's input and a high level of learners' L2 proficiency. In other words, the two obstacles to the automatic interpretation of the products of the decoding process in the L2 classroom have been removed: an incomplete knowledge of the L2 code, and the irrelevance of semantic interpretation of utterances. Let us further explain how these two obstacles cease to play their negative role in the above exchanges (142–144).

In (142) the teacher first makes sure that the learners understand the reading passage: *read this to understand [...] it's nothing new for you, you have already had this word, you must have remembered it [...] when you understand the text* .... The teacher puts an emphasis on the process of understanding, she explicitly removes the aforementioned obstacles in treating the reading passage in a superficial way and reading for gist only (the first obstacle), and in disregarding its meaning and treating it only as a task to complete (the second obstacle). While reading the passage, the learners are aware that they will be required soon to answer comprehension questions, and that is the reason why they focus not only on the general meaning but also on the details. Thus, the teacher's talking about the learning content (the passage) supports the content in making it relevant for the learners on the expected (intended by the teacher) level of relevance. The learners' L2 proficiency level is an underlying condition: they have to be able to decode the meanings on the basis of the provided forms, and the teacher skilfully matches the level of her classroom interaction and of the teaching materials with the learners' proficiency level.[10]

Real classroom communication in talking about the learning content is also clearly seen in L2 subject-matter teaching (Mazur, 2000). The learning content is the non-linguistic, factual content of the lessons. The difficulty of the L2 code, in particular of the new and difficult lexical items, makes the teachers focus on them. A characteristic feature of L2 subject-matter teaching, as has been said before, is regular code-switching from L2 to L1 and *vice versa*. Let us compare Example (142) from an EFL class with the following excerpt from a subject-matter class.

The history teacher introduces the topic of the lesson, pre-teaches new vocabulary and asks comprehension questions on the reading passage. The text is in English and more difficult lexical items are translated into L1:

(145) T: Dobra, proszę państwa. Dzisiaj piszemy sobie temat. Nazywa się *A Medieval Town*, dobra? Dzisiaj będziemy o stanie mieszczańskim sobie mówić. Stan mieszczański nie pojawił się w Europie tak od razu. To jest XI wiek, czyli około 600 lat musiało upłynąć od upadku Rzymu, żeby odrodziło się miasto w prawdziwym tego słowa znaczeniu. Proszę sobie to zobaczyć. Pięć minut na przeczytanie i zastanowienie się nad tym problemem. Jest tu jedno słówko, którego nie przetłumaczyłem, a mianowicie 'pillory'. Co to jest? [...] To jest takie urządzenie, które było na środku rynku. No, po prostu pręgierz, był to pręgierz. /OK, ladies and gentlemen, today our topic is *A Medieval Town*, OK? Today we are going to talk about townspeople. Townspeople did not reappear in Europe for a long time. That was in the 11th century, which means that six centuries must have passed since the fall of the Roman Empire before the town in the proper sense reappeared. Have a look, please. You have five minutes to read and to reflect on this problem. There is one word I have not translated, 'a pillory'. What is it? [...] It's such a device which was in the middle of the market square. Simply a pillory, it was a pillory/.
(The learners read the text).
T: OK, so these were only questions concerning the vocabulary, apart from these explained under the text?
S: Perpetual?
T: Perpetual?
Ss: Constant.
T: Perpetual, constant.
S: Stały? /constant/.
T: Stały

S: Upbraided?
T: To criticize, so 'The Mayor upbraided the citizens for doing something wrong'.
S: Municipal?
T: Proszę państwa, miejski /ladies and gentlemen, municipal/. Concerning the town.
[...]
(The teacher asks questions on the reading passage.)
T: Apart from running the town what did they do?
S: They fixed wages.
T: Yes, they fixed wages.
S: They fixed prices.
T: Yes, they fixed prices.
S: Organising defence.
T: Organising defence. Organising defence to też ważna funkcja cechu albo gildii w mieście. /... is another important function of a craft guild or guild in town/. Let's return to English [...].
T: If you want to be a craftsman, what steps do you have to go through to become a craftsman?
Ss: Apprentice, journey-man.
T: Why are they called 'journey-men'?
S: Because they had to travel.
T: Yes, they had to travel to obtain training. After such a training the journey-man returned to a town and passed an examination to obtain rights. (Mazur, 2000: 84)

What can be noticed in (145) is the teacher's focus on the factual content. He makes it explicit in his introduction to the topic of the lesson. What could be inferred from the teacher's input in a history class taught in L2 is his intention to implicitly teach English, while explicitly focusing on historical facts.

The teacher is aware of it when he reminds himself that he should use L2: *Let's return to English.* However, it is interesting to observe how the teacher introduces his lesson topic in L1. We can only speculate why he uses L1. The reason is probably his limited fluency in L2 to be able to talk at length in the target language. Another reason, in line with Puchała's (1993) speculations, is that the teacher does not switch to the L2 speaking mode until he is supported by the L2 input provided by the reading passage. His own general introduction to the topic of the lesson (*A Medieval Town*) might have been useful L2 input for the learners had it been delivered in English. According to RT, it would have raised the level of expected optimal relevance to the simultaneous focus on L2 forms and factual meanings.

On the other hand, lack of L2 input does communicate to the learners an important message. The teacher informs them through his L1 use in the introduction of the topic that the most important information on the historical processes in the course will be delivered in L1, and that, consequently, their paying attention to L2 input is not essential for the understanding of the factual material of the course. In his introduction in L1 the teacher has communicated to the learners that he is, first of all, a history teacher, who will be using an L2 English text on a medieval town.

In the second part of the lesson, after the learners have read the text, the teacher assumes his other role of an L2 teacher, and he explicitly makes sure whether the learners have understood difficult vocabulary items included in the text.[11] The teacher's use of L2 and L1 at that stage of the lesson seems to be inconsistent, he uses L1, L2 or both languages to explain the vocabulary items or to elicit them from the learners. By saying in L1 *miejski* /municipal/ and adding immediately *concerning the town*, the teacher communicates to the learner the irrelevance of the level on which they could try to guess the meaning of the L2 lexical item *municipal* on the basis of its L2 paraphrase.

In the third part of the lesson, when the teacher asks questions on the text, the discourse resembles one in (142), except that again what we can observe is lack of consistency in language use. After two exchanges in which a grammatical pattern and a lexical item are repeated (*They fixed wages. They fixed prices.*), which could indicate that the teacher combines factual teaching with L2 practice, he does not respond on the same level of relevance to the next student's turn (*organising defence*). The case in point merits consideration because it provides us with an example of language use not made relevant on the desired level of relevance.

Let us first quote from the original text read in class: [...] *in Florence, for example, the seven major guilds* [...] *practically ran the city, fixing wages, prices and hours of work, organizing defence and holding all the important municipal offices.*

The student who answers the teacher's question *Apart from running the town what did they do?*[12] uses the phrase *organising defence* derived from the text input. The teacher, however, does not provide a recast matching the grammatical pattern of the previous answers, e.g. *Yes, they organised defence*, which would probably be done by an L2 teacher. Using the same RT framework, we can say that the form of the learner's answer is irrelevant for the history teacher, because what matters for him is only the semantic interpretation of the learning content. Consequently, the teacher's attention is focused on the meaning only, and in his next move he code-switches to L1 (*organising defence* to też ważna funkcja cechu albo gildii w mieście /... is another important function of a craft guild or guild in town/). Thus, the teacher communicates to the learners the irrelevance of L2 forms.

In the final part of the excerpt, however, the teacher is inconsistent again. This time, he pays attention to the L2 form *journey-man*. By asking the question: *Why are they called journey-men?*, the teacher refers directly to the lexical item *journey*, and makes the L2 form again relevant for the learners.

The above detailed analysis of a fragment of a subject-matter lesson has served the purpose of demonstrating how the teacher's L2 or L1 input and his/her focus on the learning content in terms of purely factual knowledge, or on factual knowledge combined with language teaching concerns, can shift the level of expected optimal relevance for the instructed learners, in other words, how the teacher's input focuses the learners' attention on meaning only, or on meaning combined with form.

Talking about organisational and social matters

Good classroom management, organisation of learning tasks and disciplined students have always been a matter of great importance in L2 teaching. In order to be able to focus on the learning content and to create a class atmosphere which would be conducive to L2 learning, the teachers must make sure that the learners know what the learning tasks involve. The teachers should also give positive or negative feedback during or following the tasks, and, if necessary, they should discipline students who do not obey classroom rules. While managing the classroom, organising learning tasks and socialising with students, L2 teachers use language in real communication. The question arises whether such language use is intended by the teachers as L2 input, and whether it is interpreted by the learners as L2 input.[13]

Let us see how the L2 teachers and learners in our corpus talk about organisational and social matters. Since giving feedback has been treated separately (in the section devoted to explicit language teaching), I will deal here only with the language use focused on the organisation of the learning tasks, and on L2 classroom small talk.

From the perspective of RT, communicative tasks are particularly interesting, because they are supposed to focus on developing learners' L2 fluency, yet they provide evidence that learners automatically pay attention to other aspects of the activities, first of all, to the completion of the tasks themselves.

The following examples (146–152) illustrate how the teachers and learners manage the learning tasks, in particular how they focus on classroom communication and on the structure and function of communicative tasks. The teachers and learners alike try to manage classroom discourse in order to reach instructional goals (e.g. to discuss a topic, to answer particular questions, etc.). The linguistic data refer both to the content of the tasks and to the required forms, most frequently vocabulary items. However, it is L1 rather than L2 which is likely to be used in this function.

The examples provided below come from Fryc's (2000) and Przebinda's (2004) data. The latter author managed to a great extent to overcome learners' code-switching to L1, due to her careful preparation of the communicative activities: providing students with L2 discussion questions and role-cards. The students knew precisely what questions they were supposed to answer, and the language of the questions and the description of the roles focused them on the required answers in L2. Yet, even in very carefully prepared activities, especially at a lower level of L2 proficiency, as in (152), the turns focused on the management of communication are frequently rendered in L1.

(146)   T: Which of the statements seems most controversial to you?
        Ss: *It's always wrong to tell lies.*
        T: OK, we can start with this one. (Fryc, 2000: 102)

(147)   S: Co jeszcze musimy powiedzieć? /What else should we say?/.
        T: Zaproś koleżankę na drinka. /Suggest that you have a drink/.
        S: Come for a drink. (Fryc, 2000: 107)

(148)   S1: Co mam teraz mówić? /What am I supposed to say now?/.
        S2: Może, że nie lubisz tych grup. Nie wiem. /Perhaps that you don't like these groups. I don't know/.
        S1: OK. I don't like this groups. No i co jeszcze? /And what else?/. (Fryc, 2000: 124)

The printed questions are given in italics.

(149)   S1: So the last question ... (reads out) *More advantages ... disadvantages of reality shows?*
        S2: I think they are good for the people who take part in them [...]. (Przebinda, 2004: 111)

(150)   S1: Tell us your opinion, Kasia.
        S2: No, I'm sorry ... Nie mam weny. /I'm not in the poetical vein/. (...) OK. I think it was a great discussion, don't you think so?
        S1: Yes, yes, it was great. (Przebinda, 2004: 112)

(151)   S1: And I think that we need reality shows to make our TV programmes more interesting [...].
        S2: Zróbmy to jeszcze raz. /Let's do it again/.

	S1:	OK. So the general idea of reality shows is to show personality of people [...]. (Przebinda, 2004: 113)
(152)	S1:	No to może tutaj kolega zacznie... /So, could you please start here/.
	S2:	OK. (reads out) *What is the general idea of reality shows?*
	S3:	TV stations do this for money.
	S1:	No tak. /That's right/.
	S2:	(reads out) *Why do people join them?*
	S1:	Dlaczego oni chcą przystępować?[14] /Why do they join them?/.
	S3:	For money and to meet new friends. Sometimes for love.
	S2:	(reads out) *Why do people watch them?* People watch them because they want to see more stupid people than they are. (reads out) *Think of more advantages and disadvantages of reality shows.*
	S1:	Czyli pozytywne i niepozytywne.[15] No, to one są głupie. /That is positive and negative. Well, they are stupid/. This shows are stupid. No, to znaczy... ja tak czuję. /That is... that's what I feel/ [...].
	S2:	I don't know what to say...
	S1:	well... people can meet new friends and earn money and...
	S3:	Love...
	S2:	And they can have good fun.
	S1:	A złe strony? /And disadvantages?/.
	S3:	Paparazzi.
	S2:	They have no private life. And everyone is talking about them. [...].
	S1:	OK. Now, (reads out) *Are reality shows a good or a bad thing? Do we really need them?*
	S2:	Some people need them. Some people always watch them.
	S1:	It's interesting for them [...].
	S2:	No ale ogólnie to chyba nie są dobre. Nie wiem. /But generally speaking they don't seem good. I don't know/.
	S1:	Ja też nie wiem. /Neither do I/. [...].
	S3:	No to kończymy. /So let's finish/.
	S2:	Yes, we can finish. Good bye. (Przebinda, 2004: 114)

Example (153) from Fryc (2000) illustrates best what is meant by the focus on the completion of the tasks of L2 classroom discourse during communicative activities. The activity has been presented in Chapter 4 without the original questions (85). Let us analyse now the activity with the original questions included in the teaching material (Soars & Soars, 1996: 71).

The pair work activity requires students to discuss on the basis of the provided questions their future and the future of the world, whether they are optimists or pessimists. The questions and optional answers in the teaching materials are given in italics. The teacher does not help the learners at that stage of the activity:

(153)
About you. Do you think ...
(1) *Your life will be similar in the future to what it has been up to now?*
    (a) *Yes.*
    (b) *No, it will change a lot.*
    (c) *No, it will change a little.*
S1: Co masz w pierwszym? /What do you have in the first question?/.
S2: Yes. A ty? /And you?/.
S1: C.
(2) *Your standard of living will:*
    (a) *get better?*
    (b) *get worse?*
    (c) *stay the same?*
S1: A standard of living?
S2: Stay the same.
S1: Ja też. /Me too/.
(3) *You will:*
    (a) *stay in the same job?*
    (b) *find a job that really satisfies you?*
    (c) *live to work or work to live?*
S1: A w trzecim? /And in the third one?/.
S2: Co to znaczy 'to live to work' i 'work to live'? /What does it mean [...] and [...]?/.
S1: To drugie chyba, że praca cię tylko utrzymuje, ale tak właściwie to jej nie lubisz. /I think in the second one that your job only makes a living, but you don't like it/.
S2: A pierwsze odwrotnie, tak? /And the first one is the opposite, right?/.
S1: Nie wiem. /I don't know/.
(4) *Your children will have a:*
    (a) *better*
    (b) *easier*
    (c) *more comfortable*
    (d) *more dangerous childhood than you did?*

S2: No dobra. /OK./. My children will have more dangerous childhood. A twoje? /And yours?/.
S1: More comfortable. No, a co z tą pracą? /And what about that job?/.
S2: Ostatnie. A ty? /The last one. And you?/.
S1: B.
(5) *About the world. Do you think ... that as we learn more, we are becoming more tolerant of people of different*
 (a) *nationalities?*
 (b) *religions?*
 (c) *colours?*
S2: About the world teraz /now/. Do you think that as we learn more, we are becoming more tolerant of people of different nationalities, religions, czy /or/ colours?
S1: Zadne z tych. Tolerancja się nie zmieni. /None of them. Tolerance won't change/.
S2: Ja mam 'religions' /I have ... /.
(5) *That many species of animals will become extinct? Which?*
S1: W drugim mam, że 'many', ale nie wiem jakie. /In the second one I have 'many', but I don't know which ones/.
S2: Ja też się na tym nie znam. /I don't know much about it, either/.
(6) *We will find new sources of energy that are*
 (a) *efficient?*
 (b) *cheap?*
 (c) *safe?*
S1: To trzecie to jest już całkiem głupie. /The third one is completely stupid/.
S2: No, ja mam 'safe', bo może nie będą szkodzić środowisku. /I have 'safe', because perhaps they won't do harm to the environment/.
S1: No to ja też mam 'safe'. /So I also have 'safe'/.
(7) *We are becoming*
 (a) *wiser?*
 (b) *more selfish?*
 (c) *more materialistic?*
 (d) *more nationalistic?*
S2: Ostatnie – 'more materialistic'. /The last one ... /.
S1: No i jeszcze 'more selfish'. /And another one ... /. (Przebinda, 2004: 111)

According to Communicative Language Teaching, the above task belongs to information-gap activities, in which the students are supposed to use L2 while inquiring about something they do not know. What is unknown are the interlocutor's answers to the survey questions. As far as the language level of the task is concerned, it is not too difficult for the learners to comprehend. Similarly, they would be able to make their short comments in L2. However, as can be seen, the comments involving real communication have been made in L1. The conclusion that can be drawn on the basis of RT is that the learners do not use L2 in their comments because they interpret organisational language as irrelevant for the ongoing classroom task and for their L2 fluency practice.

Apparently, the authors of the teaching materials had designed the activity for an audience in which students do not share an L1. In the monolingual foreign language context, without careful monitoring on the part of the teacher, the relevant input in L2 is only the task itself. Any linguistic data beyond the task are likely to be perceived as irrelevant to the L2 classroom language use. Consequently, the learners use L1 throughout the activity while discussing their questions and answers.

As has been argued throughout this chapter, the teacher's instructional input can shift the level of expected optimal relevance. Let us see how such input works in organisational language use in more teacher-centred classes. We will look at the discourse in which the teacher herself uses L2 and insists on learners' L2 use. In the following examples, the teacher's L2 use communicates to the learners that they should use L2 while communicating their messages:

(154) T: Bożena.
S: Pani profesor, ale ja nie wiedziałam, że to trzeba opowiadać. /Professor X (a honorific used by students to address secondary school teachers). I didn't know that we were supposed to give a talk on it/.
T: Bożena, speak English. You can say what you like, but in English. It is an English lesson. (Kusibab, 1984: 126)

(155) T: (addressing students who are late for class): Isn't it too late?
S: My byliśmy na obiedzie. / We have been having our lunch/.
T: In English, please.
S: We are late because of dinner. (Kusibab, 1984: 125)

(156) T: (asking a student to read out her home assignment) Małgosia, next exercise, please.
S: Ja nie mam. /I haven't got it/.

T: In English, please.
S: I have only Exercise C. I haven't other exercises.
T: Why haven't you excused yourself before the lesson? (Kusibab, 1984: 94)

(157) S: (asking the teacher about a special school test called *Olimpiada* /literally: Olympic Games/. Chcieliśmy się jeszcze dowiedzieć, czy będzie Olimpiada, bo dzisiaj przyszła. /We would like to know if we'll be having the *Olimpiada*, because it has arrived today/.
T: But you forgot your English. (Puchała, 1993: 81)

By communicating to the learners that she wants them to use L2, the teacher does not, however, focus them on the accuracy of particular L2 forms. The message she communicates is *use L2* but not *use accurate L2*. It seems that for the teacher to communicate to the learners her intention to focus both on meanings and accurate forms, it is necessary to correct inaccurate forms explicitly. As is the case in the following example:

(158) S: (asking about the performance of the school choir) You think, do you think was the choir good?
T: Co te dwa pytania tutaj znaczą? /What do these two questions mean here?/.
S: Co Pan myśli? /What do you think?/.
T: Do you think...
S: ... That the choir was good?
T: Good. Repeat.
S: Do you think that the choir was good?
T: I think it was very good. It is a pity that Mr X has given up, has resigned. He is tired. (Puchała, 1993: 88)

The learner in (158) asks a real communicative question using L2. He makes a language error, which, however, does not interfere with the teacher's understanding of the question. The teacher decides to combine real communication with explicit language teaching (*Co te dwa pytania tutaj znaczą?*/What do these two questions mean here?/). By asking the question, he intends to communicate to the learner the information that he has made a language error in asking his question. The teacher's question, however, is ambiguous. The teacher refers to the form, but the learner understands it at the level of meaning (*What did you mean by asking these questions?*), and he starts translating his question (*Co Pan myśli?*). The teacher, in turn, interprets the student's question at the level of form and elicits error correction (*Do you think...*). It is only now that the learner realizes that the teacher focuses him on the correct form of the question, and he corrects himself (... *that the choir was good?*). The teacher provides the feedback *Good*, communicating to the learner that he has produced a correct sentence. The level of expected relevance is stressed by the teacher's request that the learner repeat the corrected utterance, which is followed by the learner's repetition (*Do you think that the choir was good?*). And it is at that point that the teacher switches to real communication and answers the learner's question (*I think it was very good. It is a pity that Mr X has given up, has resigned. He is tired.*)

The above analysis enables us to see the two layers of communication in L2 instructional discourse: real communication and explicit language teaching. What can also be observed is that raw (primary) and secondary linguistic data become blurred. When the learner asks a real communicative question, it is primary linguistic data. However, if the question is repeated by the teacher in order to elicit self-correction, it becomes secondary linguistic data.

The above exchange is highly artificial and hardly resembles everyday out-of-classroom communication, and only some L2 teachers have been observed to act as in (158), in other words, to link real communication with explicit language teaching. Others let the students communicate at the level of organizational language use or small talk without providing any explicit or implicit feedback on their errors, as in (159).

The teacher elicits real language use by asking students to say something which is true:

(159) **T:** Now, let's listen to a conversation about a bomb. And after the first listening, I'll want you to say one true sentence.
S: Why don't you ask us any time of saying any false sentences? /=Why don't you ever ask us to say ... /.
T: Because I prefer true sentences. I'm a truthful person.
S: But it's boring. (Puchała, 1993: 86)

In (159) the teacher does not indicate to the learner that he has made a language error. We may only wonder whether it is a conscious strategy (focus on meaning only) on his part. Whatever the reason, the learner is not given a chance to notice the error and to self-correct.

Our real communication data also include highly routinised discourse, as in the case of checking the register, checking homework assignments or managing various classroom routines, such as watering flowers, cleaning the board, etc. In those cases, probably because of the repetitive pattern of such exchanges, the teachers use L2, e.g. *Who is absent today? Why haven't you excused yourself?* or *Please, water the flowers.* The answers the students give are usually in L2 as well, which may indicate that the students recognise the teachers' intention to make them use L2 in a highly predictable way.

Real communication in the L2 classroom, if not focused on classroom routines, the organisation of the learning process or particular learning tasks, is also elicited by the learners. In fact, some teachers require that the learners ask them real questions or say something 'true', as in (159) above and in the following excerpt (160):

(160) S: You know that Mr X is going to finish [teaching at school]?
 T: He is not going to finish but he has finished. And this is a pity.
 S: Oh, why? Do you know?
 T: Because he is fed up with you. (Puchała, 1993: 88)

What can also be noticed in L2 classroom communication interpreted from the RT perspective, particularly in real communication exchanges in organisational language use, is that even if the teachers themselves speak L2, they do not make it clear to the learners that they are required to use L2 as well.

(161) T: The break is over. Renata, bring the map, please.
 S: Z gabinetu geograficznego? /From the geography lab?/.
 T: Yes. (Kusibab, 1984: 115)

The teacher could say *Yes, from the geography lab*. If she does not say that, it may mean that at the very beginning of the lesson she does not pay enough attention to implicit language teaching through L2 classroom discourse. She tolerates the learner's communicative use of L1, although she speaks L2. Such lack of consistency is common in our corpus. We could say, in line with RT that the teachers' L2 use does not communicate overtly (ostensively) that the L2 classroom discourse should be conducted in L2. The teacher's use of L2 is not sufficiently effective in making students notice the requirement. The learners do not recognise the teacher's intention, or, even if they recognise it, they seem to be purposefully denying it. Example (162) illustrates the case in point:

(162) T: The topic of the lesson today is ...
  (Two students enter the classroom late).
 S1: Bo nie było dzwonka i się zagapiłyśmy. /Because the bell did not ring and we forgot about the time/.
 T: What!?
 SS: Nie było dzwonka. /The bell did not ring/.
 T: Why?
 S1: Myśmy nie słyszały. /We did not hear it/.

T: You must be deaf.
S1: Ja byłam u pani higienistki i tam nie było słychać. /I went to see the school nurse and one cannot hear it there/.
T: Oh, really?!
S1: No naprawdę. /Really/. (Puchała, 1993: 76)

The teacher in (162) seems to be acting out a comedy, and the students follow in the convention. The teacher communicates her intention to engage in a playful exchange of bilingual turns, where she speaks L2 while the students use L1. The two parties understand each other, and there is no need to switch to a common language code. Such teachers' behaviour can be observed in our corpus from time to time. It seems as if the teachers resigned from their role of instructors and indulged for some time in the role of playful conversationalists. In Excerpt (162) the teacher's exaggerated exclamations (*What!? Why? Oh, really!?*) and her non-verbal behaviour communicate to the learners a different level of relevance of classroom interaction.

Simulated communication (fluency practice)

As has been said before, besides real communicative language use, L2 classroom communication, particularly in the Communicative Approach, involves a stage, traditionally called 'language production', when learners, usually in pairs or small groups, simulate real communication. The main aim of this lesson stage is fluency practice, and the learners' language use at this lesson stage is considered by L2 teaching methodologists as particularly beneficial for language learning. Such an opinion coincides with the Input and Interaction Hypotheses in SLA theory in their claims concerning the impact of comprehensible and negotiated input on L2 acquisition.

Simulated communication activities engage learners in interactions which resemble real communication, but which are rather focused on following communicative patterns than on communicating one's own ideas in L2. Communicative activities involve setting up group work tasks in which students are supposed to talk for a while on suggested topics, those talks being prepared beforehand, their language being frequently modelled on textbook dialogues. In other words, simulated communication, particularly in role-plays, involves supplying students with ready-made ideas. Consequently, students concentrate on the demands of the textbook tasks and not on the exchange of their own ideas. Teachers are frequently satisfied with students' communicative fluency practice rather than with their authentic exchange of ideas.

In terms of RT, in simulated L2 classroom communication the level of expected optimal relevance does not engage the whole knowledge of the learners, especially when the teachers make it explicit to them that what matters in the communicative activities is only speaking practice.

Let us consider, as hypothesised in Chapter 1, the two obstacles to the automatic interpretation of the products of the decoding process in the L2 classroom: an incomplete knowledge of the code and the irrelevance of the semantic interpretation of the utterances. In the case of communicative activities, I would like to claim that the goal of fluency practice can be reached without an adequate understanding of the requirements of the tasks. Obviously, I do not argue that the task descriptions and requirements are not understood at all, and that they are totally misinterpreted. Yet, the communicative tasks included in the textbooks or on teachers' role-cards, which give outlines of the communicative situations and their goals, as well as some necessary phrases and grammatical structures, are frequently understood as if at their face value, without considering realistic aspects of the situations and goals, or the appropriateness of the language used. Thus, in simulated communication, the completion of the tasks becomes the goal in itself, while real communicative asides (frequently in L1) are focused on how to accomplish the tasks in a quick and smooth way (as has already been demonstrated in (153).

Our corpus illustrates such cases in numerous excerpts coming from Fryc's (2000) and Przebinda's (2004) data. In order to enable comparisons each of the following classroom interactions is preceded by a description of the task from the corresponding teaching material (given in italics).

(163) Description of the task: Role-play (Soars & Soars, 1996: 5) (see 83 Chapter 4)
Student A: You have just arrived in London for the first time. You have come for a holiday to learn English. London seems a little strange and you need to ask for help. These are some of your problems:

(1) *You need to change some travellers' cheques, but you don't know where to find a bank, or what time the banks open and close.*
(2) *You need to buy some stamps and postcards.*
(3) *You would like to buy a newspaper from your country.*
(4) *You want to find a good English language school.*

You meet someone who lives in London and who seems friendly, so you ask for information. Prepare what you are going to say. Add any other questions you want to ask (e.g. about accommodation, shops, etc.)
Begin like this: Excuse me. Could you help me, please?
Student B: You live in London and know it quite well. You meet a foreigner who has just arrived and who seems to have some problems. Look at the information here and try to help him/her.

S1: Excuse me. Could you help me, please? I need to change some travellers' cheques. Where can I find bank? What time do the banks open and close?
S2: (reads out the information from the textbook) *Barclay's Bank. Opening hours: Monday–Friday 9:30 to 3:30. Closed all day Saturday.*
S1: I need to buy stamps. Where can I find post office? (The teacher approaches the students).
T: No, na czym skończyliście. Proszę kontynuować. /Where have you finished? Please, carry on/.
S1: Teraz mówimy o poczcie. /Now we are talking about the post office/.
T: No, to dalej. /Carry on, please/.
S2: (reads out the information from the textbook) *High Street Post Office. Opening hours: Monday, Tuesday, Thursday and Friday from 9 to 5:30, Wednesday and Saturday from 9 to 1.*
S1: I need a newspaper from Poland. Where can I get?
S2: (reads out the information from the textbook) *Rachman's International. 174 Bank Street opposite the Police Station.*
T: No, dobra, idźcie dalej. /OK, carry on/. (The teacher leaves the students).
S1: Co teraz? /What shall I say now?/.
S2: No, ta szkoła. No, pytaj. /About the school. Ask me a question/.
S1: Where can I find a good English school?
S2: (reads out the information from the textbook) *101 Dover Street, W1. Phone: 4912596.*
S1: W książce to wszystko, no nie? /That's all there in the book?/.
S2: Uhum. (Fryc, 2000: 77/100)

(164) Description of the task: Improvisation (Swan & Walter, 1992: 47) (see 84 Chapter 4)
Instruction: work in groups of three, and act out the following situation. Mrs. Smith is annoyed because her neighbours play loud music late at night. She goes next door to complain, but they won't turn the music down. So she calls the police and a three-sided argument develops.

S1: They play loud music at night. I can't fall to sleep. And my husband also. And he is ill.
S2: You can't play so loud music after 10 [p.m.]. This is law. You live with ... mieszkańcy /inhabitants = neighbours/.

S3: You know this is a crazy woman. We are not playing loud. She is crazy skrzypaczka /violinist/. She will listen even no, ten szept, jak jest szept? /She will even hear ... whispering, how do we say whispering?/

S1: No co ja mam mówić dalej? /What shall I say next?/.

S2: No mów byle co, że masz męża chorego. /Say whatever you want. Say that your husband is ill/.

S1: No dobra. /OK/ But my husband is very ill. It's not me. He can't sleep.

S2: And do you often play the violin?

S1: No, only on day, not at night.

S3: Trele morele! /Rubbish!/ She plays all the day and in morning also. I can't sleep in morning.

S2: No dobra, koniec. /OK. The end/.

S1: No, ale musisz powiedzieć co mamy zrobić. /But you must tell us what we are supposed to do/.

S3: No mów, bo ona na pewno nas weźmie. /Say something, because it's sure she (the teacher) will ask us/.

S2: No dobra. To obydwie musicie sobie zapłacić karę. /OK. You will pay each other a fine/. (Fryc, 2000: 78/101)

(165) Description of the task: Role-play (see 88 Chapter 4)
Role cards: the head teacher, B. Brown, J. Small
The head teacher
You are the head teacher of the best language school in the country. The school belongs to the international network of schools with a very high level of language education. You have to and you want to do everything to keep the highest standard possible in your school. This year what happened is that there are too many candidates and not enough places in the groups. You are going to speak to two people but you must choose only one student for the remaining place. Talk to them and decide. Think of the things to ask – for example, why they want to join your school. Think of what makes the best student – like high motivation, good ability to learn languages. Try to find as much as you can about them, their experience with learning. Decide who will be a better student, who will help your school and not only wait for school to help him/her.
B. Brown
You are going to speak to the head teacher of the best language school in the country. You want to learn English as soon as possible because

your girlfriend/boyfriend is English and this is the only way for you to communicate. What is more, you are going to go to England next year together, so you really need to speak good English in order to get a good job there. Because this school is so good, you are absolutely sure that you want to join it because you want to learn good English as quickly as possible. You know you can do it only if you attend a good school. The problem is that there is only one place left in the group which you would like to join and the head teacher will have to choose either you or another person. Think of as many arguments as possible to convince him/her that you are a better candidate for this place and that you can actually help the school somehow. You have learnt English for six years and you know basic French and Latin.
J. Small

You are going to speak to the head teacher of the best language school in the country. You know that the school is known almost to everyone because it is good. You want to join it because the certificate from this school would help you a lot in getting a job. You want to be a teacher of English in this country or maybe abroad. You have already attended several language schools but none of them was ideal. In fact you are not sure if any school is perfect, but the point is that the certificate from this school is valid around the world and you really want to have it. The problem is that there is only one place left in the group you would like to join, and the head teacher will have to choose either you or another person. Think of as many arguments as possible to convince him/her that you are a better candidate for this place and that you can actually help the school somehow. You have learnt English for four years, you also know German very well and Spanish.

Group A (secondary school female students: S1 – the head teacher, S2 – B. Brown, S3 – J. Small)

S1: Good morning and welcome to the language school.
S2: Good morning.
S3: Hello.
S1: I'd like you to tell me something about you because we have only one place left in one of the groups, so one of you will have to leave ... so ... just tell me something about you and then we will decide. So maybe you can start?
S2: OK ... so my name is Barbara Brown and ... I've learned English for six years and I know also French and Latin very well.
S1: Why do you want to learn English?
S2: My boyfriend is English and I want to communicate with him.

S1: OK, I have a question for you – could you tell me why do you want to study at our school?
S2: Just like I said. I've learned English for six years and I still don't speak it very well. We're going to England next year and my girlfriend ... boyfriend (laughs), and we will work there, so I want to study hard.
S1: OK, thank you. Now, what about you Ms J.J. Small?
S3: My name is J. Small and I want to study at your school because I want to be an English teacher.
S1: Yes ... and what about your experience with learning languages? Do you have any experience?
S3: I've studied in many language schools and it was ... it was not good. They were not good schools and now I'd like to study at your school because it's the best school of English and I think that it could be a good chance for me.
S2: And I want to say that I'd like to study English for one year and I want to speak English very well and my communication must be also very well.
S1: So I think I'm a better person because I already speak English so ...
S2: I speak English too. And I've studied English for six years and I want to ...
S1: OK, but let's talk about other languages now. Do you think that you have ... when you study other languages, do you think that you learn them easy? Or is it quite difficult to learn them?
S3: For me it's easy. I speak also German and Spanish and ... I think that's all I can really say ...
S2: For me too. I like learning languages and it's easy for me.
(pause)
S3: I think that studying other languages is very important because we have to communicate with people from other countries and it's very important. So because of it I study German and I can speak German very well and a little bit in Spanish.
S1: OK ... well ... do you have anything to add?
S3: I think that my person is really good for this place and I think you should choose me.
S1: OK, thank you very much for coming. And I guess I will be back in five minutes and then I will decide who gets the place.
S2: OK, thank you.
S3: Thank you and see you later.

(166) (see 89 Chapter 4)
Group B (technical secondary school male students: S1 – the head teacher, S2 – B. Brown, S3 – J. Small)

S2: Good morning. I wanna join this best English school. I have learnt English for 6 years.
S1: Yes, OK. And you?
S3: I also want to learn in this school. I want to learn English because it's so good here.
S1: All right. Tell me something more. My problem is that I must choose you. I have one place in my school so try to ... well ... tell me something more.
S3: I have learnt English for 4 years and I know German also and Spanish very well.
S1: Oh, that's good. That's very interesting. Do you like German?
S3: Yes, yes. I love German. But I think English is more easy.
S1: Yes, it's true. And what about you? Do you know any languages?
S2: I know French basic and Latin also. I am really the best person for this place.
S1: But why do you think so?
S2: I want to learn English because I am going to England ...
S3: And I ... I also want to go to this school. I will be a teacher in the future.
S2: I can pay for this place. I can pay big money. 4000 pounds.
(pause)
S1: Why do you want to come to my school? There are other schools too.
S2: Because this school is really the best. I heard it in television. It's the best in the country.
S3: But you are not the best candidate in this country. Remember it.
S1: Have you learnt any other languages?
S3: Yes, I know German and Spanish. I said this.
S1: Why do you need our school? Show me that you are the better candidate.
S3: Because this school will give me a dyplom /certificate/ and I need it because it will help me to get a better job.
S2: And I need it because I must communicate with my girlfriend. And when I go to England I must get a good job there.
S1: Yes, I get it. But how can I choose? I don't know who is better. I think I will take you all because you are great and you are the best. And I will make a big group for this year.

S3: OK, thank you very much, Mr. Head teacher.
S1: Thank you very much. And see you on the lesson. Good bye.
(Przebinda, 2004: 98/125/127)

The learners' language use in (163) is close to the description of the task, in fact S2 reads out the information from the role-card. What seems to be irrelevant for the learners is the interactional function of the role-play (see Chapter 3). In other words, the information is sought for and received without any politeness markers or concern if the stranger has understood the provided information. The teacher, who monitors a fragment of the interaction, seems to be interested only in a smooth progress of information transfer on the basis of the teaching material. The learners switch to real communication in L1 (comments on the task) as soon as the teacher leaves them.

In the improvised speaking task (164), which is not monitored by the teacher, the focus on task completion is evident as well, although lack of a clear scenario what to say next, seems to give the learners some mental space to fill with their own ideas. It is interesting to note how some background knowledge from the learners' home environment is integrated into the interaction (*You can't play so loud music after 10 p.m.*) and how S3 develops a line of defence by accusing S1 of the same offence she is accused of (*She plays all the day and in morning also. I can't sleep in morning*). Consequently, the improvised fluency interaction becomes more creative as the more resourceful learner imagines a development to the described situation (*To obydwie musicie sobie zapłacić karę*/You will pay each other a fine/). Organisational language, in other words, communicating each other what to say requires less effort in L1, and the learners, in the absence of the teacher monitoring the interaction, fall back on their native language.

As has been said before, Przebinda (2004) has been very careful in planning and monitoring her communicative activities. Consequently, what one notes comparing her data with Fryc's (2002) data, is that her subjects did not use so much L1 to comment on what they should say. Przebinda's excerpts are longer, apparently her learners were more fluent.

What is striking is that more proficient learners (in 165) playing the roles of the candidates did not think of any valid arguments to convince the head teacher, in spite of an explicit indication that they should think of as many arguments as possible. None of them mentioned what was explicitly said on the role-card that they could help the school somehow. The learner playing the role of the head teacher did not act according to her role-card, either, because she did not take the final decision. In the less proficient group (166), the students seemed to understand their roles better and they were more imaginative (one of the candidates tried to help the school by paying a large sum of money, and the head teacher decided to admit both candidates).

Indeed, it seems that role-plays can develop learners' fluency, understood as the ability to fill time with talk, and also understood as having relevant things to say (in the non-RT sense of the word). Why some learners have such relevant ideas and others do not is beyond the scope of our discussion.

The linguistic data in the role-plays viewed from the RT perspective are optimally relevant on the level of superficial communication, without paying attention to the accuracy of L2 forms, because the learners are totally preoccupied with enacting their roles, but they do not take responsibility for providing their peers with corrective input.

Besides, role-play descriptions frequently place the learners in the situations they are ignorant of, e.g. the students in (165) and (166) could have found the interview situation quite difficult cognitively, because they had never taken part in a competitive interview. As a result, learners superimpose their own knowledge of the world upon the situations outlined in role-cards and they say whatever they can think of in order to fill their turns with talk rather than to enact their roles as realistically as possible.

Having said that, let us stress that simulated L2 classroom communication may resemble everyday naturalistic communication whenever the situations and goals of communication are close to the learners' experience and they are inherently interesting. In our data, there are some examples in which the learners apparently treated simulated communication as real communication:

(167) Description of the task: Information-gap activity (Bell & Gower, 1995: 9)
Instruction: Choose someone in the class who you do not know much about. *Interview them remembering to mix direct and less direct questions and trying to keep your questions polite. Ask them at least five questions about where they live, their job, their studies, their family and the languages they speak. Find out about their favourite things – their hobbies and interests.*
S1: Where do you live?
S2: In Nowa Huta.
S1: Where exactly?
S2: Przecież byłaś u mnie. /But you've been to my place/.
S1: No, dobra. / Well, OK/ Could you tell me what's your job?
(Fryc, 2000: 85/110)

The above comment in L1 (*Przecież byłaś u mnie* /But you've been to my place/) is optimally relevant on the level of real communication. On the level of simulated classroom communication, however, the learner should have given her exact address, although her interlocutor knew it.[16] Another example of an apparently real communicative remark can be observed in the emotional exclamation in the improvised task (164): *Trele morele!* /Rubbish!/ *She plays all the day and in morning also.*

It seems that general discussions, which are inherently more interesting because they involve learners personally, are more conducive to real communicative remarks during simulated activities, as in the following L1 aside during a discussion on advantages and disadvantages of going to public schools in Great Britain:

(168) (see 80)
　　　S1: I think that it is very positive to go to schools like Eton, because it's good quality teaching.
　　　S2: But it's not a nice company there.
　　　S1: Company?
　　　S2: No, the friends /well ... /. People who go there are snobs. They think they are the best.
　　　T: What do the others think?
　　　S3: I think that you can go to other places to meet friends, not in school.
　　　S4: Ciekawe gdzie? /I wonder where?/. (Fryc, 2000: 119)

The above L1 comments (*Przecież byłaś u mnie* /But you've been to my place?; *Trele morele!* /Rubbish/; *Ciekawe gdzie?* /I wonder where/) show the communicator's wish to be perceived as a real person rather than as a discussant in a classroom activity. In other words, in terms of RT, when the communicator communicates at a different level of expected optimal relevance.

Let us finally illustrate this point with two excerpts from Przebinda's (2004) data. These are group discussions presented before in Chapter 4 (86 and 87), concerning advantages and disadvantages of education in South Korea and Poland.

(169) Group discussion
　　　Group A (the same as in 165)
　　　S1: (reads the questions provided by the teacher).
　　　S2: *What do you think? Which system is better?*
　　　S3: OK, so let's talk about the Korean one. Probably they are more educated.
　　　S2: They get better job, opportunity to study later at university and ... I don't know ...
　　　S1: How long?

S3: Probably the same.
(It is not clear from the transcript what the students mean).
S2: 17 hours (of studying per day). It's stupid. Naprawdę jakiś beznadziejny system. /It must be an awful system/.
(pause)
S1: So they have seven hours to have a shower, sleep, eat breakfast and ... 17 hours ... so they sleep almost 5 hours. This is the disadvantage.
S2: It's stupid, you can't relax, talk to your parents ... they have no private time. I don't like it.
S1: And they are more intelligent in the classes but their life ... They don't know how to live.
S3: I agree.
(pause)
S2: OK, so *which system is more effective?*
S1: I think this system have more advantages and disadvantages and Polish system have advantages and disadvantages so we must put them ... together ... choose ... I think that ... that the Korean system ... with this system you could receive better job but the problems you will be ... have ... I mean in ... I think that in Korean system you get a better job so better life, but it's not so good life if you don't have the ...
S3: Private life.
S1: Private life and ... and ...
S2: You don't know how to ...
S3: How to behave, how to act.
S2: Yes, so I think that our system is better.
S3: It's not better but it's more for people as to say. / = it's more humane, so to speak/.
(pause)
S2: No one is the best but I think our is better than the Korean system.
S1: So that's all?
S2: That's all.
S3: The end. Koniec. /The end/. (Przebinda, 2004: 121)

(170) Group discussion
Group B (the same as in 166)
S4: Dobra, no to zaczynamy. /OK, let's start/.
S5: (reads out one of the questions) *What are the advantages of the Polish system?*

S4: Polish system is better. We don't have to stay in school for 17 hours a day. And we don't have to study so much.
S5: Yes. In Korea people must study too much ... But they know more things when they finish school.
S4: But they are so tired ... they can't do nothing. They don't have time for playing sport or something like this. All the time they study. It's stupid ...
(pause)
S5: No, to w ogóle jest bez sensu. /It's total nonsense/.
S6: (reads out a question) *But which one is better?*
S4: Polish is better. We are not tired ... We have more time.
(pause)
S5: A praca? Oni mają szansę dostać lepszą pracę i kasę. /And work? They have a chance to get a better job and more dough/.
S6: No tak, ale przecież na nic nie mają czasu. To nienormalne. /That's right, but they have no time for anything. It's not normal/.
S5: In Korea you can get a good job.
S6: A w Polsce nawet jak dużo umiesz, to nie możesz dostać dobrej pracy. /And in Poland even if you know a lot, you cannot get a good job/.
(laughter)
S5: (reads out a question) *Which system gives you better opportunity to get a better job?*
S6: No to ten w Korei. /The Korean one/.
S5: *Better life?*
S4: I think Polish.
S6: We have more time ... and we have time for fun.
S5: Tak, i na imprezki. /Yes, and for little parties/.
(laughter)
(pause)
S6: No to co? Wszystko już? /So what are we doing? Is that all?/.
S4: Dobra, koniec. /OK., the end/. (Przebinda, 2004: 123)

In the above group discussion tasks, the learners are not monitored by the teacher. However, as has been said before, the author has carefully prepared the task in terms of its organisation, introducing a reading passage on education in South Korea and the discussion questions. In other words, although the communicative activity involves implicit L2 teaching, the instruction and the materials accompanying it focus the learners on specific information in the text and in the questions (*Which system is better? Which* system is more effective? What are the advantages of the Polish system? Which system gives you better opportunity to get a better job?). It is interesting to note, however, levels of expected optimal relevance in each group.

In Group A, the three co-operating students are able to formulate some kind of justification of their answer in L2 (*I think that in Korean system you get a better job so better life, but it's not so good life if you don't have the [...] private life [...] You don't know how to [...] how to behave, how to act.*) There is also a clear interference of the L1 phrase *jest bardziej dla ludzi* / *it's more for people = it's more humane*/. The students provide one another with some help in communicating the required arguments, but the cognitive difficulty of the task seems to affect the accuracy of the language they use. On the other hand, except for one comment in L1 (*Naprawdę jakiś beznadziejny system.* /It must be an awful system/) they use only L2 during the activity.

In Group B the participating students use the teacher's questions to support their discussion, which, however, becomes an L1 discussion. In terms of RT, it could be said that they treat it more as real communication than as simulated communication, and that is the reason why they switch to L1 (*No, to w ogóle jest bez sensu* /It's total nonsense./ *A praca? Oni mają szansę dostać lepszą pracę i kasę.* / And work? They have a chance to get a better job and more dough./ [...] *No tak, ale przecież na nic nie mają czasu. To nienormalne.* /That's right, but they have no time for anything. It's not normal/ [...] *A w Polsce nawet jak dużo umiesz, to nie możesz dostać dobrej pracy.* / And in Poland even if you know a lot, you cannot get a good job/).[17]

The students in Group B (Excerpts 166 and 170) seem to be more creative than Group A (Excerpts 165 and 169) both in role-play and in group discussion, and their L2 accuracy level, although formally much lower (pre-intermediate versus upper intermediate), does not seem to differ much from accuracy in Group A. As has been said before, the reasons are beyond the scope of our discussion.[18]

Thus, it seems that RT can account for an apparently paradoxical situation in monolingual classrooms, when real communication automatically involves L1 use, and it is only when students are more focused on simulated communication in L2 learning tasks that they use L2.

In the following final section of this chapter, I would like to present a proposal for an RT-theoretical approach to the role of instructional input in the L2 classroom, based on the data analysed above.

Input for Instructed L2 Learners in the Light of RT: Raw (Primary) and Corrective (Secondary) Linguistic Data Revisited

In SLA theory a distinction has been made between *raw* (*primary*) *linguistic data*, or *positive input*, and *corrective* (*secondary*) *linguistic data*, or *negative input* (see Carroll, 1995). Raw (primary) linguistic data have been defined as the language the learners hear in the naturalistic environment, which according to some models of language acquisition is internalised and drives restructuring of the learner language system on the basis of Universal Grammar. According to those models, as has been said in Chapter 1, raw (primary) linguistic data are sufficient linguistic input for the L2 learners to enable them to acquire L2.

Corrective (secondary) linguistic data, or negative input, are defined as the language that the learners hear in the instructional environment, and which is specially focused on those features of the learners' interlanguage they are not able to correct by themselves on the basis of raw (primary) linguistic data, since they do not receive enough information about those features in it. Secondary linguistic data, according to other models of language acquisition, are necessary to enable the learners to acquire native-like L2.

Carroll (1995) claims that recognising the essential role of secondary linguistic data (negative input) in L2 acquisition has serious consequences for our thinking about the architecture of the mind. She also claims, as has been said before, that secondary linguistic data are *largely irrelevant to the ongoing communicative event in which they may occur* (Carroll, 1995: 76).

This is precisely what I want to question in the light of RT. I would like to claim that the distinction between raw (primary) and corrective (secondary) linguistic data is much less clear-cut in the L2 classroom input than in naturalistic communication. On the basis of their experience with L2 teachers' language use, the learners interpret it as instructional input, in which communicative and corrective functions are much more closely linked than in everyday communication. The teachers are granted the right to interrupt and correct learners' utterances, but the learners are also allowed to inquire about formal correctness.

The linguistic data learners hear: teacher talk, peer talk, as well as spoken or written teaching materials, focus their attention not only on the meaning, but also on the unknown forms, first of all on unknown vocabulary items. The teacher either anticipates those moments of ignorance and provides additional information beforehand in pre-listening or pre-reading activities, or she provides corrective input more or less explicitly after the errors have been made. L2 corrective feedback, stemming from *ad hoc* situations, learners' errors and language problems, focuses the learners' attention on the form of the messages, which otherwise may be disregarded.

On the other hand, L2 classroom discourse may frequently raise doubts about the viability of raw (primary) linguistic data as positive L2 input, especially if the input is simplified in terms of language functions, structures and vocabulary provided by the teacher and the teaching materials.

I would like to argue that Relevance Theory sheds light on the L2 classroom discourse conflicts: those between fluency and accuracy practice, between real and simulated communication, and between L2 and L1 use.

As has been said in Chapter 1, there are two main obstacles in L2 communication in the L2 classroom to accurately interpret L2 messages:

(a) Incomplete knowledge of the L2 code.
(b) Irrelevance of the semantic interpretation of utterances.

In the monolingual L2 classroom, where L2s were taught according to the grammar-translation method, teacher talk was completely explicit. The teachers tried to explain grammatical problems in L1, to translate unknown vocabulary items into L1, and they talked in class in L1, except when they presented L2 as the subject-matter of the lessons.

In the monolingual L2 classroom, where L2s are taught according to the Communicative Approach,[19] teacher talk cannot be totally explicit, because it has a double purpose: first, its purpose is to teach L2 explicitly, to present its structure and its lexicon, as well as to provide corrective feedback at certain stages of the teaching process; second, however, its purpose is to provide raw (primary) linguistic data, in other words, to communicate with learners in L2, and to organise special activities which are supposed to develop the skill of communicating in L2 (communicative activities).

How can the learners distinguish between the teacher's focuses at a particular moment? I would like to claim that it is the relevance of the instructional input (both primary and secondary linguistic data) that automatically focuses them either on the meaning or on the form of classroom discourse.

If the teacher is focused first and foremost on factual information, as in content lessons, the learners are likely to disregard formal accuracy. Similarly, if the teacher is concerned only with the completion of the tasks in communicative activities, learners will not pay attention to correctness of forms. However, when the teacher combines fluency practice with accuracy practice by asking clarification questions, or by explicitly correcting erroneous forms, the learners focus their attention on those forms and are likely to remember them.

The teacher's input in the role of corrective feedback provides information which prevents a superficial focus on the completion of the communicative tasks in communicative activities, and, on the other hand, real and simulated communication in the L2 classroom prevents learners from focusing too much on form. Thus, I would like to argue that in spite of the obvious limitations of the L2 classroom instructional input as raw (primary) linguistic data, its most important function is using primary linguistic data (classroom L2 use) as potential secondary linguistic data, to reflect on its meanings and forms.

In other words, what teachers communicate in their input can be formulated as follows: *what we say has a double purpose, to communicate meanings and to focus you on the language in which these meanings are being communicated.* Thus, L2 classroom input should defocus an automatic tendency to search for meaning and disregard form.

However, in view of the natural tendency to focus one's attention on the most relevant information, whatever is in focus in the classroom discourse, becomes automatically optimally relevant. That is why in order to become facilitative in L2 learning processes, instructional input must be interpreted as raw (primary) linguistic data used as corrective feedback (secondary linguistic data). Anything that helps learners in such an interpretation is conducive to L2 learning. On this view, language awareness helps learners in interpreting teachers' input, as well as an active approach to L2 learning, and using active communication strategies, e.g. clarification requests and appeals for help.

From what has been said before, it follows that instructional input is an indispensable part of the L2 classroom discourse and it might play an important role in speeding up L2 learning/acquisition, in the sense of developing fluency combined with accuracy. The facilitating role of instructional input is upset if either fluency or accuracy becomes its only focus. Thus, input focused only on the development of fluency, as in communicative activities aimed at filling time with talk, or only on the development of accuracy, as in form-oriented corrections, is not facilitative for balanced L2 development.

In monolingual contexts, an automatic process of code-switching to L1 in real communicative exchanges may seriously limit primary linguistic data. However, teachers' insistence on L2 use in real communicative exchanges (organisational and social language) can considerably enlarge L2 linguistic resources. Well-prepared and monitored simulated communication (communicative activities) can also provide well-balanced instructional input for learning/acquisition. If learners are personally involved in communicative activities and trying to express their own ideas, at the same time their L2 use being carefully monitored by the teachers, peers or self-monitored, there is a very good chance that they will pay more attention to form and will learn/acquire L2, admittedly not to reach the native speaker competence, but to attain a high working knowledge of the target language.

Thus, it has been possible on the relevance-theoretical grounds to account, at least partially, for the observed paradoxes and conflicts of the L2 classrooms: fluency and accuracy practice, real and simulated communication, L1 and L2 use.

Notes

1. A relevant anecdote: While trying to elicit the name of a teaching method (*Community Language Learning*) an English teacher trainer began to write the name on the board (*Com* . . .). The trainees in a post-communist country jumped to the conclusion that the name was the *Communist Language Learning Method*.
2. Czekajewska's (1999) study findings point to teacher elicited and self-corrected (rather than teacher-corrected) forms that are most readily recalled by the corrected learners after a teaching period.
3. From what we know about effectiveness of verbal feedback, elicited self-corrections are most effective for delayed production of the corrected forms (Havranek & Cesnik, 2001).
4. Non-native teachers in monolingual settings are used to learners' implicit clarification requests which involve making a pause immediately before the required item.
5. The teacher's recast was inaccurate, she should have said *terminally ill*.
6. The teacher did not correct the error in the use of the grammatical tense.
7. The English word *recipe* and the Polish *recepta* /prescription/ are juxtaposed by the teacher as false friends. But it seems that the learners do not perceive their affinity.
8. We do not know, however, if the teacher asked the real question on purpose to illustrate her metalinguistic comment with implicit teaching, or whether it was a coincidence. Even if it was, the learners might have noticed the structural similarity, especially if the teacher repeated and made the learners repeat the required structure side by side with asking them the real questions with the same structure.
9. Articles are frequently omitted in interlanguage production. Even if the teacher corrects utterances without articles, in the spoken discourse they are not salient enough to be noticed. In teaching learners whose L1s do not use articles as a separate grammatical category, using articles seems to be one of the most difficult aspects of English grammar to teach, and errors in the use of articles constitute about 50% of all errors made by the learners (Król, 2004).
10. In saying this, I do not want to determine the level of teachers' input. Krashen's well-known, and equally vague, $i + 1$ level assumes that the level of the input which may become a source of language acquisition should be slightly above the learners' current level of proficiency. Such a general statement, even if true, is impossible to verify, since Krashen does not specify in L2 teaching and learning terms what he means by a slightly higher level.
11. The authentic text provided by the teacher contained a number of vocabulary items and phrases which were not explained during the lesson, and which probably were not known to the learners. On the whole, considering the time allotted to reading it (five minutes), the aim of the reading task was reading for gist.
12. In their answers, the learners disregard the literal meaning of the teacher's question *Apart from running the town what did they do?* It follows from the text that running the town involved all the activities mentioned by the learners, and that is what the teacher wants the students to say. It is not clear why the teacher uses *apart from* in his question. The learners, however, do not pay attention to the literal meaning of the teacher's question, because in line with RT the literal semantic interpretation of the teacher's question is irrelevant for them. They interpret

the question as referring directly to the text, where the activities of the guilds are included in running the town.
13. According to Ellis (1984) L2 used to achieve framework (organisational) and social goals of classroom interaction can be a rich source of L2 input.
14. The Polish (L1) translation of *join* (przystępować) does not collocate with *a show*.
15. It is interesting to note how L2 (advantages and disadvantages) affects L1. *Niepozytywne* (non-positive) is not used in Polish, it should have been translated as *negative*.
16. In the task description, the learners were supposed to choose someone they did not know much about.
17. The above remarks should be particularly appreciated in the context of a very high unemployment rate, spoken by 17-year-old boys, for whom the prospect of unemployment is imminent.
18. Students' formal L2 proficiency level frequently does not match their real proficiency level, because it is described globally in terms of the level of the course book currently used to teach a given group of students. Consequently, students may start every school grade with a formally higher proficiency level, or, conversely, they may be formally at the same level of proficiency for two or three years.
19. For the sake of clarity of exposition, I leave out other methodological approaches to L2 teaching.

Chapter 6
L2 Teaching Implications

In the projects described in Chapters 4 and 5, I have tried to explore L2 classroom discourse as a source of knowledge about language use and language learning. In Chapter 5, I have attempted to reinterpret the role of the teachers' and peers' input in L2 classroom discourse in the light of RT, as the language which facilitates shifts in the learners' attention from meaning to form and *vice versa*, and which changes the level of expected optimal relevance of classroom communication.

In this final chapter, I would like to formulate some L2 teaching implications of the relevance-theoretic approach to L2 classroom discourse, in particular on the basis of a comparison of the instructional input in more teacher-centred discourse with more learner-centred discourse. I claim that relevance theory sheds new light on the role of the teacher both during more teacher-centred and more learner-centred activities.

As has been said in Chapter 2, socio-political, economical and educational changes in Central Europe at the beginning of the 1990s brought about a shift in the methodological approach to L2 teaching in those countries. Communicative Language Teaching, first of all in teaching L2 English, but also in teaching other L2s, has become an official L2 teaching policy, additionally strengthened in some countries, for example in Poland, by a national system of school-leaving exams. One of the most important positive outcomes of the changes is more learner-centred teaching, which means that the learners are given more freedom to express their own meanings, and to communicate in pairs and groups. On the other hand, one of the negative outcomes of the changes has been the apparent lack of target-like (accurate and appropriate) L2 instructional input to classroom learners, linked with some degree of uncertainty on the part of L2 teachers, whether it is their role to provide corrective input during classroom activities.

As has been said before, SLA theory distinguishes two types of L2 input: raw (primary) linguistic data, that is, positive input and secondary linguistic data, that is, negative, corrective input. Primary linguistic data is the language of real communication, usually heard in the naturalistic environment. Secondary linguistic data, on the other hand, is the language focused on some features of the language produced by L2 non-native speakers, including L2 learners, to provide them with a more or less explicit metalinguistic explanation or a model concerning the features which are not target-like in the learners' speech, and which the non-native L2 speakers are unable to correct by themselves, only on the basis of primary linguistic data.

The main conclusion which has been drawn in Chapter 5 is that the distinction between primary linguistic data and secondary linguistic data cannot be maintained with reference to instructed L2 teaching/learning contexts on account of the fundamental purpose of language instruction: focusing the learners' attention on L2 forms in order to enable them to fluently express meanings. Consequently, positive input in communicative activities does not only have a real communicative purpose, but it also serves as an L2 model. On the other hand, negative input provides corrective information, but this information is frequently implicit. Such a combined focus can be facilitated by the teacher's skilful shifts of the learners' attention from meaning focus to form focus, and *vice versa*.

I have concluded my speculations in Chapter 5 on the role of instructional input in the L2 learning/acquisition process by saying that in order to be facilitative, instructional input must be recognised by the learners as serving both functions: communication of real meanings and providing corrective information. I have also claimed that the learners who are more language aware (sensitive to form) and more active in inquiring about unknown forms, are more able to recognise these functions.

If communication (real or simulated) becomes the sole focus of classroom activities, and the teachers refrain from monitoring the activities and providing corrective input, L2 learners, focused on classroom communication, may disregard incompleteness or incorrectness of the L2 forms, as long as they seem to be successful communicators, in other words, as long as they complete communicative tasks. In monolingual contexts, in the absence of the teacher's monitoring presence and corrective feedback, learner communicators are more likely than in multilingual contexts to code-switch to L1, and to carry out their communicative exchanges in their native language.

Moreover, teachers who do not make L2 learners pay attention to L2 formal correctness may unwittingly undermine their trust in the teachers' role as L2 experts and instructors. In consequence, the learners may disregard not only L2 forms but also the meanings they are supposed to communicate in communicative activities. Disregard for formal accuracy may lead to taking no heed of the content of communication, and to the development of superficial fluency, in the sense of filling time with talk in a distorted and mixed code.

To achieve balance between meaning-oriented and form-oriented instruction, it seems that L2 teachers should never lose sight of potential explicitness of their implicit instructional input, in order to provide, if necessary, explicit corrective input. On the other hand, teachers should not disregard the meanings learners wish to communicate. If formal correctness is given too much stress, the learners lose interest in real (or simulated) classroom communication.

In the following part of this chapter further L2 classroom discourse excerpts will be analysed[1] in order to demonstrate the above postulates of potential explicitness of teachers' input during L2 classroom communication, as well as pitfalls connected with an inadequate level of explicitness of teachers' or peers' input.

In the first example (171), the teacher makes the learner focus too much on the formal correctness of his real communicative question, in other words, according to our interpretation of the L2 classroom discourse in the light of RT, the teacher unnecessarily shifts the learner's attention to form, and makes his corrective intention too explicit, which can result in the learner's losing interest in the information he wants to obtain.

(171) (see 158)
- S: (asking about the performance of the school choir) You think, do you think was the choir good?
- T: Co te dwa pytania tutaj znaczą? /What do these two questions mean here?/.
- S: Co Pan myśli? /What do you think?/.
- T: Do you think ...
- S: ... that the choir was good?
- T: Good. Repeat.
- S: Do you think that the choir was good?
- T: I think it was very good. It is a pity that Mr X has given up, has resigned. He is tired. (Puchała, 1993: 88)

As has been said before in Chapter 5, the learner asks a real communicative question about the performance of the school choir. He repairs his first error (*you think, do you think*) and then he makes a relatively unimportant language error, which does not interfere with the comprehension of the question (*do you think was the choir good?* instead of *do you think that the choir was good?*). The teacher, however, decides to immediately elicit a totally correct question, and he switches to L1 to make the learner focus on the form of his question. He does it in an ambiguous way, since *Co te dwa pytania tutaj znaczą?* /What do these two questions mean here?/ may also mean *What do you mean by asking these questions?* Instead, the teacher could have answered immediately the learner's question (*I think it was very good*), as he finally did, but at the time when the learner could have lost his initial interest in finding out the teacher's opinion about the school choir.

How could the teacher focus the learner on real communication, while maintaining potential explicitness of his implicit instructional input? The teacher could have repeated the learner's question (recast), as if reflecting on the answer (*Do I think that the choir was good?*), which would provide implicit instructional input, and after giving a real communicative answer in the form parallel to the corrected question (*I think that the choir was very good*), he could have asked the same learner or other learners what they thought about the performance, reiterating the question form in real communicative questions. If the learners made more errors, the teacher could have made his correction explicit by providing L1 structural translation equivalent of only one lexical item (*I think że* /that/ *the choir was very good*). It was not necessary to make the learner repeat the corrected question (*Good. Repeat*), since the learner could have done it by himself. Conversely, the enforced repetition may not have served its purpose of making the learner remember the corrected structure. The enforced repetition (*Do you think that the choir was good?*) was interpreted by the learner(s) as formal practice only, and the teacher's answer with an elaboration (*I think it was very good. It is a pity Mr X has given up, has resigned. He is tired*) may not have had the communicative effect the teacher could have achieved had he immediately answered the learner's question.

By refusing to be real communicators in seemingly communicative classrooms, suspending or postponing their answers, and insisting on the formal accuracy of the learners' questions, the teachers communicate to the students their disregard for real communication, which is possibly the greatest methodological error of L2 classroom communication.

However, a momentary explicit focus on the L2 code and providing explicit correction, eliciting self-correction from the learners through implicit correction, or briefly commenting on some aspect of L2, without totally shifting the learners' attention to formal accuracy, seems to be a necessary condition for the learners to interpret the L2 classroom instructional input as corrective. That is what I mean by potential explicitness of instructional input.

In the following excerpt (172) the teacher briefly comments on the learner's error, but she does not shift the learner's attention only to the formal features of her answer. Although the exchange is part of the learner's assessment, and she is supposed to talk about a topic which was assigned before (the weather), the teacher seems to be genuinely interested in meaning-oriented communication.

(172) (see 90)
    T: What was the weather yesterday?
    S: Yesterday it was bad weather because it was cold and it rained.
    T: All the day?
    S: No, with breaks. It rained in the morning from six a.m. o'clock.
    T: If you use *a.m.*, do not use *o'clock*. (Kusibab, 1984: 125)

The above learner's answer (*Yesterday it was bad weather because it was cold and it rained*) could have been treated in a similar way as the learner's question in (171) (*You think, do you think was the choir good?*), and the teacher could have commented in L1 that the learner's answer had not been quite correct, or she could have tried to elicit its correction by providing the beginning of the required utterance, e.g. *Yesterday the weather* . . . . Instead, the teacher showed her genuine interest in the weather the day before, because she asked a real communicative question (*All the day?*). And it seems that it was enough to focus the learner on real communication. In consequence, the teacher's explicit comment (*If you use a.m., do not use o'clock*) was interpreted as only a momentary focus on form in otherwise meaning-focused communication. The teacher's instructional input was potentially explicit, because the learners realised that the teacher was paying attention to formal accuracy and could correct their errors, but, nevertheless, they were aware that the teacher asked communicative questions or engaged them in communicative activities, because she was first and foremost interested in real communication.

Other examples of potentially explicit teachers' input are given below:

(173) (see 97)
    T: Now let's think about Poles.
        [...]
    S: They are hostile.
    T: Could you explain what you mean?
    S: They like people when they come to them.
    T: You mean they like having guests, they are not hostile, but ...
    S: Oh, yes, hospitable, zawsze to mylę /I always mix them up/. (Fryc, 2000: 113)

The teacher elicits self-correction through a clarification request followed by an explicit feedback comment (*Could you explain what you mean?* [...] *You mean they like having guests, they are not hostile, but* ...). The teacher may have guessed the intended meaning before, but she makes the student focus on the incorrect lexical item. By repeating the lexical item (*hostile*), the teacher places it in focus, and facilitates the learner's search for an item beginning with the same sounds (*hospitable*). Had the teacher provided the required word herself (*You mean they like having guests, they are not hostile, but hospitable*), she may not have shifted the learner's attention to the form for a sufficient time to be noticed. The learner's L1 comment (*zawsze to mylę* /I always mix them up/) shows her momentary focus on the two similar forms she has realized she is likely to confuse. It seems plausible that after the above teacher's intervention, the learner will not confuse the two forms any more.

(174)   (see 132)
S: I don't know if I would get succeed.
T: What do you mean?
S: (hesitates)
T: You mean you are not sure if you would succeed?
S: Yes! (Czekajewska, 1999: 89)

In the above meaning-oriented exchange, the teacher attempts to elicit self-correction through a clarification request (*What do you mean?*), but the learner is not certain what he should say. Consequently, the teacher provides a recast, that is, an implicit corrective feedback in the form of a comprehension check question, inquiring the learner whether she has understood him correctly (*You mean you are not sure if you would succeed?*). After the form of the student's utterance has been implicitly corrected by the teacher, the student confirms both the formal correction and the clarification of his intended meaning (*Yes!*). Although the teacher provides only implicit corrective input, the teacher's corrective intention is clearly communicated to the learner in what we can again call potentially explicit input. The teacher may reiterate and elicit the problematic structure in her next question, e.g. *Why aren't you sure that you would succeed?* Probably, however, it is easier to focus the learners' attention on an incorrect lexical item, as in (173), than on an interlanguage structure, as in (174).

(175)   (see 24)
S: I should have written 'War and Peace'.
T: Written 'War and Peace'? Are you Leo Tolstoy?
S: Sorry, read. (Puchała, 1993: 38)

In the above example the teacher's focus on the sentence meaning: *Written 'War and Peace'? Are you Leo Tolstoy?*, simultaneously focuses the learner on the mistaken lexical item and elicits self-correction. Such input could also be called potentially explicit, because it is clear to the learner what the teacher wishes to communicate in it.

(176) (see 42)
    S: There is information about closing museums.
    T: So the tourists wouldn't come.
    S: No, do której są czynne muzea. /Well, how long museums are open/.
    T: Ah! About the closing times of the museums.
    S: Yes. About the closing times of the museums. (Czekajewska, 1999: 89)

Again in (176) the teacher' implicit feedback focuses the learner's attention on the form of his incorrect utterance. It is not clear if the learner has rightly interpreted the teacher's intention, because the implicit correction does not elicit self-correction on the learner's part. Instead, he code-switches to L1 (*No, do której są czynne muzea* /Well, how long museums are open/). The teacher acts as if she had only then comprehended the utterance (*Ah! About the closing times of the museums*). However, the teacher's recast is explicit enough to make the learner confirm and repeat the clarified and corrected version of his original utterance (*Yes. About the closing times of the museums*).

As has been said before, the Communicative Approach has contributed to both positive and negative changes in the use and role of L2 classroom instructional input. Let us compare what the contemporary secondary school English L2 teachers think about their role in providing corrective feedback with the actual input they provide in the L2 classroom (Fryc, 2000; Przebinda, 2004).

For the sake of this comparison, let us first consider the opinions of five teachers from Fryc's research, who according to the author's observations followed the Communicative Approach most closely. In the Opinion Survey, they all agreed with the statement that the teacher should correct only those student errors that distorted communication, unless the activity was to focus on form only, and four of them agreed that the teacher should allow the students to self-correct their errors, because that would help them remember the correct phrases better, and would prevent them from making the same errors again.[2]

Let us see how those teachers provided input during real L2 classroom communication (general discussions). Teacher A has asked her students to walk blindfolded in the school building, and to report afterwards in the classroom on their experience:

(177) **S1:** I didn't know how many stairs in the school and it was difficult to move.
S2: The school shouldn't be equipped into the flower ... no, doniczki /well, flower pots/.
T: Flower pots, yes?
S2: Yes.
S1: Our school isn't fit enough for blind.
T: The school is not suitable for the blind. What would you do to improve the situation?
S1: First, to take this flower pots from corridor.
T: OK, to remove flower pots from the corridor. What do the others think?
S3: I think heating should be ... I don't know how to say it.
T: You mean radiators should be protected [...].
T: So I hope now that it's useful to put yourself in somebody else's situation to try it and understand how the person feels.
Ss: Yes. (Fryc, 2000: 98)

During the above real classroom communication, Teacher A provides the learners with implicit corrective feedback (*Flower pots, yes? The school is not suitable for the blind. OK, to remove flower pots from the corridor. You mean radiators should be protected*).

On the one hand, the teacher's recasts may not have been treated as implicit corrective input, even in the case when the learners appealed for help (*no, doniczki /well, flower pots/* or *I don't know how to say it*), because of the real communicative focus of the activity. Had the teacher reiterated the corrected items, and had the learners repeated them in their subsequent turns, there would have been a better opportunity for them to focus their attention on form.

On the other hand, however, it is difficult to claim that the corrected items have not been noticed at all, because at least one of them was immediately used: *First, to take this flower pots from corridor*. As can be seen, and in agreement with her opinion expressed in the survey, the teacher has not corrected all errors, focusing only on those which distorted communication. All in all, it seems that the teacher's input can be called potentially explicit, since the teacher took heed of formal correctness, and provided implicit corrective input, while she had engaged learners in a real communicative situation. Besides, the collected data does not allow us to claim that the teacher disregarded the remaining errors. She could have postponed their correction to an accuracy-oriented stage of the lesson. The teacher seemed to be fully in control of the classroom discourse, and yet giving learners enough initiative to let them engage in real L2 classroom communication.[3]

A similar pattern of using implicit corrective input during a general class discussion on national stereotypes is demonstrated by Teacher B (see above Excerpt 173).

However, another teacher in the group of the teachers who were observed to adhere most closely to the Communicative Approach, Teacher C, does not provide implicit corrective input, since she accepts everything the students say without comments, and her role is limited to maintaining discussion (*What do the others think? How about boys? What do you think about it? What do you think about our school in comparison with Eton?*).

(178) (see 80)
    T: OK. We've read the text about Eton college, what do you think about going to such a school?
    S1:   I think that it is very positive to go to schools like Eton, because it's good quality teaching.
    S2:   But it's not a nice company there.
    S1:   Company?
    S2:   No, the friends. /well ... / People who go there are snobs. They think they are the best.
    T: What do the others think?
    S3:   I think you can go to other places to meet friends, not in school.
    S4:   Ciekawe gdzie? /I wonder where?/
    S5:   Yes, it's not easy. School is best for knowing friends.
    S1:   But what with job? You can get better job if you go to Eton.
    T: How about boys? What do you think about it?
    S6:   I wouldn't mind. The school may be cool.
    S7:   And the prospects of career are better.
    S4:   Yeah, you later earn more money. And you are best professional in your ... dziedzina? /discipline/.
    S8:   Field.
    T: Yeah. Now, what do you think about our school in comparison with Eton?
    S1:   Our is nicer. It's not stiff.
    S2:   We have better direct relation with teachers.
    S6:   It's not hard. (Fryc, 2000: 119)

The impression that the above communicative activity makes is that the teacher has given up her corrective role to the learners. One of the learners provides the required lexical item (*... dziedzina? /discipline/ field*), another rephrases her utterance (*But it's not a nice company there. Company? No, the friends* / well, the friends/).

Yet, the peers' input is not quite adequate, and the teacher should have provided implicit corrective input at least twice. Let us analyse the above exchange in detail. First, when one of the students makes a real communicative comment in L1 (*Ciekawe gdzie?* /I wonder where/), the teacher misses an opportunity to provide an L2 translation equivalent e.g. *You wonder where? Perhaps on holiday.* The teacher does not facilitate the L2 learning process as she seems to have given up her role of a tutor and a counsellor, who should provide support in problematic situations.

Second, the other opportunity of providing implicit correction which was missed by the teacher was the learner's question *But what with job?*, showing a direct interference of L1 (*A co z pracą?*). The teacher could have said, for instance, *What are the prospects of getting a job after graduating from Eton?* She could have also commented on the learners' opinions. In other words, Teacher C has placed herself outside the discussion, instead of being one of its participants. The reason is not quite clear, but we can speculate that it was the teacher's lack of teaching experience (Teacher C – only one year of teaching experience, in comparison with Teacher A – 11 years of teaching experience).

Let us now look at two excerpts from the classrooms taught by Teachers D and E, who were also among the five teachers most closely adhering to the Communicative Approach. Neither exchange was monitored by the teachers at the moment of recording. It is interesting to note marked differences between the two exchanges, first of all, in the involvement of the students in the simulated communicative activities. In the first excerpt (179), the learners are focused on the completion of a simple task: interviewing a stranger on her life and interests.

(179) (see 167)
Description of the task: Information-gap activity (Bell & Gower, 1995: 9)
Instruction: Choose someone in the class who you do not know much about. Interview them remembering to mix direct and less direct questions and trying to keep your questions polite. Ask them at least five questions about where they live, their job, their studies, their family and the languages they speak. Find out about their favourite things – their hobbies and interests.
S1: Where do you live?
S2: In Nowa Huta.
S1: Where exactly?
S2: Przecież byłaś u mnie. /But you've been to my place/.
S1: No, dobra. /Well, OK/ Could you tell me what's your job?
S2: I learn at school.

S1:	Have you got big family? Powiedz coś o tych braciach. /Say something about your brothers/.
S2:	One is younger and other is older.
S1:	Co jeszcze? /What else?/.
S2:	Jeszcze iloma językami mówią. /About how many languages they speak/.
S1:	OK, so how many languages they speak?
S2:	English and French.
S1:	Aha, jeszcze hobbies.
S2:	I like reading books, good music and swimming. I often go for basen /a swimming-pool/.
S1:	Books, swimming, i co? /and what else?/.
S2:	Music.
S1:	What music?
S2:	Pop and jazz.
S1:	No dobra, to chyba wszystko. /OK. fine, that's all/. (Fryc, 2000: 85/110)

As has been noted before, the information-gap condition has been disregarded by Teacher D, who has used a communicative task which is unsuitable for people who know each other very well (*Choose someone in the class who you do not know much about*). It also seems that Teacher D has neglected another point in the task instruction (*Interview them remembering to mix direct and less direct questions and trying to keep your questions polite*), because the learners do not pay any attention to the directness and politeness of their questions.

The teaching material instructions provide important information for the communicative activities they accompany. They should be treated as the context of communicative exchanges, which must take into account such aspects of communication as directness and politeness. In the L2 classroom communication, it is the teacher's responsibility to focus the learners' attention on the instructions, to enable them to understand the context before they start communicating, and to provide them with necessary phrases, if they are not included in the instructions, as is the case of the above task. The reason why Teacher D has neglected her role may be her lack of experience. Similarly to Teacher C, she has had only one year of teaching experience.

In Excerpt (179) there is no corrective input, either on the part of the teacher or the conversational partners. The learners code-switch to L1 in all instances of organisational language use (real communication), because what they are doing is not real or simulated communication for its own sake, but preparing for a future speaking presentation (probably in front of the teacher). Their focus is clearly seen when the Interviewer asks for the repetition of the Interviewee's favourite pastime, because she has not managed to write it down (*Books, swimming, i co /and what else?/*).

Information-gap activities in monolingual contexts should be very carefully monitored by the teachers. Otherwise, in line with the principle of the least processing effort, the learners will probably code-switch to L1 in all instances of real communication. A further example of such communication during an information-gap activity (a pair-work survey) has been presented in Chapter 5 (153).

In the second excerpt (180), recorded in the class taught by Teacher E, the learners do not use any organisational language (real communication), and they are much more involved in the simulated activity (role-play) they are engaged in.

(180) Description of the task. Role-play: getting a bank loan (Soars & Soars, 1996: 40)
Instruction: Student A wants to get a bank loan to start a small business. He/she is to decide what the business is. He/she is to explain to the bank manager their business experience, the preparation they have already done, the competition, how much capital they already have, what exactly they want to do with the loan, and how soon they can pay it back.
Student B is a bank manager. When Student A is asking him/her for a bank loan, they should prepare to ask about their business experience, preparation, market research, the competitors, the capital they already have, the reasons why they want the loan and how soon they want the loan repaid. At the end of the interview, the bank manager should decide if he/she is ready to give the loan.

S1: Good morning. I would like to borrow 25,000 pounds to start a small business.
S2: What business?
S1: A hotel.
S2: Where have you worked? What experience have you got?
S1: I have worked as a hotel manager in South Poland.
S2: Have you found an office?
S1: Yes. I want to wynająć /rent/ a building.
S2: Have you done any market research?
S1: Yes, the competition is not big and I think I can be rich.
S2: How much capital do you have?
S1: 50,000 pounds.
S2: So why you want loan?

S1: Żeby wynająć ten /in order to rent this/ building.
S2: And if you zbankrutujesz? /go bankrupt/.
S1: I earn a lot and I can soon pay it back.
S2: I must think about it. Come again.
S1: OK. (Soars & Soars, 1996: 90/116)

The learners' involvement in the role-play can be easily observed, because they do not use any metalinguistic language, asking each other what to say. In other words, they have been prepared by the task instruction and by the teacher for the role-play, and they know what to say as far as the content of the activity is concerned. On the other hand, they seem to be unaware of the level of directness of their conversation and lack of politeness markers. If they cannot find an appropriate L2 lexical item, they provide an L1 translation equivalent, without trying to paraphrase, or to help each other. Had the teacher monitored the role-play, she would have provided the missing L2 lexical items (*to rent a building, to go bankrupt*), and she could have recast the interlanguage structure (*so why you want loan?*).

The conclusion that can be drawn from the above communicative activities (179) and (180) about the teachers' role in learner-centred activities, is that such activities should be very carefully prepared and monitored by the teacher, who should provide the learners with corrective input. If the teachers are unable to monitor all the groups engaged simultaneously in communicative activities, they should train their students in the use of active communication strategies.

Let us look at a group discussion on reality shows:

(181) (see 105)
S1: The general idea of reality shows is ... is ... jak jest 'zarobić pieniądze'? /How do we say 'earn money'?/.
S2: To earn big money.
S1: Wow! And it's a good business (turns to the teacher). Jak jest 'reklama'? Bo po niemiecku to jest 'Werbung'. /How do we say 'advertisement'? In German it is .../.
T: Advertisement.
S2: Advertisement. OK.
[...]
S1: No a jak powiedzieć, że jest dużo przemocy i seksu? /How should we say that there is a lot of violence and sex?/.
S2: There is a lot of violence and sex. (Przebinda, 2004: 113)

In the above excerpt the learners use some communication strategies, asking in L1 for teacher and peer help (*jak jest ... ?* /how do we say/). On

L2 Teaching Implications

the other hand, the teacher does not take an active part in the discussion and does not provide corrective input.

The question arises concerning the impact of more learner-centred activities: group-work, pair-work, or even whole class discussions, in which L2 teachers do not take an active part. Most teachers in our research (Fryc, 2000) believe that:

(1) *The learner-centred approach to language teaching encourages responsibility and self-discipline of the students and allows each student to develop his/her full potential.*
(2) *Group-work activities are essential in providing opportunities for cooperative relationship to emerge, and in promoting genuine interaction among students.*
(3) *Group-work allows students to explore problems for themselves, and thus have some measure of control over their own learning. It is, therefore, an invaluable means of organizing classroom experience.* (Karavas-Doukas, 1996, in Fryc, 2000)

Let us then ask the following questions:

(a) What kind of responsibility is being developed?
(b) What kind of cooperative relationship and genuine interaction emerge from group-work?
(c) What measure of control over their own learning do students possess in group-work?

If we look again at some fragments of the communicative group-work activities (182–187), we can note the students' responsibility for speaking L2 and for enacting their roles according to their role cards, but they do not seem to feel responsible for providing one another linguistic support in the form of implicit or explicit corrective input.

(182) (see 165)
    S2: And I want to say that I'd like to study English for one year and I want to speak English very well and my communication must be also very well.
    S1: So I think I'm a better person because I already speak English so ... (Fryc, 2000: 125)

S1 does not pay attention to S2's error, because her focus is entirely on the meaning – the arguments of the person she is enacting. An interlocutor playing this role and at the same time assuming the responsibility of a corrector, apart from being a conversational partner, would probably provide S2 with implicit corrective input, e.g. *And my communication is already very good, so I think I am a better candidate.* S2 might have noticed her error, and could have repeated the corrected utterance.

(183) **S1:** OK, but let's talk about other languages now. Do you think that you have ... when you study other languages, do you think that you learn them easy? Or is it quite difficult to learn them?
S3: For me it's easy. I speak also German and Spanish and ... I think that's all I can really say ... (Fryc, 2000: 125)

S3 avoids S1's erroneous form (*Do you think that you learn them easy?*), but as above, she is not focused on formal correctness, so instead of providing a recast (*I learn them easily*) to help her friend, she further enacts her role. The lexical problem faced in the previous turn by S1 has not been solved either (*Do you think that you have ...*). An interlocutor ready to provide corrective feedback would probably guess that the learner is searching for the lexical item *special abilities to learn languages*, and would use the appropriate phrase (given in the role-card) in her answer.

(184) **S3:** I think that studying other languages is very important because we have to communicate with people from other countries and it's very important. So because of it I study German and I can speak German very well and a little bit in Spanish.
S1: OK ... well ... do you have anything to add?
S3: I think that my person is really good for this place and I think you should choose me.
S1: OK, thank you very much for coming. And I guess I will be back in five minutes and then I will decide who gets the place.
S2: OK, thank you.
S3: Thank you and see you later. (Fryc, 2000: 125)

The head teacher (S1) has nothing else to say except a set phrase (*Do you have anything to add?*). On the one hand, she does not try to ask additional questions to find out if the candidates could help the language school somehow (Instruction for the candidates: *Think of as many arguments as possible to convince* [the head teacher] *that you are a better candidate for this place and that you can actually help the school somehow*). On the other hand, S1 is trying to use in her answer some pragmalinguistic rules of indirectness and politeness, which can also have some influence on S2 and S3's behaviour.

I would like to claim that the cooperative relationship students develop, and the corrective feedback they provide for one another in role-play activities refer more to the use of set phrases and pragmalinguistic formulae than to helping the peers by providing implicit or explicit feedback in order to fill in gaps in their lexical or grammatical knowledge.

(185) (see 166)
    S1: All right. Tell me something more. My problem is that I must choose you. I have one place in my school so try to ... well ... tell me something more.
    S3: I have learnt English for four years and I know German also and Spanish very well.
    S1: Oh, that's good. That's very interesting. Do you like German?
    S3: Yes, yes. I love German. But I think English is more easy.
    S1: Yes, it's true. And what about you? Do you know any languages?
    S2: I know French basic and Latin also. I am really the best person for this place.
    S1: But why do you think so?
    S2: I want to learn English because I am going to England ...
    S3: And I ... I also want to go to this school. I will be a teacher in the future.
    S2: I can pay for this place. I can pay big money. 4000 pounds.
(Fryc, 2000: 127)

In the above excerpt (185), the same phenomena can be observed as in (182), (183) and (184). The male students enacting the same roles as those enacted by their more L2 proficient female peers (at least, according to the teaching level), as has been said in Chapter 5, seem to be more creative in finding arguments how they can help the school (*I can pay for this place. I can pay big money. 4000 pounds*). However, when the head teacher cannot find the right lexical item (*so try to ... well ... tell me something more*), the candidates (S2 and S3) do not help him, in spite of the fact that the verb *to convince* is included in their role cards. A conversational partner taking responsibility for providing corrective input, would probably say, e.g. *I will try to convince you that I'm a better candidate*. Similarly, the head teacher (S1) does not recast an erroneous S3's form (*English is more easy*), by saying, e.g. *Yes, it's true, it's easier*.

However, at the level of discourse, S1 makes some attempts to remind S2 and S3 that they are supposed to provide more arguments (*Why do you want to come to my school? There are other schools too [...]. Why do you need our school? Show me that you are the better candidate*).

(186) **S1:** Why do you want to come to my school? There are other schools too.
S2: Because this school is really the best. I heard it in television. It's the best in the country.
S3: But you are not the best candidate in this country. Remember it.
S1: Have you learnt any other languages?
S3: Yes, I know German and Spanish. I said this.
S1: Why do you need our school? Show me that you are the better candidate.
S3: Because this school will give me a dyplom /certificate/ and I need it because it will help me to get a better job.
S2: And I need it because I must communicate with my girlfriend. And when I go to England I must get a good job there.
S1: Yes, I get it. But how can I choose? I don't know who is better. I think I will take you all because you are great and you are the best. And I will make a big group for this year.
S3: OK, thank you very much, Mr. Head teacher.
S1: Thank you very much. And see you on the lesson. Good bye.
(Fryc, 2000: 127)

Although it is hardly possible that in a real interview a candidate would address another candidate as S3 addresses S2 (*But you are not the best candidate in this country. Remember it.*), the interactional discourse in the above role-play is vivid and imaginative, and the students seem to present genuine arguments[4] (*Because this school is really the best. I heard it in television.* [...] *Because this school will give me a dyplom* /certificate/ *and I need it because it will help me to get a better job.* [...] *And I need it because I must communicate with my girlfriend. And when I go to England I must get a good job there.*) No doubt that the head teacher does not want to reject anybody, and in a gesture of solidarity with his peers, he admits both of them, admittedly, using the phrase inappropriate in an interview for a job situation (*I think I will take you all because you are great and you are the best*).

Had the teacher been present at the scene, she could have provided the lexical item S3 did not know (*certificate*), and she could have explained that the head teacher would probably use a less direct expression, e.g. *I think I will admit both of you, because it seems that you both have good reasons to study at our school.*

In the following excerpt (187), the same female students as in (182), (183) and (184) discuss in group-work which system of education is more

L2 Teaching Implications

effective: the Polish one or the South Korean one. They are supposed to answer the question about system effectiveness on the basis of a reading passage on education in South Korea and their own experience.

(187) (see 169)
> **S2:** OK, so *which system is more effective?*
> **S1:** I think this system have more advantages and disadvantages and Polish system have advantages and disadvantages so we must put them ... together ... choose ... I think that ... that the Korean system ... with this system you could receive better job but the problems you will be ... have ... I mean in ... I think that in Korean system you get a better job so better life, but it's not so good life if you don't have the ...
> **S3:** Private life.
> **S1:** Private life and ... and ...
> **S2:** You don't know how to ...
> **S3:** How to behave, how to act.
> **S2:** Yes, so I think that our system is better.
> **S3:** It's not better but it's more for people as to say / = it's more humane, so to speak /.
> **S2:** No one is the best but I think our is better than the Korean system. (Fryc, 2000: 121)

As far as their cooperative relationship is concerned, the students try to build up a common argument and to help each other in finding necessary lexical items (... *if you don't have the ... private life* [...] *you don't know how to ... how to behave*). However, their linguistic means are seriously limited, in terms of both interlanguage grammar and lexical repertoire. If the L2 teacher had participated in the discussion, he could have clarified some points. For instance, after S2 and S3 say: *you don't know how to ... how to behave, how to act*, the teacher could have said: *you don't know how to live with other people, in the society*. Further, when S3 says: *It's not better but it's more for people as to say*, the teacher would certainly ask a clarification question: *Do you mean that our system is more suitable for human beings?*, which would probably be confirmed and repeated by the learner, giving her an opportunity to focus on the lexical item. The concluding statement could be explicitly corrected by the teacher, which would focus the learners on the target forms (*No system is ideal, but we think that our system is better than the Korean one*).

Coming back to the last question we have asked above, on the basis of Karavas-Doukas's Opinion Survey (Fryc, 2000), we could conclude that the students in Przebinda's research did not have much control over their own learning during communicative activities they were engaged in. Although, admittedly, they were much more active and independent than the students in teacher-centred classroom discourse (see Kosiarz, 1985; Kusibab, 1984), they were so preoccupied with the meanings they tried to express that they were not able to control the accuracy of the language they used. Besides, the groups were homogenous as far as L2 proficiency is concerned. Consequently, the learners were not in the position to provide one another with the corrective input at the problematic moments during the interaction.

Conclusion

It seems that the teacher in the role of a monitor and a judicious corrector (or a more proficient peer in the same role) is an indispensable participant of L2 classroom communicative activities, if the learners are to achieve full control over their learning process, i.e. over the development of fluency and accuracy. The teacher's role seems to involve the following:

The L2 teacher should be a mediator between meaning and form in classroom communication

Comments: In traditional L2 teaching it was believed that incomplete and inaccurate learners' knowledge of the L2 code should be first completed and improved before the learners could focus on real communication in L2. That was the reason why L2 teachers used to focus their attention, first of all, on the development of accuracy (linguistic competence). In the traditional L2 classroom communication, such an approach resulted in the teachers' disregard for real L2 communication, treating L2 only as the teaching content, and code-switching to L1, whenever the teacher wanted to communicate with the students.

Nowadays, Communicative Language Teaching has put stress on the development of students' L2 fluency (communicative competence), and learner-centred L2 teaching. Most L2 teachers follow the Communicative Approach in its postulate to give learners more independence to communicate in group work activities. However, the problem which has become most conspicuous in contemporary L2 classroom simulated communication (communicative activities) is disregard for L2 accuracy, and treating fluency development as the completion of trivial speaking tasks and *filling time with talk*.

Thus, the L2 teacher's most important role in classroom communication is to mediate between a general focus on real L2 communication and temporary focuses on accuracy of L2 forms, facilitated by implicit or explicit corrective input provided by the teacher or elicited from the learners.

The L2 teacher should communicate with her students in the target language, unless the affective or instructional circumstances make her momentarily code-switch to L1

Comments: Code-switching to L1 should never become an L1 speaking *mode* during long periods of class time. Nevertheless, in monolingual L2 classroom communication, momentary switches to L1 facilitate teacher–student rapport and help explaining difficult concepts (e.g. grammatical problems). However, the teachers should insist on real classroom communication in L2, by using the target language themselves, and providing translation equivalents for the learners who use L1.

Teaching other school subjects in L2 in monolingual countries is largely at an experimental stage. It seems that the effort involved in introducing such L2 content courses is incommensurate with their effects. Most non-native teachers of L2 content courses provide only L2 specialist vocabulary, while L1 remains the language of classroom communication.

Teacher-centred classroom communication can develop communicative competence if the teacher's main focus is real communication, and not only accuracy practice

Comments: Real communication can refer to the real world, as well as to the teaching materials or the L2 code. The role of the teacher in teacher-centred communication may be abused, if the teacher monopolises the floor, focuses only on learners' L2 accuracy and disregards real communication. However, in large, undisciplined classrooms, particularly in teaching younger learners at lower L2 proficiency levels, teacher-centred class communication seems to be a better solution than learner-centred group activities, when the teacher is unable to monitor all the groups.

Group work activities should be carefully prepared and monitored by the teacher

Comments: In group work discussions, learners are more likely to express their own opinions, but, on the other hand, they may be more reluctant to speak. They may also code-switch to L1, particularly when they are focused only on the completion of the tasks. Well-prepared and monitored role-plays allow the learners to get more involved in simulated situations and to enact their roles. In consequence, in role-plays learners are likely to speak more and to be more creative than in discussions. In group work activities L2 teachers should play the role of potential providers of corrective input, and of tutors or counsellors, who can also provide new ideas and commentaries. A total withdrawal of the teacher from the scene of group work activities does not allow learners to achieve full control over their L2 learning process, particularly as far as L2 accuracy is concerned, and additionally, it can undermine the learners' trust in teachers as educators. Peers at the same L2 level are usually unable to provide corrective input for one another, although group work can contribute to the development of their cooperative relationship.

L2 teacher training institutions should include in their courses a teaching module which would specially focus on training future teachers how to communicate in the L2 classroom, and how to provide learners with potentially explicit corrective input

Comments: Teachers' input can have a facilitating role in the L2 learning process if it is interpreted by the learners as real target language, and momentarily, as corrective feedback. To be able to provide such input, teacher trainees should be first given many opportunities to observe real situations in which experienced teachers provide instructional input. Video materials seem to be ideal in this respect, because they allow for multiple viewing of the same scenes. Later, teacher trainees should practise classroom communication, in particular monitoring group-work communication, during their L2 teaching practice. Special L2 refresher courses for non-native L2 teachers are especially useful in building up their L2 communication skills and confidence.

Notes
1. Most of the examples analysed in this chapter have already been included in previous chapters. To enable quick reference, the original excerpt number is given.
2. One of the five teachers was uncertain about her opinion.
3. Unfortunately, Teacher A is rather an exception than a rule in our corpus of classroom discourse data, as far as her imaginativeness in designing real classroom communication is concerned.
4. As has been noted before, the male technical secondary school students, who enacted the analysed role-play, seemed to be aware of their own future problems with finding a job. It could be one of the reasons why genuine interaction emerged during a simulated communicative activity.

References

Allen, P., Frochlich, M. and Spada, N. (1984) The communicative orientation of language teaching: An observation scheme. In J. Handscombe, R. Orem and B. Taylor (eds) *On TESOL'83: The Question of Control* (pp. 231–52). Washington, DC: TESOL.

Allwright, R. (1980) Turns, topics and tasks: Patterns of participation in learning and teaching. In D. Larsen-Freeman (ed.) *Discourse Analysis in Second Language Research* (pp. 165–87). Rowley, MA: Newbury House.

Allwright, R. (1988) *Observation in the Language Classroom*. London: Longman.

Atkinson, D. (1993) *Teaching Monolingual Classes*. London: Longman.

Austin, J. (1962) *How to Do Things with Words*. Oxford: Clarendon Press.

Bell, J. and Gower, R. (1995) *Intermediate Matters*. London: Longman.

Bellack, A., Kliebard, H., Hyman, R. and Smith, R. (1966) *The Language of the Classroom*. New York: Teachers College Press, Columbia University.

Bialystok, E. (1978) A theoretical model of second language learning. *Language Learning* 28, 69–83.

Bialystok, E. (1990) *Communication Strategies. A Psychological Analysis of Second-Language Use*. Oxford: Blackwell.

Bialystok, E. and Sharwood-Smith, M. (1985) Interlanguage is not a state of mind: An evaluation of the construct for second language acquisition. *Applied Linguistic* 6, 101–17.

Breen, M. (1985) The social context for language learning – a neglected situation? *Studies in Second Language Acquisition* 7, 135–58.

Breen, M. (2001) Overt participation and covert acquisition in the language classroom. In M. Breen (ed.) *Learner Contributions to Language Learning: New Directions in Research* (pp. 112–40). London: Longman.

Brown, H. (1994) *Principles of Language Learning and Teaching*. Englewood Cliffs: Prentice Hall.

Brumfit, C. and Johnson, K. (eds) (1979) *The Communicative Approach to Language Teaching*. Oxford: Oxford University Press.

Canagarajah, A. (1999) *Resisting Linguistic Imperialism in English Teaching*. Oxford: Oxford University Press.

Canale, M. (1983) From communicative competence to communicative language pedagogy. In J. Richards and R. Schmidt (eds) *Language and Communication* (pp. 2–25). London: Longman.

Canale, M. and Swain, M. (1980) Theoretical bases of communicative approaches to second language teaching and testing. *Applied Linguistics* 1, 1–47.

Carroll, S. (1995) The irrelevance of verbal feedback to language learning. In L. Eubank, L. Selinker and M. Sharwood-Smith (eds) *Interlanguage: Studies in Honour of W.E. Rutherford* (pp. 73–88). Amsterdam: John Benjamins.

Carroll, S. (1999) Putting 'input' in its proper place. *Second Language Research* 15, 337–88.

Celce-Murcia, M. and Olshtain, E. (2000) *Discourse and Context in Language Teaching. A Guide for Language Teachers.* Cambridge: Cambridge University Press.

Chaudron, C. (1988) *Second Language Classrooms. Research on Teaching and Learning.* Cambridge: Cambridge University Press.

Cohen, A. (1985) Bilingual education. In M. Celce-Murcia (ed.) *Beyond Basics: Issues and Research in TESOL* (pp. 167–92). Rowley, MA: Newbury House.

Cook, V. (1985) Universal Grammar and second language learning. *Applied Linguistics* 6, 2–18.

Czekajewska, A. (1999) The effectiveness of spoken error correction in secondary school L2 classes. Unpublished MA thesis, Jagiellonian University, Kraków.

Dakowska, M. (2003) *Current Controversies in Foreign Language Didactics.* Warszawa: Wydawnictwa Uniwersytetu Warszawskiego.

Doughty, C. (2001) Cognitive underpinnings of focus on form. In P. Robinson (ed.) *Cognition and Second Language Instruction* (pp. 206–57). Cambridge: Cambridge University Press.

Doughty, C. and Williams, J. (eds) (1998) *Focus on Form in Classroom Second Language Acquisition.* Cambridge: Cambridge University Press.

Duff, P. (1995) An ethnography of communication in immersion classrooms in Hungary. *TESOL Quarterly* 29, 505–37.

Edmondson, W. (1985) Discourse worlds in the classroom and in foreign language learning. *Studies in Second Language Acquisition* 7, 159–68.

Edmondson, W. and House, J. (1981) *Let's Talk and Talk About It.* Munich: Urban and Schwanzenberg.

Eldridge, J. (1996) Code-switching in a Turkish secondary school. *ELT Journal* 50, 303–13.

Ellis, R. (1984) *Classroom Second Language Development.* Oxford: Pergamon.

Ellis, R. (1985) *Understanding Second Language Acquisition.* Oxford: Oxford University Press.

Ellis, R. (1990) *Instructed Second Language Acquisition.* Oxford: Blackwell.

Ellis, R. (1994) *The Study of Second Language Acquisition.* Oxford: Oxford University Press.

Faerch, C. (1985) Meta-talk in FL classroom discourse. *Studies in Second Language Acquisition* 7, 184–99.

Faerch, C. and Kasper, G. (1983) Plans and strategies in foreign language communication. In C. Faerch and G. Kasper (eds) *Strategies in Interlanguage Communication* (pp. 20–60). London: Longman.

Faerch, C. and Kasper, G. (1986) The role of comprehension in second language learning. *Applied Linguistics* 7, 257–74.

Fanselow, J. (1977) Beyond 'Rashomon' – conceptualizing and describing the teaching act. *TESOL Quarterly* 11, 17–39.

Ferguson, C. (1971) Absence of copula and the notion of simplicity: A study of normal speech, baby talk, foreigner talk, and pidgins. In D. Hymes (ed.) *Pidginization and Creolization of Languages* (pp. 141–50). Cambridge: Cambridge University Press.

Fillmore, C. (1979) On fluency. In C. Fillmore, D. Kempler and W. Wang (eds) *Individual Differences in Language Ability and Language Behavior* (pp. 85–101). New York: Academic Press.
Firth, A. and Wagner, J. (1997) On discourse, communication and (some) fundamental concepts in SLA research. *Modern Language Journal* 81, 286–300.
Fisiak, J. (1994) Training English language teachers in Poland: Recent reform and its future prospects. In C. Gough and A. Jankowska (eds) *Directions Towards 2000* (pp. 7–14). Poznań: Instytut Filologii Angielskiej UAM.
Flanders, N. (1970) *Analysing Teaching Behavior*. Reading, MA: Addison-Wesley.
Flanigan, B. (1991) Peer tutoring and second language acquisition in the elementary school. *Applied Linguistics* 12, 141–58.
Fryc, A. (2000) Using communicative activities in Polish secondary schools. Unpublished MA thesis, Jagiellonian University, Kraków.
Gaies, S. (1977) The nature of linguistic input in formal second language learning: Linguistic and communicative strategies in ESL teachers' classroom language. In H. Brown, C. Yorio and R. Crymes (eds) *On TESOL '77* (pp. 204–12). Washington DC: TESOL.
Gass, S. (1997) *Input, Interaction and the Second Language Learner*. Mahwah: Lawrence Erlbaum.
Gass, S. (1998) Apples and oranges: or why apples are not oranges and don't need to be. A response to Firth and Wagner. *Modern Language Journal* 82, 83–90.
Giles, H. (ed.) (1977) *Language, Ethnicity and Intergroup Relations*. New York: Academic Press.
Goffman, E. (1959) *The Presentation of Self in Everyday Life*. New York: Doubleday.
Goffman, E. (1967) *Interactional Ritual. Essays on Face-to Face Behavior*. New York: Anchor Books.
Gozdawa-Gołębiowski, R. (2004) Relevance defocus in teaching the L2 system. In E. Mioduszewska (ed.) *Relevance Studies in Poland* (Vol. I) (pp. 285–306). Warszawa: Institute of English Studies, University of Warsaw.
Gremmo, M., Holec, H. and Riley, P. (1977) *Interactional Structure: The Role of Role*. Melanges Pedagogiques, University of Nancy: CRAPEL.
Gremmo, M., Holec, H. and Riley, P. (1978) *Taking the Initiative: Some Pedagogical Applications of Discourse Analysis*. Melanges Pedagogiques, University of Nancy: CRAPEL.
Grice, H. (1975) Logic and conversation. In P. Cole and J. Morgan (eds) *Syntax and Semantics* (Vol. 3) (pp. 41–58). New York: Academic Press.
Harbord, J. (1992) The use of the mother tongue in the classroom. *ELT Journal* 46, 350–55.
Harder, P. (1980) Discourse as self-expression – on the reduced personality of the second language learner. *Applied Linguistics* 1, 262–70.
Hatch, E. (1978) Discourse analysis and second language acquisition. In E. Hatch (ed.) *Second Language Acquisition. A Book of Readings* (pp. 401–35). Rowley, MA: Newbury House.
Havranek, G. and Cesnik, H. (2001) Factors affecting the success of corrective feedback. In S. Foster-Cohen and A. Niżegorodcew (eds) *EUROSLA Yearbook* (Vol. I) (pp. 99–122). Amsterdam: John Benjamins.
Henzl, V. (1973) Linguistic register of foreign language instruction. *Language Learning* 23, 207–22.
Henzl, V. (1979) Foreigner talk in the classroom. *IRAL* 17, 159–65.

Hoffman, E. (1989) *Lost in Translation*. New York: Penguin Books.
Hymes, D. (1972) On communicative competence. In J. Pride and J. Holmes (eds) *Sociolinguistics: Selected Readings* (pp. 269–93). Harmondsworth: Penguin Books.
Jarvis, G. (1968) A behavioral observation system for classroom foreign language skill acquisition activities. *Modern Language Journal* 52, 335–41.
Jodłowiec, M. (1991) The role of relevance in the interpretation of verbal jokes – a pragmatic analysis. Unpublished PhD dissertation, Jagiellonian University, Kraków.
Johnson, K. (1995) *Understanding Communication in Second Language Classrooms*. Cambridge: Cambridge University Press.
Karavas-Doukas, E. (1996) Using attitude scales to investigate teachers' attitudes to the communicative approach. *ELT Journal* 50, 187–94.
Kasper, G. (1985) Repair in foreign language teaching. *Studies in Second Language Acquisition* 7, 200–15.
Kasper, G. (1997) 'A' stands for acquisition: A response to Firth and Wagner. *Modern Language Journal* 81, 307–12.
Kellerman, E., Bongaerts, T. and Poulisse, N. (1987) Strategy and system in L2 referential communication. In R. Ellis (ed.) *Second Language Acquisition in Context* (pp. 100–12). Englewood Cliffs: Prentice Hall.
Komorowska, H. (1978) *Sukces i niepowodzenie w nauce języka obcego*. Warszawa: Wydawnictwa Szkolne i Pedagogiczne.
Komorowska, H. (1994) English teaching in Poland. In C. Gough and A. Jankowska (eds) *Directions Towards 2000* (pp. 19–21). Poznań: Instytut Filologii Angielskiej UAM.
Komorowska, H. (2000) New tendencies in the work of the Council of Europe. Common European Framework for language teaching and learning. Implications for curriculum development. In J. Arabski (ed.) *Studies in Foreign Language Acquisition and Teaching* (pp. 24–41). Katowice: Wydawnictwo Uniwersytetu Śląskiego.
Korpaczewska, I. (2000) Komunikacyjne nauczanie języka angielskiego w szkołach ogólnokształcących. Unpublished PhD dissertation, Uniwersytet Szczeciński, Szczecin.
Kosiarz, A. (1985) Teachers' questions at two levels of foreign language proficiency. Unpublished MA thesis, Jagiellonian University, Kraków.
Kramsch, C. (1985) Classroom interaction and discourse options. *Studies in Second Language Acquisition* 7, 169–83.
Kramsch, C. (1993) *Context and Culture in Language Teaching*. Oxford: Oxford University Press.
Krashen, S. (1981) *Second Language Acquisition and Second Language Learning*. Oxford: Pergamon.
Krashen, S. (1982) *Principles and Practice in Second Language Acquisition*. Oxford: Pergamon.
Król, A. (2004) Teaching English articles to Polish learners – a cognitive perspective. Unpublished MA thesis, Jagiellonian University, Kraków.
Kusibab, E. (1984) The contribution of classroom interaction to the development of communicative competence. Unpublished MA thesis, Jagiellonian University, Kraków.
Larsen-Freeman, D. (ed.) (1980) *Discourse Analysis in Second Language Research*. Rowley, MA: Newbury House.
Levelt, W. (1989) *Speaking: From Intention to Articulation*. Cambridge: Cambridge University Press.

Lightbown, P. (2000) Classroom SLA research and second language teaching. *Applied Linguistics* 21, 431–62.
Littlewood, W. (1981) *Communicative Language Teaching*. Cambridge: Cambridge University Press.
Long, M. (1983) Linguistic and conversational adjustments to non-native speakers. *Studies in Second Language Acquisition* 5 (2), 177–93.
Long, M. (1985) Input and second language acquisition theory. In S. Gass and C. Madden (eds) *Input in Second Language Acquisition* (pp. 377–93). Cambridge, MA: Newbury House.
Long, M. (1991) Focus on form: A design feature in language teaching methodology. In K. de Bot, R. Ginsberg and C. Kramsch (eds) *Foreign Language Research in Cross-cultural Perspective* (pp. 39–52). Amsterdam: John Benjamins.
Long, M. (1996) The role of linguistic environment in second language acquisition. In W. Ritchie and T. Bhatia (eds) *Handbook of Second Language Acquisition* (Vol. 2) (pp. 413–68). New York: Academic Press.
Long, M. (1997) Construct validity in SLA research: A response to Firth and Wagner. *Modern Language Journal* 81, 318–23.
Long, M. and Crookes, G. (1991) Three approaches to task-based syllabus design. *TESOL Quarterly* 26, 27–55.
Long, M. and Robinson, P. (1998) Focus on form: Theory, research and practice. In C. Doughty and J. Williams (eds) *Focus on Form in Classroom Second Language Acquisition* (pp. 15–63). Cambridge: Cambridge University Press.
Long, M. and Sato, C. (1983) Classroom foreigner talk discourse: Forms and functions of teachers' questions. In H. Seliger and M. Long (eds) *Classroom-Oriented Research in Second Language Acquisition* (pp. 268–86). Rowley, MA: Newbury House.
Majer, J. (2003) *Interactive Discourse in the Foreign Language Classroom*. Łódź: Wydawnictwo Uniwersytetu Łódzkiego.
Majer, H. and Majer, J. (1996) Teacher talk: Theory and classroom realities. In J. Field, A. Graham and M. Peacock (eds) *Insights 1* (pp. 13–22). Whitstable, Kent: IATEFL.
Mazur, J. (2000) Bilingual education at the secondary school level in Kraków. Unpublished MA thesis, Jagiellonian University, Kraków.
McLaughlin, B. (1987) *Theories of Second Language Learning*. London: Edward Arnold.
McTear, M. (1975) Structure and categories of foreign language teaching sequences. In R. Allwright (ed.) *Working Papers: Language Teaching Classroom Research* (pp. 97–130). Essex: University of Essex.
Medgyes, P. (1994) *The Non-native Teacher*. London: Macmillan.
Mehan, H. (1979) *Learning Lessons: Social Organization in the Classroom*. Cambridge: Cambridge University Press.
Mercer, N. (1995) *The Guided Construction of Knowledge*. Clevedon: Multilingual Matters.
Moon, J. and Nikolov, M. (eds) (2000) *Research into Teaching English to Young Learners*. Pecs: University Press Pecs.
Moskovitz, G. (1971) Interaction analysis: A new modern language for supervisors. *Foreign Language Annals* 5, 211–21.
Munby, J. (1978) *Communicative Syllabus Design*. Cambridge: Cambridge University Press.
Musiał, A. (2004) Teacher trainees' personal theories of EFL teaching and learning. Unpublished PhD dissertation, Jagiellonian University, Kraków.

Newmark, L. (1966) How not to interfere with language learning. *International Journal of American Linguistics* 32. Reprinted in C. Brumfit and K. Johnson (eds) *The Communicative Approach to Language Teaching* (pp. 160–66). Oxford: Oxford University Press.

Nęcka, E. (2000) Procesy uwagi. In J. Strelau (ed.) *Psychologia* (pp. 78–96). Gdańsk: Gdańskie Wydawnictwo Psychologiczne.

Niżegorodcew, A. (1980) The role of aptitude in foreign language learning in secondary grammar school pupils. *Glottodidactica*, 13, 37–48.

Niżegorodcew, A. (1983) A Polish child's learning of English. Paper presented at SLE XVI Annual Meeting. Poznań, August 1983.

Niżegorodcew, A. (1986) Interlanguage strategies – a foreign language learner's perspective. *Zeszyty Naukowe Uniwersytetu Jagiellońskiego* 64, 85–94.

Niżegorodcew, A. (1989) Fluency in speech production of advanced foreign language learners. In J. Arabski (ed.) *On Foreign Language Learning; Selected Papers* (pp. 175–80). Wroclaw: Zaklad Narodowy im. Ossolińskich, Wydawnictwo PAN.

Niżegorodcew, A. (1991) *Dyskurs interakcyjny a kompetencja komunikacyjna w języku obcym*. Kraków: Uniwersytet Jagielloński.

Niżegorodcew, A. (1993a) The structure of foreign language discourse and the use of communication strategies by low proficiency foreign language learners. In B. Katteman and W. Wieden (eds) *Current Issues in European Second Language Acquisition Research* (pp. 349–57). Tubingen: Gunter Narr.

Niżegorodcew, A. (1993b) Foreign language teacher training – where are we now? *The Polish Teacher Trainer* 1, 14–18.

Niżegorodcew, A. (1995) The communicative approach in the Polish context: Strengths and weaknesses. In I. Przemecka and Z. Mazur (eds) *Studies in English and American Literature and Language. Studies in Honour of the Memory of J. Strzetelski* (pp. 271–78). Kraków: Universitas.

Niżegorodcew, A. (1997) First language use in the second language classroom in the light of SLA research. In Z. Mazur and T. Bela (eds) *New Developments in English and American Studies: Continuity and Change* (pp. 631–42). Kraków: Universitas.

Niżegorodcew, A. (1998a) Second language acquisition research and foreign language teacher education. In M. Smoczyńska (ed.) *Studia z psychologii rozwojowej i psycholingwistyki: Studies in Honour of the Memory of M. Przetacznik-Gierowska* (pp. 263–72). Kraków: Universitas.

Niżegorodcew, A. (1998b) Teaching English culture in the Polish EFL classroom. In L. Dobosiewicz, L. Piasecka and J. Zalewski (eds) *Crossing the Borders: English Studies at the Turn of the Century* (pp. 19–28). Opole: Uniwersytet Opolski.

Niżegorodcew, A. (2001) Foreign language oral performance assessment or opening Pandora's box. In J. Arabski (ed.) *Insights into Foreign Language Acquisition and Teaching* (pp. 187–98). Katowice: Wydawnictwo Uniwersytetu Śląskiego.

Norton, B. (1997) Language, identity and the ownership of English. *TESOL Quarterly* 31, 409–29.

Nunan, D. (1989) *Designing Tasks for the Communicative Classroom*. Cambridge: Cambridge University Press.

O'Neill, R. (1991) The plausible myth of learner-centredness: Or the importance of doing ordinary things well. *ELT Journal* 45, 293–304.

Parks, S. and Maguire, M. (1999) Coping with on-the-job writing in ESL: A constructivist-semiotic perspective. *Language Learning* 49, 143–75.

Pawley, A. and Syder, F. (1983) Two puzzles for linguistic theory: Nativelike selection and nativelike fluency. In J. Richards and R. Schmidt (eds) *Language and Communication* (pp. 191–226). London: Longman.
Phillipson, R. (1992) *Linguistic Imperialism.* Oxford: Oxford University Press.
Pica, T. (1987) Second language acquisition, social interaction, and the classroom. *Applied Linguistics* 8, 3–21.
Porter, P. (1983) How learners talk to each other: input and interaction in task-centered discussions. Paper presented at TESOL Conference, Toronto, Canada.
Poulisse, N. (1997) Some words in defense of the psycholinguistic approach: A response to Firth and Wagner. *Modern Language Journal* 81, 324–28.
Przebinda, A. (2004) Discussion or role-play? Helping secondary school learners develop their speaking skills. Unpublished MA thesis, Jagiellonian University, Kraków.
Puchala, D. (1993) EFL classroom uses of Polish (L1) and English (L2) by non-native teachers of English. Unpublished MA thesis, Jagiellonian University, Kraków.
Richards, J. and Nunan, D. (eds) (1990) *Second Language Teacher Education.* Cambridge: Cambridge University Press.
Richards, J. and Rogers, T. (1986) *Approaches and Methods in Language Teaching.* Cambridge: Cambridge University Press.
Richards, J. and Schmidt, R. (eds) (1983) *Language and Communication.* London: Longman.
Robinson, P. (1995) Attention, memory and the 'noticing' hypothesis. *Language Learning* 45, 283–331.
Robinson, P. (2001) *Cognition and Second Language Instruction.* Cambridge: Cambridge University Press.
Rossner, R. and Bolitho, R. (eds) (1990) *Currents of Change in ELT.* Oxford: Oxford University Press.
Sachs, H., Schegloff, E. and Jefferson, G. (1974) A simplest systematics for the organization of turn-taking in conversation. *Language* 50, 696–735.
Savignon, S. (1983) *Communicative Competence: Theory and Classroom Practice.* Reading, MA: Addison-Wesley.
Scollon, R. (1976) *Conversations with a One-year Old.* Honolulu: The University of Hawaii Press.
Schegloff, E., Jefferson, G. and Sachs, H. (1977) The preference for self-correction in the organization of repair in conversation. *Language* 53, 361–82.
Schmidt, R. (1990) The role of consciousness in second language learning. *Applied Linguistics* 11, 129–58.
Searle, J. (1969) *Speech Acts.* Cambridge: Cambridge University Press.
Searle, J. (1976) A classification of illocutionary acts. *Language in Society* 5, 1–23.
Seliger, H. (1977) Does practice make perfect? A study of the interaction patterns and L2 competence. *Language Learning* 27, 263–78.
Selinker, L. (1972) Interlanguage. *IRAL* 10, 209–31.
Selinker, L. and Douglas, D. (1985) Wrestling with 'context' in interlanguage theory. *Applied Linguistics* 6, 190–204.
Shohamy, E. (1996) Competence and performance in language testing. In G. Brown, K. Malmkjaer and J. Williams (eds) *Performance and Competence in Second Language Acquisition* (pp. 138–51). Cambridge: Cambridge University Press.

Siek-Piskozub, T. (2002) Kompetencja językowa ucznia szkoły średniej. *Neofilolog* 21, 6–13.
Sinclair, J. and Brazil, D. (1982) *Teacher Talk*. Oxford: Oxford University Press.
Sinclair, J. and Coulthard, M. (1975) *Towards an Analysis of Discourse: The English Used by Teachers and Pupils*. Oxford: Oxford University Press.
Skehan, P. (1989) *Individual Differences in Second Language Learning*. London: Arnold.
Skehan, P. (1998) *A Cognitive Approach to Language Learning*. Oxford: Oxford University Press.
Slimani, A. (1987) The teaching/learning relationship: learning opportunities and the problem of uptake – an Algerian case study. Unpublished PhD dissertation, University of Lancaster, Lancaster.
Snow, C. and Ferguson, C. (eds) (1977) *Talking to Children: Language Input and Acquisition*. Cambridge: Cambridge University Press.
Soars, L. and Soars, J. (1996) *New Headway English Course*. Oxford: Oxford University Press.
Solarczyk, J. (2004) Training compensatory and cooperative communication strategies in the EFL classroom. Unpublished MA thesis, Jagiellonian University, Kraków.
Sperber, D. and Wilson, D. (1986/1995) *Relevance: Communication and Cognition*. Oxford: Blackwell.
Stone, M. (1999) The influence of teacher's use of L1 (Polish) and L2 (English) on the learners' listening comprehension in L2 (English). Unpublished MA thesis, Jagiellonian University, Kraków.
Swan, M. (1985a) A critical look at the Communicative Approach (1). *ELT Journal* 39, 2–12.
Swan, M. (1985b) A critical look at the Communicative Approach (2). *ELT Journal* 39, 76–87.
Swan, M. and Walter, C. (1992) *The New Cambridge Course*. Cambridge: Cambridge University Press.
Swain, M. (1985) Communicative competence: Some roles of comprehensible input and comprehensible output in its development. In S. Gass and C. Madden (eds) *Input in Second Language Acquisition* (pp. 235–53). Cambridge, MA: Newbury House.
Swain, M. (1995) Three functions of output in second language learning. In G. Cook and B. Seidlhofer (eds) *Principle and Practice in Applied Linguistics: Studies in Honour of H.G. Widdowson* (pp. 125–44). Oxford: Oxford University Press.
Swain, M. and Lapkin, S. (1998) Interaction and second language learning: Two adolescent French immersion students working together. *Modern Language Journal* 82, 320–37.
Tarone, E. (2000) Still wrestling with 'context' in interlanguage theory. *Annual Review of Applied Linguistics* 20, 182–98.
Tarone, E. and Liu, G. (1995) Situational context, variation, and second language acquisition theory. In G. Cook and B. Seidlhofer (eds) *Principle and Practice in Applied Linguistics: Studies in Honour of H.G. Widdowson* (pp. 107–24). Oxford: Oxford University Press.
Tomlin, R. and Villa, V. (1994) Attention in cognitive science and second language acquisition. *Studies in Second Language Acquisition* 16, 183–203.
Truscott, J. (1998) Noticing in second language acquisition: A critical review. *Second Language Research* 14, 103–35.

Ur, P. (1996) *A Course in Language Teaching. Practice and Theory.* Cambridge: Cambridge University Press.
Van Lier, L. (1988) *The Classroom and the Language Learner.* London: Longman.
Van Lier, L. (2000) From input to affordance: Social-interactive learning from an ecological perspective. In J. Lantolf (ed.) *Sociocultural Theory and Second Language Learning.* Oxford: Oxford University Press.
VanPatten, B. (1996) *Input Processing and Grammar Instruction.* New York: Ablex.
Vygotsky, L. (1978) *Mind in Society.* Cambridge, MA: Harvard University Press.
Vygotsky, L. (1986) *Thought and Language.* Cambridge, MA: MIT Press.
Wajnryb, R. (1992) *Classroom Observation Tasks. A Resource Book for Language Teachers and Trainers.* Cambridge: Cambridge University Press.
Wesche, M. (1994) Input and interaction in second language acquisition. In C. Gallaway and B. Richards (eds) *Input and Interaction in Language Acquisition* (pp. 219–50). Cambridge: Cambridge University Press.
Wesche, M. and Ready, D. (1985) Foreigner talk in the university classroom. In S. Gass and C. Madden (eds) *Input in Second Language Acquisition* (pp. 89–114). Cambridge, MA: Newbury House.
Widdowson, H. (1978) *Teaching Language as Communication.* Oxford: Oxford University Press.
Wilkins, D. (1976) *Notional Syllabuses: A Taxonomy and its Relevance to Foreign Language Curriculum Development.* Oxford: Oxford University Press.
Willis, J. (1992) Inner and outer: Spoken discourse in the language classroom. In M. Coulthard (ed.) *Advances in the Spoken Discourse Analysis* (pp. 162–82). London: Routledge.
Willis, J. (1996) *A Framework for Task-Based Learning.* London: Longman.
Wilson, D. and Sperber, D. (2004) Relevance theory. In L. Horn and G. Ward (eds) *Handbook of Pragmatics* (pp. 607–32). Oxford: Blackwell.
Witalisz, E. (2004) An analysis of the written English produced by Polish EFL learners applying to the English Department of the Jagiellonian University. Unpublished PhD dissertation, Jagiellonian University, Kraków.
Zawadzka, E. (2004) *Nauczyciele języków obcych w dobie przemian.* Kraków: Impuls.

Index

Authors

Allen, P., 56, 79
Allwright, R., 27, 39, 41, 63
Atkinson, D., 37
Austin, J., 43

Bell, J., 138, 157
Bellack, A., 39
Bialystok, E., 4, 8, 11, 17, 21, 33
Bolitho, R., 29
Brazil, D., 43
Breen, M., 27, 43
Brown, H., ix, 25
Brumfit, C., 27

Canagarajah, A., 32
Canale, M., 28, 33
Carroll, S., 9, 18, 96, 97, 110, 143
Celce-Murcia, M., 45
Cesnik, H., 6, 36, 38, 146
Chaudron, C., 44, 49
Cohen, A., 71
Cook, V., 21
Coulthard, M., 39-41
Crookes, G., 29
Czekajewska, A., 38, 53, 55, 56, 57, 67-70, 105-110, 146, 153, 154

Dakowska, M., 17, 21
Doughty, C., 5, 6, 95
Douglas, D., 43
Duff, P., 25

Edmondson, W., 42, 43
Eldridge, J., 37
Ellis, R., ix, 2, 4, 5, 11, 39, 40-44, 47, 49, 51, 55, 63, 147

Faerch, C., 7, 17, 34, 43, 48
Fanselow, J., 39
Ferguson, C., 35, 47
Field, J., 83, 156
Fillmore, C., 33

Firth, A., 10
Fisiak, J., 24, 29, 54
Flanders, N., 39
Flanigan, B., 49
Fryc, A., 46, 53, 55-57, 62, 78-86, 97, 99-101, 110-113, 122, 123, 131-133, 137-139, 152, 154-156, 158, 161-165

Gaies, S., 35, 48
Gass, S., 1, 3, 4, 10
Giles, H., 47, 49
Goffman, E., 17, 35
Gower, R., 138, 157
Gozdawa-Gołębiowski, R., 16
Gremmo, M., 42
Grice, H., 12

Harbord, J., 37
Harder, P., 27
Hatch, E., 11, 35, 50
Havranek, G., 6, 36, 38, 146
Henzl, V., 48
Hoffman, E., 27
House, J., 43
Hymes, D., 28

Jarvis, G., 39
Jodłowiec, M., 15, 16
Johnson, Karen., 40, 47
Johnson, Keith, 27

Karavas-Doukas, E., 46, 80, 161, 165
Kasper, G., 7, 10, 17, 34, 44
Kellerman, E., 17
Komorowska, H., 25-27, 29, 54, 57
Korpaczewska, I., 26
Kosiarz, A., 53-57, 60-62, 102, 103, 166
Kramsch, C., 25, 43, 45
Krashen, S., 2-4, 146
Król, A., 48, 146
Kusibab, E., 53-59, 95, 115, 117, 126, 127, 129, 152, 166

Index

Lapkin, S., 10, 22
Larsen-Freeman, D., 45
Levelt, W., 34
Lightbown, P., 30
Littlewood, W., 30, 116
Liu, G., 10
Long, M., 2-5, 10, 29, 30, 39, 42, 44, 48, 50, 51, 54, 94, 95

Maguire, M., 10
Majer, H., 47
Majer, J., 27, 37, 38, 40, 41, 44, 46-52
Mazur, J., 53, 55-57, 70-78, 97-99, 110, 118, 119
McLaughlin, B., 2
McTear, M., 41, 42
Medgyes, P., 24, 25
Mehan, H., 49
Mercer, N., 37
Moon, J., 44
Moskovitz, G., 39
Munby, J., 28
Musiał, A., 36, 41, 46

Newmark, L., 32
Nęcka, E., 18
Nikolov, M., 44
Niżegorodcew, A., 7, 8, 17, 25-27, 29, 31, 33, 34, 37, 38, 42, 46, 51, 62
Norton, B., 27
Nunan, D., 29, 45

Olshtain, E., 45
O'Neill, R., 29

Parks, S., 10, 22
Pawley, A., 11, 22
Phillipson, R., 32
Pica, T., 45, 50
Porter, P., 50
Poulisse, N., 10
Przebinda, A., 27, 46, 53, 55-57, 62, 80, 86, 87, 89-92, 101, 102, 122, 123, 125, 131, 137, 139-141, 154, 160, 165
Puchała, D., 53, 55-57, 62-67, 103, 104, 119, 127-130, 150, 153

Ready, D., 49, 67
Richards, J., 23, 44, 45
Robinson, P., 7, 8, 22, 23, 30, 94
Rogers, T., 23

Rossner, R., 29

Sachs, H., 41, 44
Sato, C., 42, 44, 51, 54, 95
Savignon, S., 28
Schegloff, E., 35
Schmidt, R., 7, 18, 44
Scollon, R., 35
Searle, J., 43
Seliger, H., 27
Selinker, L., 21, 43
Sharwood-Smith, M., 4, 21, 33
Shohamy, E., 33
Siek-Piskozub, T., 26
Sinclair, J., 39-41, 43
Skehan, P., 6, 23, 26, 30, 31, 34, 38
Slimani, A., 55, 67
Snow, C., 35, 47
Soars, J., 123, 131, 159, 160
Soars, L., 123, 131, 159, 160
Solarczyk, J., 34
Sperber, D., ix, x, 4, 12-17, 19, 22
Stone, M., 37
Swain, M., 2, 3, 5, 10, 22, 28
Swan, M., 28, 132
Syder, F., 11, 22

Tarone, E., 10
Tomlin, R., 7
Truscott, J., 7, 8, 18

Ur, P., 23, 25, 29, 30, 31, 32, 33, 35

Van Lier, L., 11, 43
VanPatten, B., 6
Villa, V., 7
Vygotsky, L., 10, 11, 37

Wagner, J., 10
Wajnryb, R., 56, 79
Walter, C., 132
Wesche, M., 46, 47, 49, 50
Widdowson, H., 28
Wilkins, D., 28
Williams, J., 5
Willis, J., 31, 43
Wilson, D., ix, x, 4, 12-17, 19, 22
Witalisz, E., 36

Zawadzka, E., 25, 27, 36, 41, 45

Subjects

Accuracy (correctness) practice, x, xi, 20, 31, 32, 94, 103, 144, 145, 167
Attention
– functions of attention, 7

Code model of verbal communication, 13
– decoding, 1, 8, 14-18, 94, 117, 131
– code-switching, 20, 25, 57, 65, 118, 122, 145, 166
Cognitive processes
– macroprocesses, 6
– microprocesses, 6
Communicative activities (teaching techniques), xi, 6, 20, 24, 27, 31, 41, 44, 46, 50, 53, 55-57, 71, 78-81, 86, 94, 100-102, 110, 111, 113, 122, 123, 130, 131, 137, 144, 145, 149, 152, 157, 158, 160, 166
– discussion, ix, x, 18, 20, 31, 32, 79, 80, 81, 82, 83, 87, 88, 94, 102, 109, 112, 122, 138, 139, 140, 141, 142, 156, 157, 160, 161, 165
– role-play, xi, 20, 33, 46, 53, 55, 57, 59, 81, 86, 87, 90, 100, 130, 137, 138, 142, 159, 160, 163, 164, 167, 168
Communicative language ability model, 34
Communication strategies, 11, 25, 34, 37, 46, 51, 62, 145, 160
Conversational analysis, 41, 44, 52
Cooperation in the L2 classroom, 35

Discourse
– L2 classroom discourse, ix, x, xi, 10, 18, 20, 21, 27, 39-46, 51, 56, 57, 62, 81, 93-96, 109, 112, 114, 116, 123, 129, 143-145, 148, 150
– features of L2 classroom discourse, 40, 56
– goals of L2 classroom discourse
    core goal, 42, 43, 63
    framework goal, 42, 43, 63
    social goal, 42, 55, 63, 147
– inner structure of L2 classroom discourse, 43
– outer structure of L2 classroom discourse, 43
– naturalistic discourse, 10, 21, 40-43

Error correction (corrective feedback), x, 18, 35, 36, 38, 44, 46, 53, 68, 79-81, 108, 110, 111, 113, 127, 143-15, 149, 153-155, 162, 163, 168
– recasts, 14, 22, 44, 48, 82, 84, 95, 111, 155
– repairs, 33, 35, 150

Fluency assessment, 33, 38
Fluency practice, xi, 19, 32-34, 36, 46, 94, 111, 112, 114, 126, 130, 131, 144
Foreign language teaching context, xi, 50

Form-focused instruction, 4, 5
Fossilisation, 21, 36

Initial learning, 32, 33
Input
– apperceived input, 3
– conceptually driven input processing, 8
– data-driven input processing, 8
– input to learning, 9
– input to processing, 9
– roughly tuned input, 2
Input for instructed L2 learners, ix, x, 142
– planned L2 input, 41
– primary (positive) input/raw input (primary linguistic data), 128, 142, 144, 145, 148, 149
– secondary (negative) input/corrective input (secondary linguistic data), 99, 101, 109, 110, 112, 128, 138, 143-145, 148-150, 153, 155-158, 160, 61, 163, 166-168
Interactional (interactive) discourse, x, 11, 18, 35, 39, 40, 43, 48, 54, 164
Interactional adjustment (modification), 2, 49
– clarification request, 2, 50, 51, 99, 109, 145, 146, 152, 153
– comprehension check, 2, 50, 51, 98, 153
– confirmation check, 2, 50, 51
Interactional analysis, 41
Interactional speech acts, 43
Interlanguage, 5, 16, 21, 35, 37, 41, 47, 49, 50, 52, 62, 113, 143, 146, 153, 160, 165
– interlanguage-talk input, 41

Knowledge
– explicit knowledge, 5
– implicit knowledge, 5
– metalinguistic knowledge, 8

L2 acquisition, xii, 2, 4-1, 20, 23, 29, 38, 48, 51, 130, 143
L2 classroom
– distribution of power in the L2 classroom, 45
– L2 classroom management, 49, 117, 121
– L2 classroom teaching, xi, 23, 29, 31
– real L2 classroom communication, 154, 155
– simulated L2 classroom communication, 130, 138
L2 competence, 24, 25
– communicative competence, xii, 7, 23, 26, 28, 33, 34, 45, 53, 54, 57-60, 166, 167

Index

- discourse competence, 28
- grammatical competence, 10, 26, 28
- sociolinguistic competence, 28
- strategic competence, 28, 34

L2 development, xii, 2, 29-32, 34, 37, 40, 42, 50, 51, 145

L2 learning, xii, 2-6, 9-13, 21-26, 29, 31, 34, 37-39, 41-43, 47-49, 51, 52, 93-95, 115, 121, 142, 145, 149, 157, 168

L2 teachers' roles, xi, xii, 3, 6, 8, 12, 13, 23-26, 35-38, 40, 41, 45, 46, 48, 49, 51, 55, 67, 95, 115, 121, 128, 143, 148, 150, 154, 161, 166-168

Language learning aptitude, 26

Language production model, 21, 22, 34, 114, 130

Learner differences, 26

Lexicalised sentence stems, 11, 22

Lingua franca, 27, 32

Meaning-focused instruction, 4, 114

Mediation/mediator, 11, 32, 38, 45, 166

Methods of L2 teaching, 23
- Audio-Lingual Method, 28
- Communicative Approach (Communicative Language Teaching/CLT), 27-31, 34, 36, 37, 40, 45, 94, 114, 126, 148, 166
- Grammar-Translation Method, 144
- Task-based Learning Approach, 29, 50

Monolingual L2 classrooms, x, 51, 62

Multilingual L2 classrooms, 36

Participation
- participation rights, 45, 46
- patterns of participation, xi, 40, 46

Personal teaching theory, 36

Presentation, 32
- explicit presentation of the linguistic data, xi, 94, 102

Questions
- display-questions, 42
- referential (real) questions, 44, 45, 59, 129, 146

Relevance Theory (RT), ix-xi, 1, 4, 8, 10-21, 80, 93, 94, 96, 97, 99, 103, 105, 107, 108, 110, 112, 114, 116, 119, 120, 121, 126, 129, 130, 138, 139, 142-144, 146, 148, 150
- Cognitive Principle of Relevance, 22
- communicative intention (communicative layer of intention), 14, 41, 105
- contextual assumption, 12, 13, 15, 18, 19, 22, 95, 105, 106
- contextual effect, 12, 15, 19, 96
- expected (level of) optimal relevance, 18-21, 54, 93, 95, 96, 103, 105, 107, 111, 114, 117, 119, 121, 126, 130, 139, 142, 148
- expected relevance (expectation of relevance), 8, 12, 105, 128
- informative intention (informative layer of intention), 14, 94
- ostensive-inferential communication, 15, 94
- presumption of optimal relevance, 15
- Principle of Relevance, x, 12, 15, 16, 20, 22
- processing effort, 12, 13, 15, 19, 96, 159
- rationality principle, 12

Scaffolding, 11, 35

Second Language Acquisition (SLA) theories, ix-xii, 1, 2, 4, 6-11, 13, 18, 19, 29, 33-35, 39, 43, 47, 94, 114, 130, 142, 148
- Accommodation Theory, 47, 49
- affordance, 11
- Cognitive Focus-on-Form (FonF) Approach, 5, 6
- Comprehensible Input Hypothesis, 2, 3, 6, 45
- Comprehensible Output (Output-as-Input) Model, 3
- Discourse Theory, 11
- Focus-on-Forms Approach, 5
- Integrated Theory of Instructed L2 Learning, 4, 6
- Interaction Hypothesis, 2, 5, 6, 39, 45, 50, 51
- Noticing Hypothesis, 7, 8
- sociolinguistic and sociocultural theories, 10
- Universal Grammar Hypothesis, 21

Secondary instructed L2 learners, 25

Skills
- communication (communicative) skills, 28, 29, 168
- language skills, 62
- productive (speaking) skills, 53, 55, 80, 86, 87
- receptive (listening) skills
  scanning, 30
  skimming, 30, 95

Speech Acts Theory, 43, 52

Strategic behaviour, 7, 17, 34
- negative strategic behaviour (avoidance), 34
- positive strategic behaviour, 7, 34

Subject-matter teaching, xi, 38, 55, 57, 118

Talk
- caregiver talk, 35, 47
- foreigner talk, 35, 46-48
- L2 teacher talk, 46-49
- metatalk, 48, 49
- peer talk (tutor talk), xi, 39, 49, 50, 143

Talking about organisational and social matters, 121

Task-based activities (practice), 30
Topic-based activities (practice), 30, 33
TEFLese, 49
TESLese, 49

Vertical structures, 11, 35

Zone of Proximal Development, 11

For Product Safety Concerns and Information please contact our EU Authorised Representative:

Easy Access System Europe

Mustamäe tee 50

10621 Tallinn

Estonia

gpsr.requests@easproject.com

www.ingramcontent.com/pod-product-compliance
Lightning Source LLC
Chambersburg PA
CBHW052130010526
44113CB00034B/1505